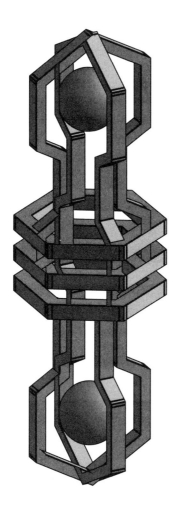

The Oracle Cookbook

For Design, Administration, and Implementation

Harry D. Liebschutz

M&T Books
A Division of MIS:Press, Inc.
A Subsidiary of Henry Holt and Company, Inc.
115 West 18th Street
New York, New York 10011

```
Liebschutz, D. Harry.
   The Oracle coobook : for design, administration, and
implementation / by Harry D. Liebschutz.
      p.  cm.
   ISBN 1-55851-454-6
   1. Oracle (Computer file)  2. Relational databases.
QA76.9.D3L536  1995
005.75'65--dc20                                95-36296
                                                  CIP
```

98 99 97 96   4 3 2 1

Associate Publsher: Paul Farrell	**Managing Editor:** Cary Sullivan
Aquiring Editor: Jono Hardjowirogo	**Copy Editors:** Shari Chappell
Production Editor: Anthony Washington	**Illustrator:** Tad Barney

Table of Contents

INTRODUCTION I

PART ONE:
Review of Relational Technology

CHAPTER 1: Relational Database Management Systems 9

Three Schema Architecture 10

    External Schema 12

    Conceptual Schema 13

    Internal Schema 17

The Relational Model and Logical Data Modeling 19

    Structure 20

Foreign Keys 25

    Integrity 26

    Entity Integrity 26

    Manipulation 29

    Implications and Benefits 29

Structured Query Language 30

Data Definition Language DDL 31

Data Manipulation Language DML 32

Data Control Language DCL 33

PL/SQL 34

CHAPTER 2: Oracle Component Overview **35**

Executable RDBMS Code—The Kernel 36

Instance 36

System Global Area 38

Server Processes 43

User Processes 47

Program Global Area 47

Program Interface 47

Background Processes 48

Database 54

Files 54

Logical structures 61

Data Dictionary 96

The Optimizer 101

Startup and Shutdown 105

Startup 106

Shutdown 108

STARTUP FORCE 109

Oracle Architectures 109

CHAPTER 3: Installation **111**

Users, Groups, and Owners 113

Directory Structures 114

Install 115

PART TWO:
Building a Physical Database

CHAPTER 4: Backups, Archiving, and Recovery 119

   Cold or Off-Line Backups 123

   Archiving and Hot/On-Line Backups 124

   Oracle Backup Manager 127

   Recovery 128

   Export and Import 129

CHAPTER 5: Getting Down to Business 135

   System Goals or Purpose 135

      Purpose 136

   System Inventory and Sizing 137

      Hardware Components 138

      Software Components 140

   Database Design 142

      Validate Logical Data Model 142

      Evaluate Processing and Transactions 146

      Stored Procedures, Triggers, Functions, and Packages 147

      Transform Logical to Physical 149

      Size Objects 154

      Group objects by tablespace 165

      Database Environments 174

   Security 178

      Grants 179

      Roles 182

      Users 184

      Audit 189

Create Database 190

    Execute Initial DDL 190

    Load Tables 197

    Execute Remaining DDL 198

Testing 200

    Database Functionality 200

    Applications 201

    Database Object and File Sizes 202

CHAPTER 6: Data Loads and Conversions **203**

SQL*Loader 205

Logistics 207

PART THREE:

Tuning, Monitoring, and Maintenance

CHAPTER 7: Tuning, Monitoring, and Maintenance **213**

Applications and SQL 214

    EXPLAIN PLAN 215

    SQL TRACE and TKPROF 219

Memory 222

    Shared Pool 222

    Database Buffers 224

    Redo Log Buffers 225

    Sort Area 226

I/O 227

Contention 228

    Rollback Segments 228

    Redo Latches 229

    Freelists 230

UTLBSTAT and UTLESTAT 232

A Quick Check List 232

Monitoring and Maintenance 233

    Alert Logs and Trace and Dump Files .234

    Database Growth 235

    Analyze Tables and Indexes 235

    Tools Again 236

PART FOUR
Other Issues

CHAPTER 8: Policies and Procedures 239

Personnel 240

    Data Administration 240

    Database Administration 244

    Systems Administration 244

Naming Standards 245

    Abbreviations and Acronyms 248

    Entities 249

    Relationships 249

    Domains and Attributes 251

    Tables 251

    Columns 252

    Indexes 255

    Constraints 256

    Directories 258

    Files 258

    Lookup Codes 259

Change Control 262

    You Control It or It Controls You 262

    Limit Access to Database Environments 263

    Full Backups Before and After Any Production Database Changes 264

CHAPTER 9: Special Issues . . . .**.265**

Project Management 265

Prototyping 269

    Phase 2 273

    Phase 3 276

CASE Tools 276

Off-the-Shelf Software 277

Very Large Databases 279

    Creating Databases, Tablespaces, and Other Objects 279

    Data Loads 281

    Backup and Archiving 282

Hardware is Cheap Relative to Labor 282

    Denormalization 282

    Obsession with Detail 285

    The Mathematics of It All 285

APPENDIX A . . . .**.287**

APPENDIX B . . . .**.293**

GLOSSARY . . . .**.305**

INDEX . . . .**.317**

Introduction

Just how do you go about "making" an Oracle database? What are the necessary and proper ingredients, how much of each is necessary, and how do you combine them so that you get the blue ribbon? My checklist for winning a blue ribbon includes the following:

- The database performs well. While this is relative, good performance means getting the job in the allotted time. A customer representative may need the much requested "sub-second" response time; a batch job should not exceed predefined time frames. In the former case, performance might be defined in seconds; in the latter, good performance may be within minutes or hours.

- The database is easy to maintain. This could mean that a lot of internal resources, both human and machine, are not dedicated to baby-sitting the database for fear of a crash. A well-designed database should work quite a while with little or no intervention or maintenance. Change, however, is inevitable. The other aspect to good maintenance is creating an environment that survives personnel, hardware, and business changes. This quality can be easily judged by the amount of time it takes an outsider (such as an outside consultant or a new employee) to figure out what a system is all about, what it's intended to do, and how it does it. Making systems obvious makes them maintainable.

- The database is secure from unwanted intrusions and operations.
- The database is protected from machine or other failures, but in the case of the inevitable failure, it can be recovered fully and promptly.

To help win blue ribbons, I provide a reference and a guide to both technical and management issues for new and experienced users. I have included a lot of detail for the experienced Oracle practitioners and background material to help novices learn how to build and maintain Oracle databases.

In addition to the technical issues, I provide a guide on how to manage the database development process and production database environment(s). One of the things you will quickly discover in working with Oracle is that there are numerous tools to help design, build, and maintain your environment(s). These include CASE tools and database monitoring products, as well as scripts that you will develop and accumulate over the years. While some of the database development tasks still require certain skills, experience, and talent, much of the actual work can be automated. Oracle development, therefore, is more about managing the development process than how to write DDL or triggers or stored procedures or any of the other technical things that too many developers get bogged down in.

I believe that database design can only begin with a good logical data model. Just as a building begins with an architect's plan, a database should have similar preparation and plans. An elegant meal needs a recipe, and any good database design must begin with a good data model.

While my style is informal, this book provides a comprehensive study of Oracle7 Server. as well as information on Parallel Query Option and Oracle7 Parallel Server. Included are numerous well-documented scripts can be used as is; others serve as templates for developing systems. The book does not cover topics related to Trusted Oracle.

This book contains information about the database architecture, tuning, policies, and procedures which should prove very useful in formulating an overall application development strategy/environment. It is not, however, intended as an application developer's guide.

The book is divided into four parts. Part One is a general review of relational technology; it covers the necessary inputs to database design. Consider this part a discussion of ingredients. Part Two moves on to the business of building a physical database, or how to cook the meal. Part Three deals with tuning and maintenance, similar to maintaining a good diet to stay fit. Part Four deals with several issues that don't fit neatly into other sections or span all of the sections. This is similar to kitchen management for a restaurant.

Part One

Chapter 1, "Relational Database Management Systems," provides background on the technology at hand and inputs into the physical database design process. If you want or need to know why you should care about relational theory and logical data modeling, this chapter review the basics. It covers logical data modeling and the relational model, the three schema architecture, Structured Query Language (SQL), and how they all relate to Oracle and the task of implementing a production database.

Chapter 2, "Oracle Component Overview," reviews the pieces that make up an Oracle database. Have you ever wondered exactly what is an instance or the SGA? If knowledge of a particular nomenclature makes an expert, then this chapter can make you an instant guru. this chapter also covers the available Oracle database architectures to clarify the difference between Oracle Parallel Query and Oracle Parallel Server and other not-so-subtle-points.

Chapter 3, "Installation," reviews various issues that need to be addressed before and during an Oracle installation. Where should Oracle go relative to the operations system? What is an appropriate directory structure? You really want to get this stuff right the first time because reinstalling Oracle can be time-consuming.

Part Two

Chapter 4, "Backups, Archiving, and Recovery," reviews options for backups, archiving, and recovery of an Oracle database, and how this option effects your database design.

Chapter 5, "Getting Down to Business," covers the issues necessary for bringing up a production database. The first topic is that of *purpose*. Just what kind of processing is intended for the new database, that is, what flavor will it be? Next, we look at some hardware and software issues and get an inventory of the target machines(s). There is a brief discussion of backups and archiving and how they will affect the database design.

These are all appetizers. For the real meat and potatoes, we move on to database design. All the ingredients come together as we get ready to create a new recipe—the physical database design. Then we can actually create our new database.

Chapter 6, "Data Loads and Connection" covers the often neglected art of loading a database. When converting legacy systems or any large systems, loading data can be a real show stopper. It's like getting ready to put your soufflé in the oven, only to find the oven isn't working.

Part Three

Chapter 7, "Tuning Monitoring and Maintenance," covers the ongoing maintenance of a production system and how to tune Oracle database.

Part Four

Chapter 8, "Policies and Procedures," review issues external to an Oracle database that affect the Oracle system. Naming standards are something that can make life easy or hard, depending on how they are chosen and implemented. A little common sense can go a long way in making the design and maintenance of database easier.

Change control policies and procedures will determine whether your environment controls you or you control it. Could you really be a master chief if you have to carry a fire extinguisher all the time? The basic issue is how can you manage the inevitable requests for changes to the system. Without formal change control, you will be in a perpetual state of fire fighting? This is more a matter of will than effort. Less effort is required to make the environment run smoothly than to let the environment run itself.

Chapter 9, "Special Issues," covers project management (PM), very large databases (VLDB), off-the-shelf software, and certain cost considerations. While change control and project management are similar and usually used together, the distinction here is the one-time project orientation of PM versus the ongoing nature of change control. A sample project plan is included.

Off-the-shelf software presents special challenges. Much of this third-party software is intended to run with different kinds of databases, such as Informix or Sybase, as well as with Oracle. This generic approach to databases (SQL is an industry standard, right?) can cause special problems.

Very large databases provide some very special opportunities to excel. These opportunities often present themselves as seemingly insurmountable problems. The Oracle Parallel Query Option (OPQ) has provided some excellent tools that are particularly effective for VLDBs. Even without these tools, there are recipes for VLDBs.

On the cost side, my experience is that few hardware and software sales people or budget managers have a good grasp of the relationships and trade-offs between buying more hardware to solve a problem and spending labor dollars to try and fix it. The problem with spending labor dollars to fix a performance issue is that the dollars are often spent to show that more hardware is required. there is a lesson here, and it can save you a lot of time and money.

Throughout most of the book, I try to use the Oracle-supplied Scott Tiger database(s) in examples. Depending on your installation, you may receive on e or several versions of this database. Each version is a small database that models a small retail sales organization. You can create the database when installing the system or by running the **DEMOBLD7.SQL** script or the **DEMOBLD.SQL** script. While small, these databases can satisfy most of the example requirements and they may make it easier for you to try some of the examples on your own. The logical and physical data models for the sample databases are included in Appendix A.

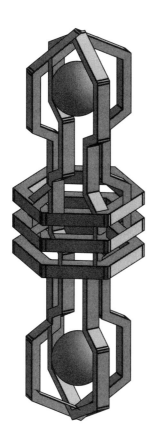

PART ONE

REVIEW OF RELATIONAL TECHNOLOGY

Chapter 1: Relational Database Management Systems

Chapter 2: Oracle Component Overview

Chapter 3: Installation

CHAPTER I

Relational Database Management Systems

This chapter reviews several issues that might be considered "background material" but the information is too important to be relegated to the background. It covers the inputs into the physical database design process. This book is not about logical data modeling *per se*, but a good data model is the primary ingredient, or prerequisite for a good database design. (This implies that one of the first steps in designing a physical database is to validate the data model that is to become the database.) The logical data model (LDM) represents the structures, rules, and information about data of interest to an organization. The LDM is usually built and presented with diagrams, and associated text which describes the structures and rules. Whatever the form of a LDM, it should conform to the rules of the relational model. The relational model, in turn, fits into a larger information architecture called the three schema architecture. The database itself is defined and manipulated with a Structured Query Language referred to simply as SQL.

I do not intend to teach you how to develop a logical data model: there are numerous texts and classes to do that. However, if you are tasked with designing and building a physical database, you should have a solid understanding of your primary input, the LDM. It is also important to understand the interaction of the LDM, the database, and the applications or programs that will execute against that database in a larger context which describes how these three components relate and interact. This larger context is the three schema architecture.

I get the impression from various developers that some of these topics are perhaps passé or old hat. Some folks feel that the relational model and three schema architecture may not be as relevant in today's fast changing world of object oriented this and that, CASE (computer aided systems engineering) tools, and client/server technology with GUI (Graphical User Interface) front ends. Oracle, however, is called a *relational* database management system (RDBMS) for a reason and, in order to get the most that the technology has to offer, it is important to understand its heritage.

I contend that, if you understand the concepts presented here, you will have a better understanding of how to design and build a solid relational database. You will also see that developing systems using Oracle's tools and capabilities can be very different than is generally practiced. It is quite possible to shift much of the functionality of many applications to the database. Therefore, work currently performed during applications development should be shifted to the database development. The greatest impacts of this shift relate to the amount of effort needed to develop applications versus the database, the skill level of those developing applications and the database, and the quality, integrity, and flexibility of the new systems.

This paradigm shift is described in general in the following three sections. Details describing how to perform this new database development are described Chapter 5 .

Three Schema Architecture

So what is a schema anyway? The *American Heritage Dictionary* defines a schema as: "A diagrammatic representation; an outline or a model." And why should we care?

The Three Schema Architecture (TSA) provides a good reference or framework around which to discuss various aspects of systems development in general and for our purposes database design and implementation in particular. It is especially important with the release of Oracle7 because of the functionality now available at the database level (these capabilities will be described in detail later.)

The TSA was the result of an effort to develop a database standard during the 1970s by the American National Standards Institute (ANSI), Special Programs and Reports Committee (SPARC). Rather than promulgate a single physical database standard to which database manufacturers should adhere, ANSI SPARC suggested an information architecture that could insulate users of information from its storage and access methods thus making systems more responsive and flexible. The report said:

- A database contains data about a selected part of the real world. This part of the real world is called an enterprise. It generally represents information about a group of people, artifacts, ideas, event, and processes organized to support collective goals. The real world concepts may be expressed in terms of any one of a number of formal schemes...

- A database management system should provide the ability to evolve by emphasizing data independence. Data independence allows the users to add new applications, to follow changes in the enterprise, to correct errors and to tune for better performance and response...The necessity for data independence cannot be avoided by choosing the right way to organize the stored data such that it never has to change. Change is inevitable. Data independence is not the capability to avoid change; it is the capability to reduce the trauma of change." (The ANSI/X#/SPACR DBMS Framework Report of the Study Group on Database Management Systems,AFIPS PRESS, p. 1.)

The report describes three realms or views of the data and each view is described or defined as a schema. Objects that are of interest to a particular user or application represent an external view and are described in the external schema. This view is usually along functional or departmental lines. The conceptual schema describes the system from an enterprise perspective that crosses all functional boundaries. The internal schema describes how the data is physically stored and accessed and is intended to make best use of machine resources.

The TSA allows an end user to look at and manipulate their data *as if* it were in a set of private files, even though many people might be using the same data for many other purposes. While this sections describes all three schemas, this book is primarily about designing, building, and maintaining the internal schema in such a way that it supports the needs and requirements of the other two schemas.

External Schema

The external schema (ES) is the end users' view of the world. It describes their individual representations of their processes, data and information. This view is usually seen through computer terminals or reports, and is generally departmental or functional in nature (Figure 1.1). Most organizations have many different ES views. Purchasing's view of the world is quite different from the sales organization, which is probably different from the view of accounting.

Figure 1.1 The External Schema

The external schema is a view that is usually driven by processes rather than data. The focus is on how the data is used, not how it is stored or structured. To the end users their particular external view *is* the database. This is why it is important to allow users to perform inserts, updates, and deletes of data *as if* they were working with their own tables or files. The sales manager should not have to care how the data is stored, but she will certainly care about how it is used. The ES looks at the processes of an organization and determines how data is used by each process and how it flows from process to process. It describes how data is seen and used by individual users, processes, or functions.

Development of the various external views of the system has generally been the purview of application developers/programmers and end users. Programmers wrote the code that produced the screens and reports. Within the programs for each view/screen, that is **each and every** program for **each and every** view, were the rules and logic that enforced the business rules for a particular function. That meant that the applications were to enforce the business rules which, might determine a customer's credit worthiness, the best supplier when entering purchase orders, or whether to take discounts when paying bills. This also meant that end users could not or should not directly access information in the database, except through the application for fear of circumventing the business rules.

There are several problems with the applications directly enforcing or applying the business rules. The biggest is getting every programmer to understand or apply every rule. Harder still, is getting them to apply the these rules uniformly and correctly. This also means that a large proportion of every program is written to enforce the rules and handle errors. In addition, a lot of time needs to be spent testing to ensure that every program has all of the rules right. If a rule should change, many programs may also have to change. This programming effort directly relates to the number of hours and the cost required to develop and maintain systems. There are big bucks involved here.

Another problem relates to the end users getting, or more likely not getting direct access to their data. Very few production systems let users jump into Oracle's SQL*Plus and execute queries directly against the database. Virtually no one considers letting end users directly manipulate or update data except by way of the application programs. This means that a knowledgeable end user, and perhaps even ones that are quite computer literate, must go through a programmer to get at the data.

Conceptual Schema

At some point, various portions of the different users' views will overlap. Data must be shared and, therefore, the meaning of the data must be shared. Where the whole is the sum of the parts, the *conceptual schema* represents the whole. It is a view of the data taken from an enterprise or organizational perspective rather than an individual department or end user perspective. While purchasing generally only cares about purchase orders, at some point the information they enter must pass in some form to accounts payable, and receiving. The sum of all of the external schemas is the whole conceptual schema.

It is important to understand what the conceptual schema is not. The conceptual schema is not about physical storage or physical access. This means that things such as files and indexes are not part of the lexicon of the conceptual schema. And while the external schema has tangible screens and reports, the conceptual schema is more of an abstraction, not something physical, but a conceptual representation.

For our purposes, the conceptual schema is defined in terms of the objects and rules that make up the relational model: relations/tables, domains, attributes/columns, primary keys, and foreign keys which are described later in this chapter. Its representation is usually in the form of a logical data model which is depicted with diagrams and documentation. The diagrams often take the form of entity relationship diagrams (ERDs) as illustrated in Figure 1. 2.

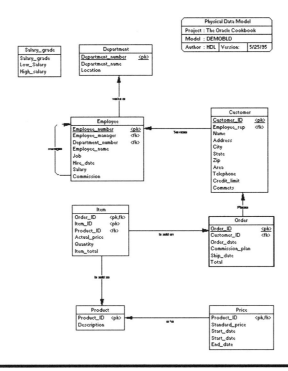

Figure 1.2 The Conceptual Schema Depicted as an Entity Relationship Diagram

The data model in Figure 1.2 represents the sample database that is provided in various forms with every Oracle installation. There were actually two sample databases that came with my copy of Oracle. The model is Oracle's not mine. I might not have chosen to model a sales order system in the exact same way but I use this model because every Oracle installation should have the script to create a similar database. This model and database is used in most of the examples/screens in this book and I thought it best to use something that you could easily reproduce on your own system.

The conceptual schema is not concerned with how the objects are implemented or accesses physically at the database level. Physical implementation is a database design issue not a logical data modeling issue. The conceptual schema should allow any authorized user to view any data in any manner they wish without regard to functional boundaries or physical storage.

There are numerous diagramming techniques and CASE tools available to depict these models, many of which elicit a kind of religious fervor as to why one is better than another. We are not here to engage in a highly stimulating debate about which CASE tools are best, or which techniques are best. The fact is, many CASE tools allow the user to choose from a variety of methods. It really doesn't matter much which one you choose; just choose one and learn how to use it. (See Chapter 9 for more on CASE tools.)

Building a conceptual schema for an entire organization can be an extremely difficult, if not impossible, task for a large organization. Where small systems may have 50 to 100 tables a large stand alone system, such as accounting, or college enrollments, may have 500 to 1,000 tables. Put together an entire organization and the numbers are even higher. Trying to combine all aspects of an enterprise into a single, cohesive, conceptual schema is at best daunting and generally overwhelming for any one person (or group of people) and beyond the capabilities of many CASE tools.

Rather than developing an entire data model up front, the conceptual schema usually grows a piece at a time as different application systems are built. Essentially, the conceptual schema is built by combining the various external schema pieces (Figure 1.3). BUT IT SHOULD NOT BE BUILT WILLY NILLY

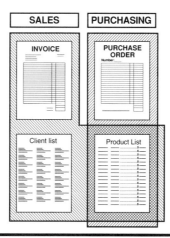

Figure 1.3 Conceptual Schema Development

While trying to build an entire data model of an organization may be overwhelming (I have never done it completely, and don't know any single person who has), what I do find surprising is that many organizations have not developed a set of core entities for their models. For any organization, there should be common definitions for important things like products, customers, employees, or departments.

Without a common definition for the core entities from which to develop the various external schemas, what should be common portions of the external schema won't match as each development groups creates its own definition of customer or product. Some of the most compelling reasons to justify developing the conceptual schema are questions like, "How does a company that has multiple definitions of their product ever get a cohesive picture of what it produces, sells, and maintains?".

This issue of common definitions illustrates the strategic nature of conceptual schema development versus the tactical nature of applications/external schema development. Too often the time and effort needed to develop a cohesive and consistent conceptual schema is sacrificed to the need to get applications out the door. The short sightedness of this approach will become painfully apparent as soon as different departments want to share data or someone wants a comprehensive picture of a common portion of the business like products. If you thought the up front or initial cost of developing these common elements was too much, wait till you start to pay for programs that try and pull it all together.

When this desire to share arises, (and of course the data can't be shared because there are four different product tables, and at least three different versions of supplier, and...well you get the picture) you will notice that it is never the applications that are inconsistent, the applications work fine—it's "the database." No one will remember that data modeling was sacrificed so the programs would be delivered faster.

In terms of allocating resources for development efforts, at least one person should "represent" the conceptual schema point of view on every project. This person, or group of people, forms an organization or function referred to as data administration (DA). DA representatives are the keepers of the conceptual schema. I recommend that people from DA plan on selling users and developers on the advantages and benefits of common definitions as well as their participation in development projects rather than acting as the data police trying to force standards. See Chapter 8, Policies and Procedures for more information on DA as well as Database Administration.

This discussion about commonality relates directly to one of the major themes of this book, which is that a good database is one designed and built to be easily maintained. Reusing a common set of objects is usually easier, less costly, and less risky than building every object from scratch for each development effort. The whole point of relational technology is to allow you to leverage your investment in work that is already completed. It's important to note that the cost of not leveraging can be more that the cost of leveraging. It can cost substantially more to write interfaces and gather and store data from different systems than planning to share right from the start. This sharing isn't rocket science; it's simple things like using common datatypes and lengths for columns.

What if we had a way to take the rules previously defined as the external schema, consolidate, and address them through modeling techniques at the conceptual schema level? Rather than define each and every rule at the application level, hoping that every programmer uses them correctly; we could define the rules at the conceptual level, so that they apply to every user and developer. This kind of shift and effort would only be worthwhile if a database could support or enforce the rules. With Oracle you have such a database and the tools and capabilities are described in Chapters 2 and 5..

Internal Schema

The *internal schema* is the definition of the physical database. It describes the size, location, and content of the physical files. It also describes physical access methods such as indexes, hash clusters, and other things we will cover later (Figure 1.4). The internal schema is often spread across many machines with different operating systems, and there are often numerous databases from several different vendors.

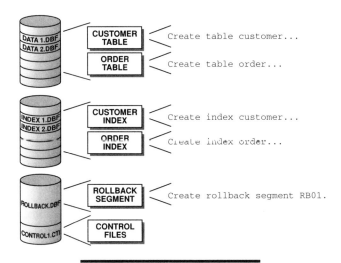

Figure 1.4   The Internal Schema

The goal for those responsible for the internal schema is to design systems that are consistent with the over all needs of the business while supporting the performance requirements of individual applications. The database should be a physical implementation of the conceptual schema that supports individual external schemas. This is not always an easy balancing act and often requires as much political finesse as technical skills. As in walking a tightrope, good balance between the external and conceptual schema has rewards. Some of the things that help achieve this balance are planning, well thought out designs, controls, training, sufficient hardware, communications, flexibility, adaptability, standards.... and everything else covered in this book.

While data administrators are the keepers of the conceptual schema, The database is the bailiwick of *database administrators* or DBAs. The DBAs are the ones who design, build, and maintain the databases.

Many shops extend the responsibilities of the DBAs beyond the internal schema definitions to include the SQL code used in programs for the external schema. While programmers may write SQL to support their programs, DBAs have final review and performance responsibility. The DBAs check tuning, reusability (are there any similar SQL queries that already exit, and if not then catalog the new one), integrity, and security. See Chapter 8, Policies and Procedures, for more information on Database Administration.

When viewed together, all of the components of the three schema look like Figure 1.5:

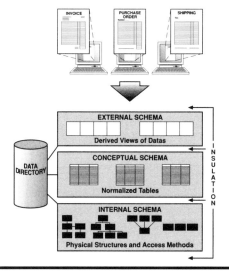

Figure 1.5 The Three Schema Architecture

Note the data dictionary to the side of the three schemas. This is when many of the definitions are stored. Oracle provides an extremely robust data dictionary and we will examine it in detail later. Most CASE tools also have a data dictionary, and some application development tools even include a dictionary of some sort.

The data independence provided by the three schema architecture is what provides the insulation between the schemas.

The Relational Model and Logical Data Modeling

The relational model has three components. There is a structural component that defines the the types of things we can use to build the model, an integrity component which defines the operational rules of the data model, and a component which describes how to manipulate the structures.

The LDM and relational model provide a representation of the data that is not machine or program oriented. This is the conceptual schema protion of the TSA. In that respect, the models are logical constructs, not physical ones. Instead of dealing with files, indexes, pointers, and access, the LDM and the relational model provide an abstraction of the organization's information that is flexible, easy to use, rigorous, yet simple. As Dr. E. F. Codd, the originator of the relational model explains, "In developing the relational model, I have tried to follow Einstein's advice, 'Make it as simple as possible, but no simpler.' I believe that in the last clause he was discouraging the pursuit of simplicity to the extent of distorting reality." Rather than talk or think of how data is physically stored, the relational model helps users see data as it is represented in terms of how they do business. (*The Relational Model for Database Management* version 2, E.F. Codd, 1990, Addison-Wesley Publishing Company, Inc., p. vi.)

For our purposes, I will refer to the LDM as something that is given as input to the database design process. The relational model is the theoretical foundation for the LDM regardless of the diagramming techniques or symbology used to represent it. The LDM should adhere to the rules of the relational model.

Structure

A model requires a structure or framework with which to describe and build it. The structure describes the allowable components and how they can fit together.

Relations, Attributes, Domains, and Tuples

The basic structural components of the relational model are relations (tables), attributes (columns), and tuples (rows). Tables, rows, and columns,that's pretty simple, isn't it? In addition, there are domains. The foundation of the relational model comes from two parts of mathematics; the theory of relations and first order predicate logic. This point is not to bore you, it's just to let you know that there is some pretty sound thinking, centuries of it actually, that went into this stuff.

Again, relations and tuples can be thought of as tables and rows, and attributes are the columns of the tables. (Through out most of the other sections of the book I will use the terms table, column, and row.) There are a few things, described below, that make relations and tuples special.

Domains describe data of interest to the organization. The domains are grouped into tables. A column is really the occurrence of a domain in a table. A domain defines the data type, length, format, or other business rules. Domains also define the set of all allowable values. Most importantly, a domain defines the meaning of the data. Columns that share the same domain can reasonably be compared to each other and joined because they mean the same thing. It would make no sense to compare a birth date to a hire date even though they are both dates because they don't mean the same thing. (While domains are not explicitly supported in the Oracle database, they are supported in the Oracle CASE tools, as well as by many other CASE vendors.)

Relations are special kinds of tables. Every row, or tuple, in a given relation must have the same structure, the same set of columns. Every table/relation must have a unique name. Every column in a table must have a unique name. Every row/tuple in the table must be unique. By specifying these unique values, we are guaranteed access to any data in the database. That is, the intersection of any row and column (tuple and attribute) in a given table will hold a single value. These rules are intended to eliminate ambiguity.

Columns are the descriptive attributes of a table. A column can appear only once in a given table. The order of the columns is not important in the relational model. If we were to describe a particular human being, we might say that he or she is 5'9" tall, weighs 150 pounds, has brown hair, and brown eyes. Similarly, if we had a table of EMPLOYEEs, they might have attributes of Employee Number, Employee Name, Employee Address, and so on. When there is data in a column of a table, it is telling us a fact about that table or object.

Tuples are rows in a table. Each row in the table represents the occurrence of data that is described by the table and columns. Tuples cannot appear more than once in a given table (otherwise it is *just* a row and not a tuple). The order of the tuples is not important in the relational model.

The following diagrams, Figures 1.6 and 1.7, show two representations of a table. One is a model of the table, the other is the table itself with data in the rows. The rows represent individual employees.

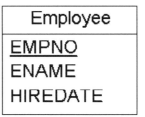

Figure 1.6 Model of Employee table

EMP

EMPNO	ENAME	HIREDATE
98721	Harry Liebschutz	7/25/85
34872	Ed Eimutis	6/30/92
47329	Tad Barney	2/18/87
76293	Robert Banner	6/30/92
87371	Elaine Friedman	10/15/91

Figure 1.7 Employee relation

Tables that have duplicate rows or columns are not relationals, they are simply tables. For example, the following table, Figure 1.8, has duplicate rows; therefore it is not a relational.

EMP

EMPNO	ENAME	HIREDATE
98721	Harry Liebschutz	7/25/85
76293	*Robert Banner*	*6/30/92*
47329	Janet Smith	2/18/87
76293	*Robert Banner*	*6/30/92*
87371	Elaine Friedman	10/15/91

Figure 1.8 Employee table with duplicate rows

The following table, Figure 1.9, has duplicate columns, therefore, it is not a relational.

EMP

EMPNO	ENAME	ENAME
98721	Harry Liebschutz	Harry D. Liebschutz
76293	Robert Banner	Stephen Banner
47329	Janet Smith	Janet Smith-Jones
76293	Robert Banner	Robert Banner
87371	Elaine Friedman	Elaine Friedman

Figure 1.9   Employee table with duplicate columns

The rule about duplicate row and columns is important because it eliminates the problem of multiple answers to a single question. For example, if we should say, show me the employee name where employee number is equal to 76293 there are four answers in the table above. Which one is correct? By following the rules of the relational model the intersection of a row and a column will give only one answer, thus controlling ambiguity.

Primary Keys

How do we tell that a row is unique? If we were to insert or update information in a relation, one way to ensure the row was unique might be to match every single column in the row with all of the columns in every other row. An easier mechanism is to specify a single column or group of columns as unique. That's the function of the primary key, which is a column or group of columns that uniquely identifies a row in a table from every other row in the table. A table can only have one primary key.

The following two diagrams, Figures 1.10 and 1.11, illustrate an entity called department. The primary key of the Department table is the Department_number. Every department must, therefore, have a unique number.

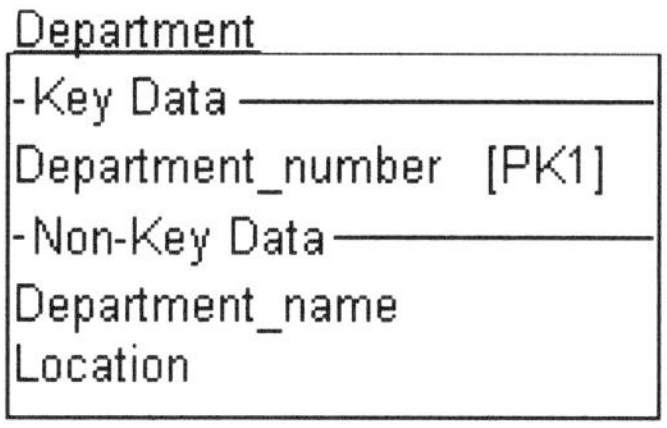

```
Department
-Key Data
Department_number   [PK1]
-Non-Key Data
Department_name
Location
```

Figure 1.10   Entity created with System Architect

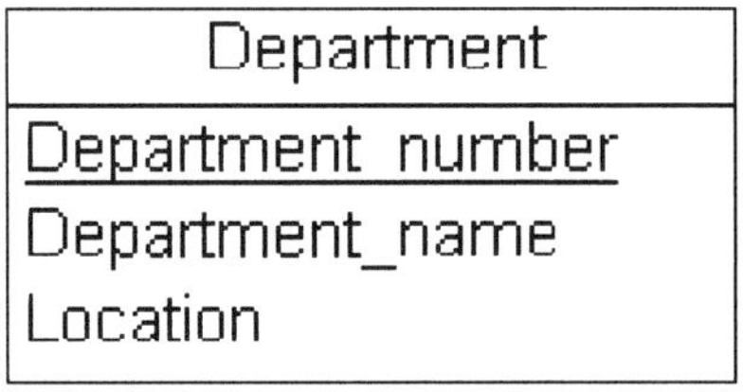

```
┌─────────────────────────────┐
│        Department           │
├─────────────────────────────┤
│ Department_number           │
│ Department_name             │
│ Location                    │
└─────────────────────────────┘
```

Figure 1.11　Entity created with S-Designor

The first diagram was produced with the System Architect CASE tool, produced by Popkin Software. The symbology illustrated here is called IDEF1X. For a comprehensive study of IDEF1X modeling techniques, see Thomas A. Bruce, *Designing Quality Databases with IDEF1X Information Models* (Dorset House Publishing).

Figure 1-11 was produced with S-Designor, produced by SDP Technologies, Inc. S-Designor is based on the Information Engineering Methodology. This methodology was developed by James Martin and is described in several of his books. The rest of the entity relationship diagrams in this book were created with S-Designor.

Many people try to embed meaning into their primary keys. An example of this might be including a state or customer type as part a customer identifier. Any information that is embed into the primary key should really be carried as an attribute of the entity. If the state is included as part of the primary key of the customer primary key, and if the state is in the customer table as well, we have a redundant field. What happens if the customer moves to another state? Do you change the primary key value? If you change the primary key do you go and update all of their old sales orders? Well, you'd better, if you want to find that customers' invoices again but, it's time wasted.

The best kinds of primary keys are those that do not have any meaning associated with them. These are called blind keys. (An associate of mine calls blind keys *bozo keys* which, I guess, is his way of indicating just how meaningless they should be.)Remember that the simple reason for primary keys is just to identify a row in a table. The primary key need not tell us anything other than this row is different from that row. This point will become more apparent and important when we discuss Oracle's *sequences* later in the book.

Foreign Keys

Foreign keys are columns in one table that point to the primary key of the same or another table. Foreign keys provide the references or links from one relation to another or one relation to itself. In entity relationship diagramming, foreign keys are shown as relationships.

The following diagram, Figure 1.12, illustrates a foreign key. Each *Customer* **is serviced by** an `Employee_rep` or employee representative. The `Employee_rep` column in the Customer table is a foreign key that points to the primary key, `Employee_number`, of the Employee table. When an `Employee_rep` is assigned to a customer, the foreign key ensures that the employee exists. The table where the foreign key resides is often called the source table. The foreign key *references* the primary key of the *target table*.

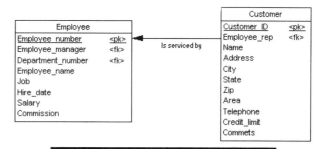

Figure 1.12 Foreign keys between tables

A foreign key can also reference the same table in which it resides. For example, every employee is assigned a manager. This means that the `Employee_manager` column is actually a foreign key that references the `Employee_number` because the manager is also an employee. The `Employee_manager` *manages* the *Employee*. When we add or update an employee, the manager that is assigned must reference a valid employee. This type of self-referencing foreign key is often called a *recursive foreign key* (Figure 1.13).

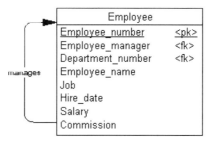

Figure 1.13 Recursive foreign key

Foreign keys are the main mechanism for enforcing the business rules relating to the interaction of tables and changes to certain data..

Integrity

The relational model describes a structure for our data. The model also provides some rules to which our data must adhere. Entity integrity describes the rules that refer to a single table and its primary key. *Referential integrity* describes the rules that relate to foreign keys and how tables that are linked with foreign keys must be maintained. Referential integrity and entity integrity are often referred to as *integrity constraints*. These integrity constraints are, in turn, often referred to as insert, update, and delete constraints.

Entity Integrity

Providing a primary key value is a good way to identify or select a row in a table. The primary key guarantees that you will select only one row. This leads us to another point, which is, you cannot identify something with nothing. This in turn leads to the concept of nulls and nothingness.

A null is the absence of information and has no value. While this may seem similar to blanks, the two are not equivalent in the relational model or relational databases. When I press the space bar on my computer keyboard to create a blank, I am actually creating a blank character which the computer stores as such . Blanks are not the same as nulls. Nulls have no values and therefore, are not stored. A column in a row can, however, be tested to see if it is null by using the SQL predicate IS NULL in a WHERE clause. This is equivalent to checking to see if there are any values, including blanks, in the column. Nulls should not be used to imply information such as zeros or blanks. The following screen illustrates these points.

The first insert into the LOCATION table adds the LOCATION_ID of 222 with no value (a null) for the REGIONAL_GROUP. The two quote marks without a space indicate a null. The second insert adds the LOCATION_ID of 333, but here there are spaces (not null) between the quote marks for the REGIONAL_GROUP. The two queries show different results when looking for columns that are null (IS NULL) and columns that are not null (NOT NULL) (see Figure 1.14).

Figure 1.14 The difference between null and blanks

Nulls lead us to a final point about primary keys - no part of a primary key can be null. As we will discuss in more detail later, Oracle has a PRIMARY KEY constraint which will ensure that every primary key column has a value and that these combined values are unique. Unfortunately, the PRIMARY KEY does not prevent someone from inserting blank characters into a primary key column.

Referential integrity

Referential integrity defines a set of rules that applies when there are inserts, updates, or deletes to the tables that involve foreign keys. For a foreign key value there must be a corresponding primary key value.

- When you insert a value into the foreign key column(s) that value must exist as a primary key referenced by the foreign key.
- If a foreign key value is updated, the new value must also point to a primary key value.
- If a primary key value is updated, its related foreign key values should also be updated. Many RDBMs, including Oracle, do not allow updates of primary keys where there are existing foreign key values.
- If a primary key is deleted perform one of the following functions:

  Restrict — Do not allow the delete if there are existing foreign key values. (Supported by Oracle as a restrict delete.)

  Cascade — Delete all rows in the foreign key table(s) that reference the deleted primary key value. (Supported by Oracle as a cascade delete.)

  Nullify — Set the foreign keys values to null.

  Default — Set the foreign key values to a valid default value.

While foreign keys may guarantee good data, they cannot guarantee good information. Take as an example the entity relationship diagram (ERD) below The diagram shows three tables that are related in the following manner: a company sells PRODUCTs which are supplied by SUPPLIERs. The table in the middle, SUPPLIER_PRODUCT, is often referred to as a cross reference or xref table. It represents a "many to many" relationship between the two entities, SUPPLIERs and their PRODUCTs. That is, a SUPPLIER sells many PRODUCTs and a PRODUCT can be purchased from many SUPPLIERs (Figure 1.15).

When we decide to purchase a particular PRODUCT from a particular SUPPLIER, we insert a row into the SUPPLIER_PRODUCT table. When the actual insert is performed, referential integrity will tell us whether we are referencing a valid PRODUCT and whether this is a valid SUPPLIER. Both foreign keys, PROD_ID and SUPPLIER_ID, must reference valid primary key values. The question that begs answering is, whether that particular PRODUCT is, indeed, sold by that particular SUPPLIER. Only the user can make that decision when adding rows to the SUPPLIER_PRODUCT table. So, while referential integrity may guarantee us that we are working with valid data, it may not be able to guarantee that we have valid information. Garbage in, garbage out.

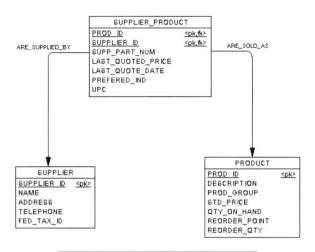

Figure 1.15 Supplier Product tables

I need to add a note here about the differences between keys and indexes. Keys are logical structures that enforce entity integrity using primary keys, or referential integrity using foreign keys. Indexes are physical structures used to locate and/or order data in a table. Special kinds of indexes, UNIQUE indexes, can also be used to enforce uniqueness. Primary keys are actually physically implemented with special unique indexes. These primary key indexes are physical structures that check the uniqueness of every value in the index, and do not allow any nulls. The index generated for the primary key actually maintains entity integrity at the database level.

Manipulation

We have described a structure for our data, and we have defined certain limits about how it can be used. The manipulative component describes how we work with the data. In Oracle, and most other relational databases there are numerous operators that are available to user to view and maintain their data. User can SELECT, INSERT, UPDATE, and DELETE data where they have proper authority.

Implications and Benefits

So just how do you benefit from the relational model and the three schema architecture? Read on reader.

- Reduce the trauma of change—Application developers should be able to make changes to their applications without requiring changes to the database. DBAs should be able to change and tune database objects without requiring changes to the applications.

- Leverage existing work—New projects do not start from scratch. They start with the conceptual schema and build from there.

- Counter entropy—Many uncoordinated development efforts will lead to disorganization. Building on the conceptual schema should make systems more similar.

- Reduce programming efforts and cost—Define the business rules in the conceptual schema and implement them in the database using primary keys, foreign keys, triggers, procedures, packages, and views. Once they are in the database several things happen; programmers do not have to put them in their applications, (See leverage above.) they cannot forget them, and they will not get them wrong. Less coding, less testing, less time, less cost. This is real important stuff here.

- Data security—The database can be secured and audited independent of or in addition to the applications.

- Data consistency—By developing consensus definitions for objects in the conceptual schema you don't end up with one system that a 15 character supplier name and another that has a 30 character name.

- You know this list gets really long. Additional points are covered through out the book.

Structured Query Language

SQL is a language used to define, control access to, and manipulate data in a database. It was originally defined by IBM and has since been standardized by ANSI and the International Standards Organization, ISO. Oracle is 100% compliant with the ANSI92 and ISO standards. In addition, Oracle has numerous extensions to the standard SQL that provide additional power and capabilities. Regardless of the language in which an application was written, Visual Basic, Powerbuilder, SQL*Forms, C, C++, SQL*Plus, or COBOL, the application only communicates with the database via SQL. Therefore, SQL must be incorporated or embedded in any application that wants to talk to an Oracle database.

There are three sets or types of SQL. Each one performs a different function. There is DDL for the data definition language, DCL for the data control language, and DML for the data manipulation language.

Each type of SQL consists of commands that must be combined to form valid SQL statements. SELECT is an SQL command, but

```
SELECT deptno ,dname FROM dept;
```

is a SQL statement.

Data Definition Language DDL

DDL is the code that is used to build databases and database objects, such as tables and indexes. In the Oracle environment, there are really two portions to most DDL commands. There is a logical portion which describes just the object structure. Except for datatypes specific to a particular RDBMS, this syntax is very common across most relational databases. This logical side relates to the objects defined in the conceptual schema. There may or may not be a one to one correlation between all of the relations/entities defined in the conceptual schema and all of the tables defined in the database. The DDL used to define a table for the entity DEPARTMENT is as shown in Figure 1.16:

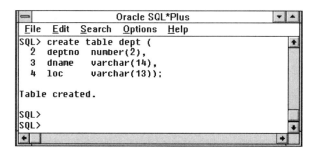

Figure 1.16 Data Definition Language

Virtually every CASE tool can generate the DDL to support object structures. Most people think of DDL as simply CREATE TABLE and CREATE INDEX statements. For Oracle, however, we need to define numerous physical parameters as well. These parameters define among other things, how large to make the object and where it should go. This book is more about the physical parameters than logical structures, because it's the physical parameters that really define the physical database, the internal schema.

Adding some of the additional Oracle specific commands (which will be covered later) to size and place the DEPT table expands the above CREATE TABLE statement into that shown in Figure 1.17:

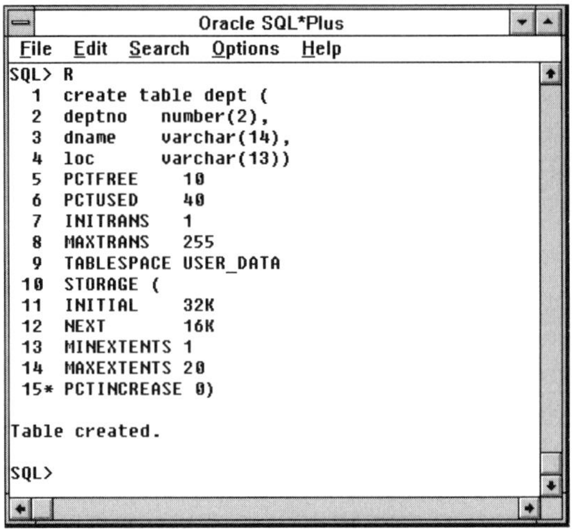

```
┌─────────────────────────────────────────────────┐
│ ─              Oracle SQL*Plus          │▼│▲│    │
├─────────────────────────────────────────────────┤
│ File  Edit  Search  Options  Help               │
├─────────────────────────────────────────────────┤
│ SQL> R                                        │↑││
│     1   create table dept (                     │
│     2   deptno    number(2),                    │
│     3   dname     varchar(14),                  │
│     4   loc       varchar(13))                  │
│     5   PCTFREE      10                          │
│     6   PCTUSED      40                          │
│     7   INITRANS     1                           │
│     8   MAXTRANS     255                         │
│     9   TABLESPACE USER_DATA                     │
│    10   STORAGE (                                │
│    11   INITIAL      32K                         │
│    12   NEXT         16K                         │
│    13   MINEXTENTS 1                             │
│    14   MAXEXTENTS 20                            │
│    15* PCTINCREASE 0)                            │
│                                                 │
│ Table created.                                  │
│                                                 │
│ SQL>                                          │↓││
├─────────────────────────────────────────────────┤
│ ←│                                           │→│ │
└─────────────────────────────────────────────────┘
```

Figure 1.17 DDL with Oracle parameters

Data Manipulation Language DML

DML is the portion of SQL that you use to manipulate data. In SQL you can SELECT, INSERT, UPDATE, and DELETE data in rows from tables.

I find it easiest to think of the SELECT command portion of DML as a problem statement language (Figure 1.18). State the problem to be solved first, then develop the SQL to solve the problem. (The questions are often harder than the answers.) For example, one may ask, "Show me all of the employees that work in department twenty."

Using SQL*Plus we can solve the problem thusly:

```
─                    Oracle SQL*Plus              ▼ ▲
 File  Edit  Search  Options  Help
SQL> select ename, deptno                            ↑
  2   from emp
  3   where deptno = 20;

ENAME          DEPTNO
----------  ----------
SMITH              20
JONES              20
SCOTT              20
ADAMS              20
FORD               20

SQL>                                                 ↓
 ←                                                 →
```

Figure 1.18 Data Manipulation Language

Data Control Language DCL

With DCL, you control access to the database. Users and roles are added with
the CREATE USER command. DCL is then used to GRANT or REVOKE privileges to
both commands and objects in the database for any of the roles or users in the
database. The following example creates a new user and grants them CONNECT
and RESOURCE privileges, meaning they can access data in the database, and
create their own objects like tables and indexes (Figure 1.19).

```
─                    Oracle SQL*Plus              ▼ ▲
 File  Edit  Search  Options  Help
SQL> create user new_user identified by new_password  ↑
  2   temporary tablespace temporary_data
  3   default tablespace user_data;

User created.

SQL> grant connect, resource to new_user;

Grant succeeded.

SQL>                                                  ↓
 ←                                                  →
```

Figure 1.19 Data Control Language

Details of DCL and database security are covered in Chapter 5 .

PL/SQL

PL/SQL is the Oracle programming language extension to the standard SQL. PL/SQL is an ADA-like language that, if you're interested, provides virtually all of the capabilities necessary for object oriented programming. This includes capabilities for such things as data encapsulation, information hiding, and overloading. PL/SQL combines procedural language flow-of-control with the data manipulation capabilities of SQL and can be used in procedures, functions, triggers, or packages which are embedded in the database. It can also be used for stand alone programs or scripts that are run like any other program against the database. (I say, "If you're are interested," because sometimes it's easier to ask for forgiveness than to ask for permission. If you were to go to your management and say you wanted to develop the new Oracle system using object oriented techniques, you might get the response, "Our shop doesn't do object oriented development; Oracle is not an object oriented database, and we don't have the time and budget for all these new fangled buzz words, etc..." However, if you were to simply use the capabilities in the Oracle database and PL/SQL, you could end up with an object oriented system.)

PL/SQL can be used in conjunction with the declarative referential integrity capabilities of Oracle to enforce business rules at the database level. This provides much greater power and flexibility than just the use of primary and foreign keys. PL/SQL can be used in trigger, functions, procedures, and packages. These capabilities are covered in more detail in Chapters 2, and 5 . This book is not intended to teach PL/SQL or even SQL for that matter.

CHAPTER 2

Oracle Component Overview

Chapter 1 covered the theoretical foundations for relational databases and presented an information architecture with which to view the various aspects of systems development, the three schema architecture. This chapter moves from the theoretical to the practical as we focus on the RDBMS product at hand— Oracle. Most of the details about how to combine, define, size, and place these components is covered in Chapter 5.

Oracle runs on more machines and more operating systems than any other database product available today. It also runs in a variety of configurations to support just about any processing requirements on the appropriate platforms.

Mention the word *database*, and most people associate the reference to a product, such as Oracle, Sybase, or DB2. In the world of Oracle, however, it is important to realize that a database is really an operational component of the product. It is the component of Oracle where data is physically stored. A database has a name and is made up of physical files located on the disk drives. In addition to the database, there is a set of memory structures and processes called an *instance*. There is also all the executable code that makes it all work together. In an Oracle environment, the database stores the data, the instance performs the work, and the executables provide the instructions.

Before discussing physical database design, it's important to have a clear and comprehensive understanding of the various Oracle components and configurations, what they are, what they do, and how they work together. The complexity of the subject is such that the initial sections of this chapter are dedicated to the various Oracle components, while the latter sections focus on how they work together.

There are many ways to monitor performance and tune an Oracle system. As we cover the individual components, tuning issues and parameters are addressed in terms of what you might look for and what impacts various components have on overall performance. For a step-by-step approach to monitoring and tuning, refer to Chapter 7.

Executable RDBMS Code—The Kernel

The Oracle RDBMS is a collection of programs, structures, and files used to store and manipulate data. There are other Oracle components that are used for application programming and reporting, as well as a comprehensive set of CASE tools. The *kernel* is the part of the RDBMS code that runs the SQL requests for the users. It performs all of the reads and writes to the database, coordinates user and background processes, and maintains the memory components.

When a user logs on or connects to Oracle (through either an Oracle tool like SQL*Plus or an application program), that user process communicates with a server process. The server process performs various tasks on behalf of the user, including retrieving data from the database. These server processes and other Oracle processes described later are executing the kernel code.

Instance

An *instance* is a set of memory structures and processes used to communicate with user processes and to control and manipulate the data stored on the disk. An instance can be associated with only a single database, but a database can be addressed by multiple instances, as with the Oracle Parallel Server. Multiple instances can run on a single machine.

Whenever you start an instance (we will cover the details of startup, shutdown, mount, open, and so on later in this chapter), Oracle reads a small file called an *init.ora* file. The **init.ora** file contains a list of *parameters*, or instructions, that determine among other things; which database to use, how large to make the various memory portions of the instance, and what kind and how many types of processes to use. (We will cover various **inti.ora** parameters later in this chapter; Appendix B lists details of many of them.)

When an instance starts, Oracle allocates a portion of the machine's memory for what is called the *System Global Area* (SGA) and other components. Oracle also builds a number of tables or lists in memory to help control and monitor performance. These are called the *dynamic performance tables*, and most are accessed with views that begin with the characters **V\$**. Many of these views are referenced throughout this chapter. There is also a section in this chapter that covers these tables and the Oracle data dictionary views.

It's within the SGA that Oracle actually works with data. This area of memory is used and shared by all user processes for accessing data. Before a user can use any data, it must be read into the SGA. Efficient use of the SGA can reduce physical reads and writes of data to and from the disks. The reading and writing is call *input/output* and is referred to as *I/O*. As you will soon see, the physical file I/O is almost an inconvenience, but it will greatly affect our design of the physical database (Figure 2.1).

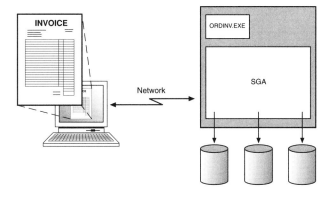

Figure 2.1 A lot of moving parts.

System Global Area

The SGA has three main components, or caches, each of which can be monitored, tuned, and sized independently. They are the shared pool, the redo buffers, and the database buffers. (There are numerous other components that you can see with the view **V$SGASTAT**. All of these components are used by Oracle to manage and process data, but many are beyond the scope of this book.)

With today's technology, disk access is measured in milliseconds, while memory access is measured in nanoseconds. A *nanosecond* is a billionth of a second (about the time it takes light to travel one foot); a *millisecond* is a thousandth of a second. The difference is six orders of magnitude, or in more technical terms, memory access is a lot faster than disk access. If you wanted to access a piece of data, would you prefer it to get it from memory—with nanosecond access—or from disk—in milliseconds?The folks at Oracle figured this one out a long time ago. If data can be accessed in memory, it's almost instantaneous. If it has to be accessed from disk, the relative wait for the data is substantially longer. This will lead us to some very detailed disussiond about memory amnagement and disk I/O.

Where all this should lead you, and where it led Oracle, is to a strategy that says: if I can access and manipulate data in memory, my system(s) should run substantially faster than if I have to always access and manipulate data by reading from and writing to disk.

Oracle can address a lot of memory. With some 32-bit machines and operating systems, Oracle can address up to 2 gigabytes of memory. With certain 64-bit machines and operating systems, Oracle can address up to 14 gigabytes of memory.

Shared Pool

The *shared pool* is an area in memory that Oracle uses to store and manipulate information about the Oracle database itself and the SQL statements processing against the database. The shared pool has two components, the data dictionary cache and the library cache or shared SQL area. A *cache* is a set of memory buffers. The size of the shared pool is determined by the **init.ora** parameter SHARED_POOL_SIZE.

Shared SQL Area

When a SQL statement is sent to the database, Oracle divides the statementinto a public, or shared, part called the *shared SQL area,* and a private portion called the *private SQL area.* The shared SQL area contains the parse tree and execution plan for a query. Parsing breaks the query into its component parts, and the execution plan is a definition of how Oracle will actually fetch data from, or manipulate the data in the database. The shared SQL area is stored in the shared pool. The private SQL area contains buffers and definitions for the data passed between the applications and the database. The location of the private SQL area will vary depending on the database configuration.

Users or processes that use the exact same query can share the query in the shared SQL area. Every query has its own private SQL area. The first thing Oracle does when it receives a query is to check the shared SQL area to see if the query is already in memory. If it is, Oracle does not have to validate and reparse the query, and thus it runs faster.

In order to reuse or share a query, the queries must match *exactly.* If two users submitted the following query, it would only be parsed once and then shared by the different users:

```
SELECT ENAME FROM EMPLOYEE;
```

The following queries, however, are not equivalent to the preceding one. Their meanings may be the same, but they are not exact matches. Similar is not the same as exact.

```
SELECT ename FROM EMPLOYEE;
SELECT ENAME FROM employee;
Select ENAME from EMPLOYEE;
SELECT  ENAME  FROM EMPLOYEE;
```

Parsing the query and developing the execution plan for the query are very CPU- and I/O-intensive operations. So, if Oracle can store the structure definitions used for parsing and the resulting execution plan in memory, the database will run faster. The shared pool is intended for just that purpose.

Dictionary Cache

Oracle stores all the information about a particular database in its data dictionary. Every Oracle database has a data dictionary, which is created when a database is created. The *data dictionary* contains information about tables and their columns, indexes, users, grants, privileges, and more, which we will cover in detail later.

When a user submits a query to the database, Oracle validates the user's authority to perform the query and the query syntax against the information stored in the data dictionary. In fact, for all commands issued against the database, Oracle goes to the data dictionary for some sort of information. When Oracle has to read dictionary information from the disk, it's called a *recursive call* to the data dictionary. Fortunately, the data dictionary is usually finite in size and extremely well organized.

Since it is faster for Oracle to access information from memory than to go to disk for every query, in order to reduce the number of recursive calls to the database, Oracle provides a special cache in the shared pool, called the *dictionary cache*, that contains information about the database. To help performance, it is best if you can cache the entire data dictionary in memory.

Database Buffers

Oracle physically stores data in units on the disk called *data blocks*, which vary in size from 512 bytes (512K) to 32 kilobytes (32K). Many rows of data can fit into a single data block. Before a user process can access data from the database, the block or blocks that contain the data must be read into the database buffers. That is, **every** piece of data that a user needs must go through the database buffers. Oracle only reads data from the disks if it is not already in the database buffer cache.

The size of the database buffer cache is determined by the number of DB_BLOCK_BUFFERS specified in the **init.ora** file. The number of DB_BLOCK_BUFFERS multiplied by the BLOCK_SIZE determines how much space in memory is allocated to the database buffers.

Most computers have much more disk space than memory. All the data in the database will generally not fit into memory, or more specifically, into the database buffers. (Although with 2 gigabytes or 14 gigabytes of memory, you can cache a lot of data.) When a request is made for data, Oracle first looks in the database buffer cache to see if the data block(s) that contain the row(s) of data is already in memory.

Because space is limited in memory, Oracle is forced to write blocks back out to disk at various points to make room for new data that is needed in memory. To optimize the reading and writing of data in the buffers, Oracle organizes the blocks in the database buffers into two lists. There is a *dirty buffer* list, which contains blocks that have been modified but not yet written to disk and a *least recently used* (LRU) list, which contains:

- Free buffers—blocks that have been accessed and are now available for use

- Buffers that are in use or pinned buffers—these are blocks that are currently being accessed

- Dirty buffers—buffers that were modified but have not yet been written to the database

The relative position of a buffer on the LRU indicates whether it was most recently used (MRU) or least recently used. The buffers on the MRU end of the list are the ones that were accessed most recently, while the buffers on the LRU end of the list have aged (Figure 2.2). (An exception to the aging of buffers is blocks that are read as part of a full table scan. When a query performs a full table scan, Oracle considers the buffers reusable immediately, and they go to the LRU end of the list.)

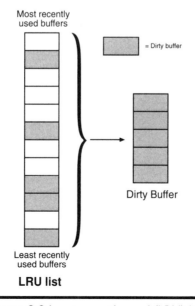

Figure 2.2 Least recently used (LRU) list.

When a user process needs data from a particular block, Oracle first looks in the buffer cache to see if the block is already in memory. If it is not in memory, then the user process scans the LRU list looking for a free buffer where it can write its data. The user process starts at the LRU end of the list, looking for free buffers. Any dirty buffers that are encountered during the search are added to the dirty buffer list. If the user process cannot find any free buffers after searching a predefined number of blocks, it will signal the database writer (DBWR, described in more detail later in this chapter) to write the dirty buffers on the dirty buffer list back to the disk. The write by DBWR will mark the dirty buffers as free buffers, which can then be accessed by another query or overwritten by new blocks that were read from disk. The number of blocks searched is determined by the **init.ora** parameter DB_BLOCK_MAX_SCAN_COUNT.

The premise behind the LRU list is that those blocks most recently used will tend to be the ones most likely to be needed again. If Oracle does not find a block it needs in memory, this is called a *cache miss*. The goal of the LRU list is to keep those blocks that were most recently used in memory so that Oracle does not have to perform I/O to the disk to retrieve data.

You should know by now Oracle likes to avoid I/O to the disks. A good question then is how does Oracle know where to insert new records without looking at the disks (performing I/O) to see where there is free space? It doesn't. Oracle has, one or more *freelists* for every table, cluster, and index. These are lists of all the database blocks that have space available for inserts. So, rather than have to look to the disk for available space, Oracle can look to the freelist for the address of a database block that has room available for inserts.

Redo Buffers

Oracle is a very safe database in terms of protecting users from loss of data in the event of a system crash or other corruption problem. Whenever there is a change to any data, Oracle records the before and after images of the data until the transaction is either committed or rolled back. The *before images* is a copy of the data before it was changed; and the *after image* is the data after the change is made. **Commit** is a command that tells Oracle to make the changes permanent. A rollback is issued when changes should not be committed and the data should be returned to its original state. These two sets of images can be used to recover the database after a crash. The recovery process is covered in Chapter 4, "Backups, Archiving, and Recovery."

The redo buffers are an area in memory that Oracle uses to write all of the after images of changes made to the database buffers. (The redo buffers can actually contain additional information, but that is beyond the scope of this book.) The following SQL commands can alter data or structures in the database: **CREATE**, **INSERT**, **UPDATE**, **ALTER**, and **DROP**. Any time data is modified, copies of the changes are written to the redo buffers. At various points, the redo buffers are copied to the on-line redo log files by the log writer process (LGWR).

The size of the redo buffers is determined by the **init.ora** parameter LOG_BUFFER and is expressed in bytes.

Figure 2.3 illustrates the three major components of the SGA.

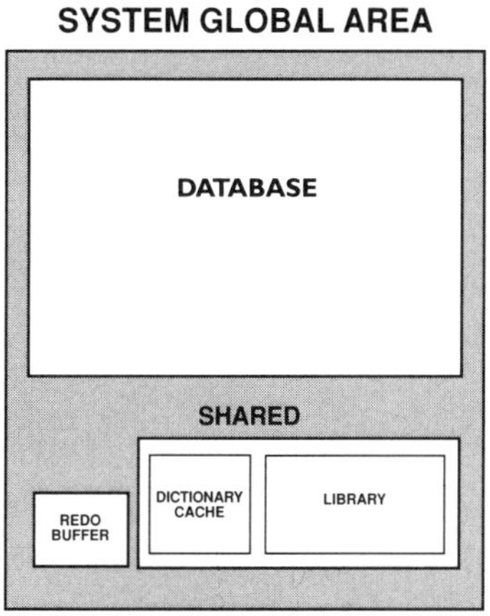

SYSTEM GLOBAL AREA

Figure 2.3 System Global Area (SGA) components.

Server Processes

Server processes communicate with connected user processes and perform tasks on behalf of the users. Server processes parse and execute SQL statements for user processes. The server process may retrieve data blocks from the disk and read it into the database buffers to satisfy a user's query. The server process will also return data to the user process in a usable form. The connection between the user process and the server process is called a session. User and server processes can be configured in a variety of ways, depending on your operating system, hardware resources, and processing requirements.

A *single-task configuration* is where the user processes and server processes are actually combined to run as a single user process. In a single-task configuration, a *program interface* maintains the separation of the RDBMS and application and handles communication between the two sets of code (Figure 2.4). This type of processing is only available with specific operating systems (such as VAX VMS and IBM's MVS) that can maintain the separation of the code within a single process. In this configuration, terminals are hard-wired to the server and all processing is done on the server machine.

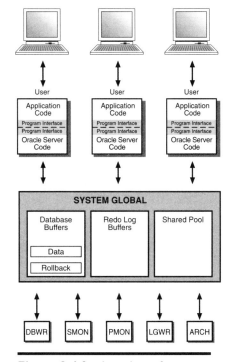

Figure 2.4 Single-task configuration.

With a *dedicated server configuration*, a separate server process is created for each user process. In this configuration (also referred to as *two-task*) the user processes can run on a different machine from the server processes (Figure 2.5). The user processes run on clients, while the server processes run on the server, thus the name *client/server*. Every client or user process has a corresponding/dedicated server process running on its behalf.

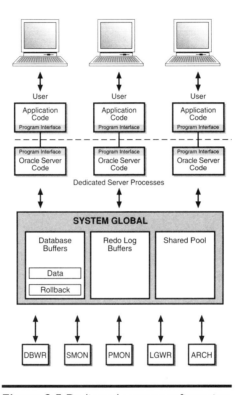

Figure 2.5 Dedicated server configuration.

If the clients and server are run on the same machine, the program interfaces communicate through the operating system's interprocess communications mechanism. If the clients and server are on different machines, they must communicate through SQL*Net (this is important).

A *multi-threaded server* (MTS) configuration allows a server process to service multiple user processes. Typically, with MTS many user processes share a small number of server processes. In addition to the server processes run on the server machine, there is a network listener process and one or more dispatcher processes.

Figure 2.6 illustrates the various processes and the flow of information from the users to the database and back again.

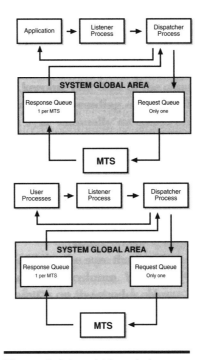

Figure 2.6 A multithreaded server.

The MTS works like this:

- A user process sends a request/query, via SQL*Net to the server.

- The listener process (which is part of SQL*Net and not the RDBMS) waits for user requests. When a request is received, the listener determines whether the request is for a dedicated server (in which case a dedicated server process is started and assigned to the request) or can be sent to a dispatcher. (SQL*Net version 2 is required to run MTS; if the request comes in via SQL*Net version 1 or 1.1, the user process is assigned a dedicated server.)

- The dispatcher sends the request to the request queue that resides in the SGA. There is a single request queue that services all dispatchers.

- The request in the request queue is picked up by the first available shared server process. The requests in the request queue are handled on a first-come, first-served, or FIFO, basis.

- Once the server process has processed the request, the data is returned to the dispatcher's response queue, also in the SGA. Each dispatcher has its own response queue.
- The dispatcher returns the data to the user process.

Once the response is sent back to the dispatcher (and from there to the user process), the shared server picks up the next request in the request queue. The user may still be connected to the dispatcher, but the shared server has moved on to other requests.

The number of shared servers can change based on demand: the longer the request queue, the greater the need for shared servers. A minimum number and maximum number of shared servers can be set with the **init.ora** parameters MTS_SERVERS and MTS_MAX_SERVERS.

User Processes

In addition to the Oracle processes running on the machine, user processes, or applications, also execute and require memory. A user process is created whenever an application or Oracle tool, such as SQL*DBA, connects to the database. The user processes communicate with the server processes.

Program Global Area

The *Program Global Area* (PGA) is a memory buffer for each server process that is allocated by Oracle when a user process connects to the database. The PGA contains session information and stack space, which is used for variables, arrays, and other information. Each PGA is read from and written to only by the Oracle code.

Program Interface

The *program interface* is the means by or through which a user process communicates with a server process. It acts as a conduit, formatting data requests, converting data types, and trapping and returning errors.

Figure 2.7 illustrates the components covered in the following pages. It is presented here to help you visulize how all the pieces fit together.

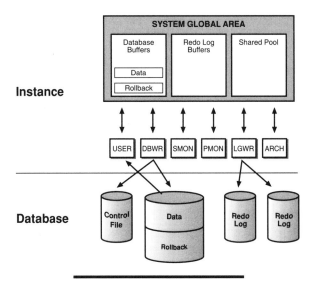

Figure 2.7 Oracle components.

Background Processes

Background processes perform tasks related to the database in general rather than any particular user. These processes begin work when an instance is started. Four of the processes—database writer, log writer, the system monitor, and the process monitor—must be running in order for an instance to function properly. Other processes are optional and support certain kinds of processing, such as the lock process, used for parallel processing, or the archiver, used when the database is in ARCHIVELOG mode. Some of the optional processes are enabled through settings in the **init.ora** file.

Database Writer—DBWR

While the server processes retrieve data for a user request, only DBWR performs writes of data to the database. Unlike the server processes, which must respond to every user request for data, DBWR writes data to the disk(s) in batches. The only data that gets written back to the disks are data buffers/blocks that have changed and been marked as dirty. DBWR is constantly trying to "clean up" the database buffer cache by writing dirty buffers out to disk. While a buffer may contain many rows of data, a change to any column in any row when it is in the SGA causes the entire buffer to be marked dirty. However, just because a buffer is marked dirty does not mean that it is immediately written to disk.

The dirty buffer list is a list of the database buffers that have been modified but no written to the database. Dirty buffers are added to the dirty buffer list as a server process scans the LRUlist looking for free buffers, or when a checkpoint occurs

When we say that Oracle writes the dirty buffer out to disk, this does not mean that Oracle actually removes the dirty buffer from the SGA and writes it to disk, leaving an empty buffer in memory. Creating empty buffers in memory would defeat the purpose of the SGA. Remember that when asked for data, Oracle first looks in the SGA to avoid having to get the data from disk. Rather than remove the dirty buffers from memory and copy them to disk, Oracle simply replaces the original data blocks on disk with the data in the dirty buffers that were changed. Once Oracle knows that the disks are updated, it marks the dirty buffer free buffer but leaves it in memory. By leaving the buffers in memory (as opposed to making empty buffers) and keeping the buffers full, Oracle increases the chance that a user request will find the data it is looking for in memory.

DBWR will write dirty buffers to disk for any of the following reasons:

- A checkpoint has occurred.
- Three seconds have elapsed since the last write—a *time-out*. This parameter is not adjustable.
- The dirty buffer list reaches a threshold value. As server processes add dirty buffers to the dirty buffer list, the number of dirty buffers increases. When the list reaches the limit of dirty buffers equal to half the **init.ora** parameter DB_BLOCK_WRITE_BATCH, DBWR will write the dirty buffers to disk. (see Figure 2.9.)
- A server process searches the LRU list for free buffers and the search is too long. When a server process has searched the LRU list for a free buffer, but has searched for an amount equal to the **init.ora** parameter DB_BLOCK_MAX_SCAN_CNT, it signals DBWR to write dirty buffers to disk to make room for free buffers. (see Figure 2.8.)

When a time-out occurs, DBWR writes a number of dirty buffers on the LRU to disk that is equal to twice the value of the **init.ora** parameter of

DB_BLOCK_WRITE_BATCH. If the system is idle, or if DBWR is not signaled otherwise, the time-outs will cause DBWR to write all the dirty buffers on the LRU list to disk. As I said earlier, DBWR is always trying to clean up the LRU list, and this automatic time-out makes sure that it doesn't sit around idle.

A checkpoint forces DBWR to write all buffers that were modified since the last checkpoint to disk. This ensures that even the dirty buffers on the most recently used end of the LRU list get written to the database. The interval of checkpoints is controlled by the **init.ora** parameters LOG_CHECKPOINT_INTERVAL, which is the number of redo buffers that have changed since the last checkpoint, and LOG_CHECKPOINT_TIMEOUT, which is the number of seconds since the last checkpoint started. A checkpoint also occurs whenever there is a redo log switch.

When called by a checkpoint, the log-writer process (LGWR covered in detail later.) makes a list of the buffers in the buffer cache that have committed changes and prompts DBWR to write these buffers to disk. DBWR writes all the dirty buffers specified by LGWR. This process makes sure that all the buffers written to the redo logs by LGWR are synchronized with the dirty buffers written by DBWR.

When signaled by server processes to write, DBWR writes batches of dirty buffers equal to the value for the **init.ora** parameter DB_BLOCK_WRITE_BATCH. Occasionally, DBWR will not find that many buffers on the dirty buffer list. In this case, DBWR will look in the LRU list for dirty buffers that have not yet been written to the dirty buffer list and will write them to disk as well.

When a server process needs a free buffer, it scans the LRU list from the bottom looking for a free buffer. If the process scans the LRU list and does not find a free buffer in the number of buffers equal to the number of buffers specified in the **init.ora** parameter, then the process signals DBWR to write the dirty buffers (Figure 2.8).

The statistic "dbwr free needed" indicates the number of times that a server process invoked DBWR because it could not find a free buffer on the LRU list within the specified quantity. The value for "dbwr free needed" should not go above zero. If it is greater than zero, it indicates that processes are having to wait for DBWR to write dirty buffers before they can perform their work. Use the **V$SYSSTAT** view to query this statistic.

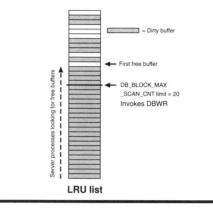

Figure 2.8 DB_BLOCK_MAX_SCAN_CNT.

As the server process scans the LRU list looking for free buffers, it will write every dirty buffer it finds to the dirty buffer list. If the process finds the number of dirty buffers on the dirty buffer list is equal to half the number of buffers specified in the **init.ora** parameter DB_BLOCK_WRITE_BATCH, then the process will signal DBWR to write the dirty buffers. The statistic "dbwr free low" indicates the number of times that DBWR was invoked because the server process found the specified number of dirty buffers on the dirty buffer list (Figure 2.9).

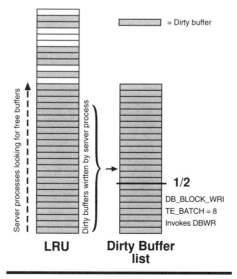

Figure 2.9 DB_BLOCK_WRITE_BATCH.

Some operating systems allow multiple DBWR processes. The number of DBWR processes created is specified by the value of the **init.ora** parameter DB_WRITER. If your operating system allows multiple DBWR processes, consider creating as many DBWR processes as there are disks on the system.

Log Writer—LGWR

LGWR writes data in the redo buffers to the redo log files on disk. LGWR will write the redo buffer to the on-line redo log for any of the following reasons:

- The redo buffers become one-third full.
- Three seconds have elapsed since the last write.
- A user commits a transaction.
- The DBWR has written dirty buffers to disk.

Checkpoint Process—CKPT

CKPT is an optional process that is used to transfer some work from LGWR during a checkpoint. When a checkpoint occurs, all the data file headers are updated with the number of the current redo log file. LGWR normally performs this task. Updating multiple files can slow LGWR down on systems with a lot of files. If this happens, enable CKPT by setting the **init.ora** parameter CHECKPOINT_PROCESS to TRUE.

Archiver—ARCH

ARCH is an optional process that writes the most recently filled on-line redo log to the archive log file destination. Archiver writes to a destination specified by the **init.ora** parameter ARCHIVE_LOG_DEST.

Process Monitor—PMON

PMON monitors individual user processes connected to the database. If a user process fails, PMON will release locks, remove the user from any active process lists, reset the status of its active transactions, and clean up buffers used by the failed process.

Occasionally, a user may simply turn off his or her client machine before logging off Oracle. In some cases, PMON may not detect the disconnect, which can cause problems especially when trying to shut down the database. These are often referred to as *hung processes*, and they must be isolated and killed (a strong word perhaps, but **KILL** is the UNIX command used to get rid of unwanted processes) from the operating system level.

System Monitor—SMON

SMON monitors the various processes associated with the database. It performs instance recovery on startup and cleans up, or coalesces, adjacent free extents to make larger blocks of free space available. SMON also manages the temporary segments.

With Oracle Parallel Server, SMON can recover an instance on another node in case of an instance or CPU failure.

There are additional background processes that depend on the configuration you are using. These include but are not limited to:

- Multithreaded Server—Snnn: When running as a multithreaded server, there will be multiple MTS processes running. Each of these shared servers can be used by more than one user process.

- SQL*Net V2 Listener—KMNLIS: The SQL*Net listener process runs to support the MTS. The listener listens for user processes trying to connect over the network. When they send a request, KMNLIS will either route them to a dispatcher or create a dedicated server process for them.

- Dispatcher—Dnnn: The dispatcher is used when Oracle in running in a multithreaded mode. It allows user processes to share a limited number of server processes by routing requests to available server processes via the request queue and the response queue.

- Recoverer—RECO: The Recoverer process is used to recover transactions that failed in a distributed environment.

- Lock—LCKn: LCKn is used with the Oracle Parallel Server to control distributed locks.

There are a variety of other processes that depend on the network drivers available and used on your platform.

Database

An Oracle *database* is a set of physical files used to store data. Each Oracle database has a name. Oracle has logical structures, which are used to group objects within the physical files. Some of the logical objects, like tables, primary keys, and foreign keys, relate to the conceptual schema. Other logical objects, like views, relate to the external schema. Some of the logical objects, like tablespaces, indexes, clusters, segments, and extents, relate to the internal schema, as they define how data is stored and accessed. These logical objects will be discussed in more detail later.

In a physical database design context, a *database* is a collection of physical files. These files contain user data and information about the database. An Oracle database is made up of the following types of files:

- One or more data files
- One or more control files
- Two or more redo log files
- An initialization (init.ora) file

There are several other type of files that may also appear with an Oracle installation:

- One or more trace/alert files
- Archive log files
- Export files
- Load files
- Backup files
- Dump files

Files

The following is a detailed description of the different files that are used in an Oracle environment. This section presents what they are and how they are used. Chapter 5 covers how to organize, size, and place the various kinds of files. An important reason to mention them all here is to be sure that you consider the space and maintenance requirements of each type during database design and operations. Consider this another list of ingredients in the database recipe.

Data Files

These files contain the user's data and Oracle's data dictionary. This data includes tables, indexes, and clusters. The data files are the catch-all; they make up the major portion of any Oracle database. The other types of files support specific types of database operations, while the data files hold data.

Redo Log Files

The redo log files are often referred to as the on-line redo log files or on-line redo logs, and sometimes simply as the redo logs. The term *online* is used to distinguish these files from the archive log files.

These redo logs contain any and all of the database changes that were written from the redo log buffers by the log writer process, LGWR. The data files contain the latest image of the database's data, while the log files contain all the changes that have been made to that data over some period of time. In fact, between the on-line redo logs and the archive redo logs, you can log and keep a record of every change to the database since the last database backup.

In the event of a crash, go to your last set of backup tapes and write them to disk. You now have an image of the database at the time of the last backup. What do you do about the ten hours of work that have occurred since the last backup? Go to your redo logs and begin to apply all those changes recorded in them. You basically rebuild all the work performed since the last backup through the transactions recorded in the redo log. If you were running your database in ARCHIVELOG mode, you can recover from the last backup to the last committed transaction before the system crashed.

ARCHIVELOG mode enables the archiver process and automatically makes copies of the on-line redo log files before they are overwritten by the LGWR. Archiver is covered in detail in Chapter 4.

Every Oracle database must have at least two online redo logs. LGWR writes to the redo logs in a circular fashion. Each redo log file (and each archieve log file) is identified with a *log sequence number*. When a redo log fills, LGWR writes to the next redo log. When that redo log file fills, LGWR writes to the next redo log (Figure 2.10). When the last redo log fills, LGWR writes to the first redo log. If there were only two redo logs, then LGWR would write to the first redo log when the second redo log in the rotation fills. If there are three redo logs, LGWR writes to the first redo log when the third redo log in the rotation fills. The change from one redo log to another is called a *log switch*.

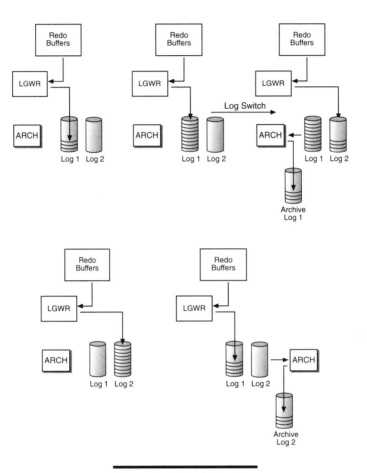

Figure 2.10 Redo log files.

All redo logs should be the same size. The size of the redo logs directly affects how much data might be lost in the event of certain types of crashes and how long a recovery might take.

To increase database safety, Oracle can *mirror* the on-line redo logs. This means that redo information is simultaneously written to two or more different files. These mirrored redo log files are called *redo log groups*, and each redo log file in the group is called a *member*. Members of each log group should be stored on different disks. Figure 2.11 shows redo data being written to mirrored redo log files.

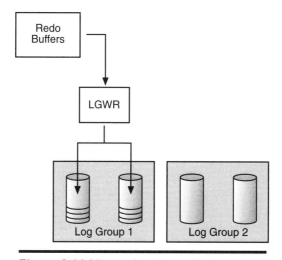

Figure 2.11 Mirrored on-line redo log groups.

The redo logs should not be stored on any disk that contains data because the redo logs contain the data that would be used to recover a database. If a data file were on the same disk as a nonmirrored redo log file and the files were lost because the disk failed, the data could not be recovered; the data is gone, and so is the redo information. When mirrored redo logs are stored away from data files, your system could lose two disk drives and still be recovered.

The preceding paragraph touches on one of the main criteria used to judge good database design. For most production systems, I believe safety of the data is one of the most important design factors. If you cannot recover your database, your organization is basically out of business (at least temporarily) and you may lose hundreds, if not thousands, of transactions, in addition to dollars. In order to prevent, or at least reduce, the chances of this kind of loss, redo logs and certain data files must be kept separate.

If data files and the redo logs should be separated, an Oracle system should have at least two disks. If we are mirroring the redo logs, that is, we have two redo log files in each group, we need at least three disks—one for data files and two for the log groups.

Since the new logs contain all of the changes for all of the data files, this makes the redo logs some of the most active files in a database system.

The activity and critical nature of the redo logs requires special attention when laying out the location of the physical files for the database. These issues and discussed in more detail in Chapter 5.

init.ora File

This is a file that lists the operating parameters for an instance. Among other things, it specifies how much memory to allocate to different buffer caches and therefore, it controls how large the SGA will be when the database starts. The file is read by Oracle whenever an instance is started, and changes to the file only take effect at startup.

There may be several **init.ora** files that are used to operate the database under different conditions. For example, one **init.ora** file may be used to support on-line data entry during the day, while another is used to support overnight reporting.

Not all parameters are valid for all machines or operating systems. Individual initialization parameters are detailed in Appendix B.

Control Files

Control files contain a list of all of the database files and redo log files and the current log sequence number. At least one control file is created with the **CREATE DATABASE** command. If Oracle cannot access the first control file listed in the **init.ora** file on startup, it will not come up. If Oracle is unable to access any of the control files specified in the **init.ora** file during operations, the instance will continue to run, but the database should be shutdown and the damaged file replaced with one of the other control files.

Every database should have multiple copies of the control file residing on different disks. The easiest way to do this is to specify multiple control files in the **init.ora** file used to create the database. The name and location of the control files are specified with the **init.ora** parameter CONTROL_FILES. These files are small and are accessed during checkpoints and operations that affect data files, such as addung or renaming files .

Oracle matches the log sequence number in the control file with the redo logs and data files to determine whether the database needs recovery.

Archive Log Files

The archive log files are created when the database is in ARCHIVELOG mode. These files may be used in conjunction with the on-line redo logs to recover the database in case of a disk crash or system failure. The archive logs are copies of the online redo logs that are created whenever there is a log switch. The archiver process (ARCH) works with LGWR to copy the redo logs once they are filled.

Because the archive logs contain data that is needed to recover the database, they should not be stored on any disk that contains data files. The location of these files is specified with the **init.ora** parameter LOG_ARCHIVE_DEST. (How many disks do we need if the redo logs are mirrored (Figure 2.12)? To support archiving while protecting the data files, four disks would be needed to keep the information separate; at least one active for data, two actives for the mirrored redo logs, and one active for the archival log files.)

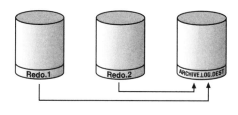

Figure 2.12 Redo log switch.

Trace, Alert, and Dump Files

Oracle writes information about certain activities or events to trace, log, and dump files. These files do not contain any user data; they are strictly information about the operations in the database. The background processes write the trace files. These files represent the DBA's "console" for each Oracle instance. The location of these files is specified by several **init.ora** parameters.

The alert log records a continuous stream of database events. Some entries in the alert log, such as errors, reference specific trace files. The trace files contain information about discreet events. If you are having problems with your database, check these files for error messages.

It is important to note that this information is available, but these files will grow until someone cleans them up. Some of the information will be of interest to the system's DBA, while other information is necessary to help Oracle support when reporting problems. I have seen directories containing more than 200MB of these files. Some of the files were more than two years old and not of much use, but no one had told the client they needed to clean up or delete these files. It is important to periodically review and delete the contents of the alert log and the trace files, lest they fill up your hard disk.

Backup, Export, and Load Files

In addition to the files listed above that are used or created in the day-to-day operation of the database, there are several other files that you need to be aware of and save room for in your database design.

For the sake of speed, many shops back up files to another disk on the system, rather than out to tape. If you plan to back up to disk, you need to save room for the backed up files.

Exports are a type of backup that include not only data, but definitions of the database as well. If you plan on performing exports you will need to plan for the space.

Many databases replace "legacy" systems, and begin their operations with data extracted from these systems. In addition, many systems are updated on a regular basis from other systems, or sources. Be sure to save space for staging the data loads. Figure 2.13 reviews the components of the Oracle database and instance.

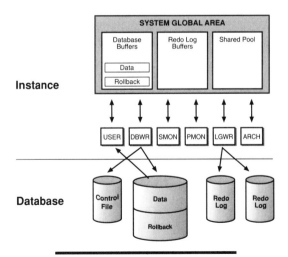

Figure 2.13 Oracle components.

Logical structures

While the files physically store data on disks, logical structures are used to define the structures and grouping of that data. The relationships between some of the structures is illustrated in Figure 2.14.

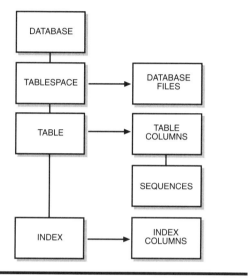

Figure 2.14 Physical and logical object relationships.

Schema Objects

At this point, the word *schema* requires some clarification. Chapter 1 covered the three-schema architecture, which described an information architecture. Oracle uses the term schema in two ways. There is a *schema* that a user can create with the **CREATE SCHEMA** command. This kind of schema must have the same name as the user creating the schema. The Oracle schema is used primarily to create the objects in a single command set and to allow grants to all the objects (the tables and indexes) in a schema to other users as a group, rather than having to perform grants for individual objects in the schema.

Schema objects are logical structures that relate or refer to data or certain PL/SQL code in the database. Schema objects are the internal schema representation of the conceptual schema objects and rules. Using triggers, procedures, and packages (which are covered later in this chapter), you can also implement certain external schema functionalities. Schema objects are also objects that you can grant/control access to when you create users and roles.

The various schema objects are covered below.

Tables

The table is the basic logical storage structure for user data. It is a two-dimensional table made up of rows and columns. Every table has a name and an owner. The *owner* is the user who created the table.

While Oracle can implement the rules of the relational model, it does not require them. Oracle does not require primary or foreign keys on tables. Without primary keys or unique constraints you can have duplicate rows in tables. There are sometimes legitimate reasons to build "nonrelational" tables, such as temporary tables that hold result sets used for reporting. Upgrading from an Oracle version 6 database may be another good reason. If you are building a new system you should use all the database power at hand including primary and foreign keys, and the other constraints, discussed here.

Indexes

An *index* is a structure created on one or more columns of a table used to improve retrieval performance, ensure uniqueness, or sort/order data.

Indexes store each distinct value for the column or columns being indexed, and the ROWID of the row or rows that contain those values. The ROWID (which is covered in more detail later in this chapter) is the physical address of the actual row in the table. Rather than scan an entire table looking for a particular value, an index can be searched to locate the value and ROWID or address of the row in the table. Once Oracle gets the ROWID from the index, it can then directly get the row from the table.

Index value	ROWID/Address
667	00000107.0000.0002
668	00000107.0001.0002
669	00000107.0002.0002
670	00000107.0003.0002
671	00000107.0004.0002

Figure 2.15. Index with ROWIDs.

Clusters

Clusters are structures that allow you additional control of how data is physically stored on the disk and accessed. There are two types of clusters available in Oracle. There are *hash clusters* and *indexed clusters*. Both types can be used to group tables that share one or more columns.

Clusters store data based on cluster keys. A *cluster key* is one or more columns from one or more tables. The cluster key in a hash cluster is used to physically place and locate data using a hashing function rather than an index. The cluster key of an indexed cluster must have an index created for the cluster key.

When there are two or more tables in a cluster, the rows for each table with the same cluster key value are stored together on the disk, usually in the same data block. Grouping the rows together effectively creates a stored join because all the rows with the same cluster key value are stored together on the disk. Each table in the cluster must share one or more columns, and these common columns make up the *cluster key* for the cluster. These multitable clusters can be indexed or hashed clusters.

Hash and indexed clusters are each described in detail here, but in general both types of clusters work well under the following circumstances:

- The tables are stable—the cluster key values are seldom updated.
- Where there are multiple tables in the cluster, there is a master-detail relationship between tables. A master-detail relationship typically involves two tables that have a one-to-many relationship. The SALES_ORDER and ITEM tables represent a master-detail relationship. For every order, there are many items, and the ORDID column appears in both tables.
- Where there are multiple tables in the cluster, the tables are predominately accessed as a group.
- The number of rows in the relationship is well known and finite. For our SALES_ORDERS we should know that there are usually five items per order and seldom more than ten.
- All the rows for a given cluster key value (whether a single table or multiple tables as in the master-detail relationship) fit into one or two data blocks.

Clusters do not work well in the following circumstances:

- The cluster key values of the cluster require updates.

- Where there are multiple tables in the cluster, one of the tables is frequently accessed by full table scans.

- You have not read the Oracle manuals in detail and therefore do not know how to perform the calculations necessary to build a cluster. Clusters are not for the uninformed or faint of heart. I do not intend to repeat all the formulas and syntax for clusters (consult the Oracle manuals).

Hash Clusters

To understand hash clusters you need to understand equality tests and hashing functions. The following query will serve as our example to illustrate these points:

```
SELECT *
FROM SALES_ORDER
WHERE ORDID = 1111
```

The WHERE clause of a SQL statement uses comparison operators to compare one expression, or one value to another. In this example, we are asking the database to compare the values for ORDID in the SALES_ORDER table to the number 1111. That is, show us any rows from the SALES_ORDER table where the ORDID is equal to 1111. When a WHERE clause uses an equal sign (=), it is called an *equality test*.

Consider the SALES_ORDER table if it were built as a "normal" table with the ORDID as the primary key. (Remember that a primary key also has an index associated with it.) If we issued the preceding query, Oracle would search the primary key index for ORDID 1111. If the number were found, Oracle would use the ROWID retrieved from the index to perform the read of the data block for that sales order. At a minimum, there are two I/Os performed to retrieve a single row—one I/O to the index to get the ROWID and another to get the row from the table.

Instead of using indexes to find data, Oracle can use *hashing functions* (sometimes called *hashing algorithms*) to place and locate data on the disk. The input to the hashing function is the value for the cluster key of the hash cluster. The output of the hash function is a file number and a data block number (two thirds of a *ROWID*), which is an address used to place or find the row on the disk. Because Oracle can get the address of the row by hashing the cluster key value, it does not need to perform the extra I/O to an index to locate the row.

Figure 2.16 How hashing really works.

To read the row from the disk, the cluster key value is input to the hash function and the address is again returned, allowing the database to directly access the data block that contains the row. With a hash cluster, rows are read from and written to the disk using a hash function rather than an index where there is an equality join.

Figure 2.17 shows the creation of the cluster, and Figure 2.18 shows the SALES_ORDER table added to the cluster.

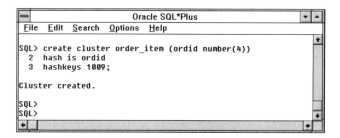

Figure 2.17 **CREATE CLUSTER** command.

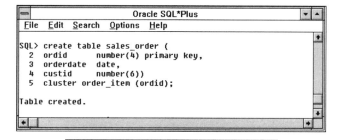

Figure 2.18 Adding a table to a cluster.

Hash clusters work best where:

- The table or tables are accessed with an equality test (=).
- You know how many records will be in the table so the cluster can be sized properly.
- If the cluster is for a single table, the cluster key is the primary key of the table.
- If the cluster is for master-detail relationships, the cluster key is the primary key of the master table.

Hash clusters do not work well where:

- There are any table scans on the table or tables in the cluster.
- Space is limited on the disks.

Indexed Clusters

Hashed cluster works best where data is accessed by the primary key column(s), and indexed clusters work well where the cluster key has multiple rows for each cluster key value. Where the hashed cluster used the cluster key to place and locate rows, the indexed cluster uses the cluster key to group rows.

Before data is added to the indexed cluster, an index must be created on the cluster key. Creating the index for the cluster is slightly different from creating a "normal" index. Instead of specifying the table and columns for the index, you simply specify the cluster name as follows:

```
CREATE INDEX index_name ON CLUSTER cluster_name
```

You will not be able to create a cluster index for a hashed cluster.

If a single table is often accessed by a column(s), other than the primary key column(s), you can create an indexed cluster to physically group the rows of the table. This is helpful for queries or applications that process the data by the cluster key. If employees were often processed by their department number, then create a cluster for the employee table with the department number as the cluster key. The rows of the employee table would be physically clustered or stored together, based on their department number. A query that requested the employees would see the rows returned grouped by their departments.

Indexed clusters work best where the cluster key is not the primary key or is only part of a primary key. Index clusters do not work well where one of the tables in the master-detail relationship is accessed often using full table scans. Index clusters are significantly more complex than hash clusters to size, build, and populate.

Sequences

Sequences, or *sequence generators*, are Oracle-supplied counters that can be used to generate numbers for items like invoice numbers or customer numbers. They are best suited for blind keys where there is no meaning intended or implied to the value of the key, other than it be unique.

A single sequence supply values used for more than one table, and its definitions and values are stored in the data dictionary.

Figure 2.19 shows a sequence that will create numbers that start with 1000, increment by 1, and continue until 1,000,000. If the MAXVALUE is not specified, the sequence will count up to 10^{27}, which is a very large number. The CACHE parameter tells Oracle to generate 50 numbers at a time and keep them in memory. With the numbers in memory, applications have almost instantaneous access to the next value. When all 50 numbers are used, Oracle will generate another fifty numbers.

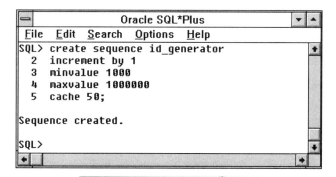

Figure 2.1 9 CREATE sequence.

There is a CYCLE option that allows the sequence to start over again when the MAXVALUE is reached. This option should not be used for any primary keys that have only one column. It could be used for part of a compound key such as in a master-detail relationship where you know the master table part of the key must be unique, as in the following example (Figure 2.20). This example will also show one of the limits of sequences.

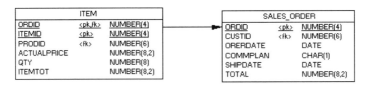

Figure 2.20 Master-detail relationship.

SALES_ORDER and ITEM make up a master-detail relationship, with SALES_ORDER the master table. For every SALES_ORDER there can be multiple ITEMS. The ITEM table really represents line items on an invoice, and the column ITEMID can be thought of as a line number. By using the ITEMID instead of the PRODID as part of the primary key, the same product can appear multiple times on an invoice, perhaps as an add-on with a different ACTUALPRICE.

If you wanted your ITEMID to begin with the number 1 for each new invoice, you cannot use a sequence. There is no practical way to restart a sequence for each user's needs. If, however, it did not matter what the value of ITEMID number was, then a sequence could be used when adding new line items. Further, because the ORDID must always be unique (it's the primary key of the SALES_ORDER table) you could CYCLE the numbers of the ITEMID and not have to worry about duplicates.

There are two **init.ora** parameters that affect sequences, SEQUENCE_CACHE_ENTRIES and SEQUENCE_CACHE_HASH_BUCKETS. These are parameters covered in Appendix B.

Views

A *view* is an object that lets us look at one or more tables as if it were a table in its own right. Views are one way to create the external schema, or user views, of the entire database (Figure 2.21). The view provides the mapping from the external schema to the internal schema. Views can also insulate programmers and users from database changes. If a table should change, the view, rather than the application code, can be modified.

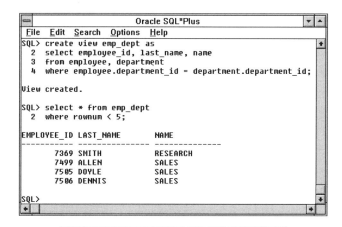

Figure 2.21 Create and select from view.

Views are also used to limit access to columns and rows in tables. The section on security illustrates how to limit row access based on a user's Oracle user name.

Program Units

Various types of program units can be stored in the database. These include triggers, user-defined functions, procedures, packages, and package bodies.

Program units are written in PL/SQL which is Oracle's procedural language extension to SQL. PL/SQL not only adds control logic to SQL, you can also develop error messages and routines. Think of them as little applications that are stored in the database.

Triggers are associated with a specific table and "fire" before or after predefined events, such as an insert, update, or delete of one or more rows in the table. The following trigger would not allow negative numbers to be added in the ITEMTOT of an invoice line. If the user did try to add a negative number, the trigger would return an error message.

```
CREATE TRIGGER check_itemtot
BEFORE UPDATE OF itemtot ON item
BEGIN
IF (:new.itemtot < 0) THEN
raise_application_error(-20225, 'Price cannot be <0');
END;
```

Where a table has one or more triggers, users or applications that access the table do not to explicitly reference or call the trigger. The triggers fire based on events that affect the table and are transparent to the users.

Procedures are also PL/SQL applications that are stored in the database, but they must be explicitly referenced by a user or application. The following code creates a procedure that would insert data into the DEPT table as long as there was not an existing value.

```
CREATE PROCEDURE add_dept
(new_deptno number, new_dname char, new_loc char) IS
BEGIN
INSERT INTO DEPT (deptno, dname, loc)
VALUES (new_deptno, new_dname, new_loc)
IF SQL%FOUND THEN
raise_application_error(-20226, 'Department exists');
ENDIF;
END;
```

Where a trigger fires automatically, a procedure must be called with an EXECUTE command. The following code would insert data into the DEPT table using the procedure above.

```
EXECUTE add_dept (1234,'NE Sales','Boston')
```

Packages are sets of one or more procedures that are grouped together. User defined functions allow users to create their own functions, in addition to those already provided by Oracle. A function is usually used to perform some sort of calculation or conversion of a number or text string.

In Chapter 1 I spoke of database programming; shifting development effort from the applications to the database. The program units provide the primary tools for doing that. For example, rather than have each application program include the SQL code to perform inserts into the database, procedures (such as the one above) chould be developed and simply executed by the program. Note that the procedure above is also providing error checking, which could also be eliminated form the application.

A detailed discussion of database programming is the topic of a future book and well beyond the scope of this text. Program units have a much greater impact on application design and development than on the actual database design.

Synonym

Synonyms are used to reference various objects in the database, such as tables, sequences, views, or program units. A synonym is an alias for an object. They can be used to limit or provide access to these objects, even across databases. Synonyms are especially useful when creating database links so that a user can actually access an object in a remote database.

A synonym can be either public or private. Public synonyms are usually used to grant access to an object to all users, the public. This eliminates the need for one user to have to prefix the owner's name of an object when accessing an object owned by another user. Figure 2.22 shows the user HARRY trying to access the table SALARY_GRADE which is owned by user SCOTT. HARRY cannot access the table unless he prefixes the table name with SCOTT.

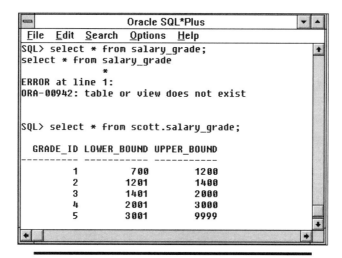

```
                          Oracle SQL*Plus
 File   Edit   Search   Options   Help
SQL> select * from salary_grade;
select * from salary_grade
                   *
ERROR at line 1:
ORA-00942: table or view does not exist


SQL> select * from scott.salary_grade;

  GRADE_ID LOWER_BOUND UPPER_BOUND
---------- ----------- -----------
         1         700        1200
         2        1201        1400
         3        1401        2000
         4        2001        3000
         5        3001        9999
```

Figure 2.22 SELECT on a table without a synonym.

Figure 2.23 illustrates a public synonym created by user SCOTT on the table SALARY_GRADE. Once the synonym is created the user HARRY can access the data without having to prefix SCOTT's name to the table. Note that the name of the synonym is different from the table name.

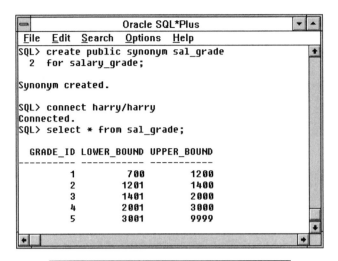

Figure 2.23 SELECT on a table with an alias.

Synonyms cannot be used like views to limit access to particular rows or columns. When you reference a synonym, you are basically accessing the table, although synonyms can have different privileges than the underlying table.

Database Links

Users or applications need not be confined to a single database in an Oracle environment. Database links are a way to point to other databases. Figure 2. 24 shows a database link that is created to connect two databases. The link is named, along with a username and password and a connect string. The link could be called humpty.dumpty but you will find it quite useful to use the global database naming conventions supported by Oracle.

Figure 2. 25 shows a query that is accessing data from the table PRODUCT on the remote database.

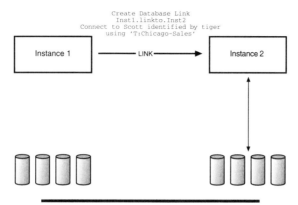

Figure 2.24 CREATE DATABASE LINK.

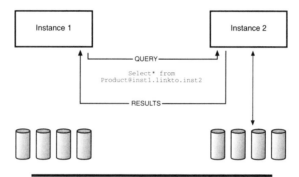

Figure 2.25 Query from a remote database.

Tablespaces

A database is made up of one or more tablespaces, and each *tablespace* is made up of one or more data files. Tablespaces are the mechanism or the means by which logical objects, such as tables and indexes are mapped or placed in the required files. Tablespaces are also used to logically group different types of database objects.

The sum of all the data files allocated for a tablespace represents the total size, or total storage capacity, of a tablespace. The sum of all of the tablespaces represents the total size, or total storage capacity, of a database.

Besides grouping applications for a single application, tablespaces can be used to group objects from different applications. This may be done to support maintenance or backup strategies. A more detailed discussion about grouping and placing objects is in Chapter 5, Getting Down to Business.

The following are common tablespace types that should be included in most database design.

System

The system tablespace is created when a database is created. It contains the Oracle data dictionary, which includes definitions of all the objects in the database, and all the code for any program units. Except for the data dictionary and the system rollback segment(s), it should not contain anything else.

The size of the system tablespace depends on the number of objects defined in the data dictionary and the number and size of stored procedures, packages, and triggers.

Tables/Data

Separate tablespaces should be created to hold tables and clusters. Tables should not be combined with other objects like indexes or rollback segments. Another goal in designing an Oracle database is to spread I/O across disk drives and controllers. Since tablespaces are made up of one or more data files that, in turn, are placed on physical disks, you can control which disk will contain which objects by creating multiple tablespaces and placing their files on the appropriate drive.

Figure 2.26 illustrates multiple table in a single tablespace.

With multiple tablespaces and disk drives, I/O can be spread across the drives, thereby reducing contention during reads and writes. Your task will be to find those tables that are accessed most often and to try to isolate them on their own disks. Also, tables that are accessed together during operations, such as SALES_ORDER and CUSTOMER, should be separated.

A single table space can have multiple datafiles (Figure 2.27). This is done where a single table or index cannot fit on a single disk or to spread I/O on a single table across multiple drives.

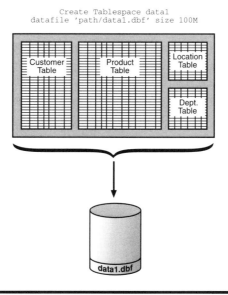

Figure 2.26 Multiple tables in a single tablespace.

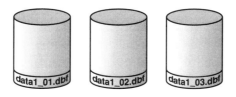

Figure 2.27 Multiple data files for a tablespace.

Indexes

Indexes should be separated from the tables they reference, so they should be placed in their own tablespace(s). Just as you try to separate tables into different tablespaces to spread I/O, indexes should be separated from their tables. If there are multiple indexes on a single table, you should try to separate them too.

Rollback

Plan to create one or more tablespaces for rollback segments. Rollback segments are very active on systems that perform a lot of INSERTs, UPDATEs, and DELETEs.

Temporary and User

The *temporary tablespace* is used by Oracle as a place for sorting data. Oracle will only point to the temporary tablespace if it is listed as part of a user definition.

If a user creates a table without specifying a tablespace, the table is placed in the users DEFAULT TABLESPACE. If there is no DEFAULT TABLESPACE for a user, the table is added to the system tablespace. The SQL statement in Figure 2.28 creates the user *james* and assigns him to a default and a temporary tablespace.

The temporary tablespace may also be subject to a lot of I/O if there are queries that perform sorts. If this is the case, then try to separate the temporary tablespace from both data and index tablespaces.

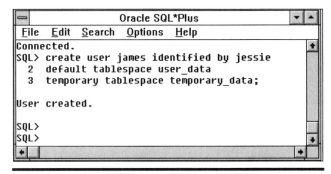

Figure 2.28 Default and temporary tablespaces for a user.

Product/Tools

Certain products, like SQL*Forms, create and use Oracle tables in building and maintaining applications. If any of the applications or products you intend to use create their own tables and indexes, consider placing them in their own tablespace(s).

Data Blocks

The information for the various schema objects is physically stored in areas on the disk called *blocks*. Oracle blocks are distinct from operating system blocks, and the sizes of the two kinds of blocks may differ. The operating system and Oracle perform I/O operations in these block units. Each block is identified by a file number and a block number within the file. Each Oracle row is numbered within the block. The combination of block number, row number, and file number (`block#.row#.file#`) is called the `ROWID`. (Figure 2.29 show the ROWID. for the row in the JOB table.)

The Oracle block size is established when the database is created. The only way to change the Oracle block size is to re-create the database. What this really means is that you cannot change the block size of an existing database. The block size is set with the **init.ora** parameter `DB_BLOCK_SIZE`. Changing this parameter after the database is created will have no effect on the database; Oracle does not even return an error if this is changed. After database creation, the parameter only serves as documentation.

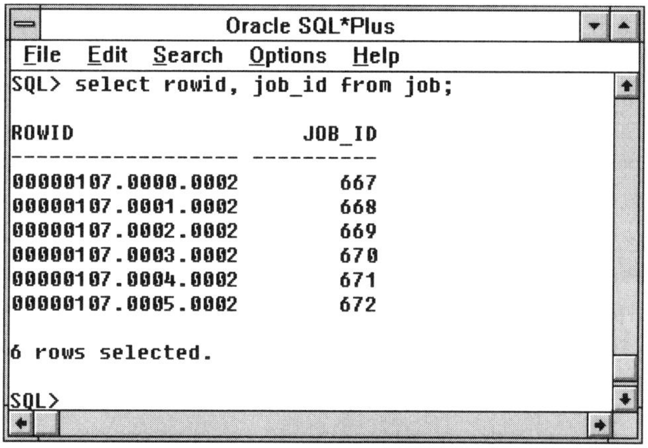

```
┌─────────────────────────────────────────────────────┐
│ ═  │            Oracle SQL*Plus              │ ▼ │ ▲ │
├─────────────────────────────────────────────────────┤
│  File   Edit   Search   Options   Help              │
│ SQL> select rowid, job_id from job;            │ ▲ │
│                                                      │
│ ROWID                    JOB_ID                      │
│ ------------------     ----------                    │
│ 00000107.0000.0002          667                      │
│ 00000107.0001.0002          668                      │
│ 00000107.0002.0002          669                      │
│ 00000107.0003.0002          670                      │
│ 00000107.0004.0002          671                      │
│ 00000107.0005.0002          672                      │
│                                                      │
│ 6 rows selected.                                     │
│                                                      │
│ SQL>                                           │ ▼ │
│ ◄                                          ►         │
└─────────────────────────────────────────────────────┘
```

Figure 2.29 ROWID .

The Oracle block size should be the same size as, or a multiple of, the operating system block size. The valid range of block sizes is platform-and operating system–specific, but generally runs from 512 to 32,768 bytes.

There is a limit of 16 million Oracle blocks for a given database. Figure 2.30 shows the maximum size of a database for a given block size.

Block size	Total database size in bytes
512	8,192,000,000
1024	16,384,000,000
2048	32,768,000,000
4096	65,536,000,000
8192	131,072,000,000
16384	262,144,000,000
32768	524,288,000,000

Figure 2.30 Database size limits.

The Oracle block size not only affects the maximum size of a database, it also affects the amount of data you can store in your database and retrieve with a single I/O. In addition to data, each block contains header information that describes what is in the block. There is a fixed and a variable portion in this header, but it typically ranges from 83 to 120 bytes, depending on the number of columns in the index or table stored in the block and the value for INITRANS, discussed later. This means a 2K block has between 1965 and 1928 bytes available to store data. If a row were 100 bytes long, then about 19 rows could fit into the 2K block. An 8K block would have between 8109 and 8072 bytes available to store data. With the 100-byte row, about 80 rows could fit into the 8K block. Multiply the number of rows in the 2K block by 4 and we see that the 2K blocks can only store 76 rows, 4 fewer than a single 8K block. This means four because of the block header space, it will take more 2K blocks to store the same number of rows than an 8K block size. For large databases, the difference may be significant.

With a 2K block size, a table that averaged 82 bytes per row would result in the total table sizes shown in Figure 2.31.

Space per block	1948			
Number of rows	Average row size	Rows per block	Total 2K blocks	Table size
100,000	82	24	4,209	8,620,945
500,000	82	24	21,047	43,104,723
1,000,000	82	24	42,094	86,209,446
5,000,000	82	24	210,472	431,047,228
10,000,000	82	24	420,945	862,094,456
100,000,000	82	24	4,209,446	8,620,944,559
200,000,000	82	24	8,418,891	17,241,889,117

Figure 2.31 Tables with a 2k block size.

The table sizes that result from a 16K block size are shown in Figure 2.32.

Block size	16384			
Space per block	16284			
Number of rows	Average row size	Rows per block	Total 8K blocks	Table size
100,000	82	199	504	8,250,356
500,000	82	199	2,518	41,251,781
1,000,000	82	199	5,036	82,503,562
5,000,000	82	199	25,178	412,517,809
10,000,000	82	199	50,356	825,035,618
100,000,000	82	199	503,562	8,250,356,178
200,000,000	82	199	1,007,124	16,500,712,356

Figure 2.32 Tables with an 8K block size.

For 200 million rows, the 16K block size results in more than 700 megabytes, or about a 4.5% savings in space, which may or may not be significant for you.

Extents

An *extent* is a contiguous set of Oracle blocks. Each extent can only contain data associated with a single object. Extents are the units used to define the size of an object. Sizing objects is covered in Chapter 5.

The Oracle block size determines the total number of extents that can be allocated for an object. The Table in Figure 2.33 gives the maximum number of extents for each object that can be created for a given block size. These maximum values have priority over the MAXEXTENTS parameter specified in a STORAGE clause.

Oracle block size	Number of extents
512 bytes	25
1K	57
2K	121
4K	249
8K	505
16K	1017

Figure 2.33 Maximum extents for a given block size.

Segments

A *segment* is a set of one or more extents allocated for a particular object. Segments are created for the followingtypes of objects:

- Data—tables and clusters
- Index
- Rollback
- Temporary

Segments are never specified as part of any DDL or DML, and they are transparent to the users. Segments are, however, used by Oracle to control space allocation and usage. The data dictionary view, DBA_SEGMENTS shows details about how much space each segment is using, among other things.

Oracle uses rollback segments to perform some special functions. Oracle does not simply modify data in the database when requested to do so. Before any data is changed, a copy of the data is written to a rollback segment. This copy of the data is called a *before image*. The rollback segments contain the before images of any data that is modified.

No changes are permanently made to the database until a user *commits* the transaction. If the user modifies data but decides not to commit the changes to the database, the changes that were made must be *rolled back* to the image of the data before the transaction began. If a transaction fails before it reaches a commit point, the data must also be rolled back. If a change is not committed, the before image can be copied from the rollback segment to restore the data to its original state.

When a transaction does commit the data, the rollback segment is freed for use by other transactions. A transaction can only use a single rollback segment. There should be one rollback segment for every four concurrent users.

Rollback segments also provide a *read-consistent image* for transactions that are trying to read rows that may be updated by other transactions. If a long transaction is reading data that has been changed since the transaction started, Oracle uses the data in the rollback segment to get the image of the data as of when the transaction started.

There are public and private rollback segments. Private rollback segments are acquired by an instance on startup. Private rollback segments are specified in the ROLLBACK_SEGMENTS in the **init.ora** file and cannot be used by any other instance. Each instance should specify every rollback segment it is going to use in the init.ora file. Public rollback segments form a pool of rollback segments from which several instances can acquire the necessary rollback segments.

To control your environment, always use private rollback segments. In an OPS environment you may want to create several public rollback segments in case an instance needs one during operation. If one of the instances does acquire a public rollback segment, consider adding additional private rollback segments for that instance.

DataTypes

Every column in a table must be assigned a data ype. The datatype determines the types of characters that can be entered into the column. The two major distinctions are between columns that allow only numeric data, and those that can accept alphabetic as well as numeric data. In addition to these two datatypes, Oracle can accept binary data in certain types of columns.

Character

A *character* datatype is a fixed-length field that accepts alphanumeric characters. When a column is specified with a character data type, that column will always take up as much space as the length of the column, whether or not there is any data in the column. For example, if a column were created as CHARACTER(10), ten spaces would always be stored in the database, even if there were only three characters in the column. Character columns can store up to 255 bytes of data.

VARCHAR2

A *VARCHAR2* data type stores data in variable-length fields. This kind of datatype can store up to 2000 characters. When a column is specified as VARCHAR2, the column will only take up as much space as the data in the column. If a column were specified as VARCHAR2(60) but there were only ten characters in the column, only ten characters would be used in the database.

Oracle will accept columns that are specified as just VARCHAR in DDL. It will, however, convert those fields to its VARCHAR2 data type as illustrated in Figure 2.34.

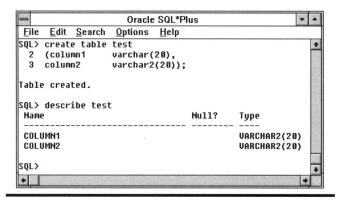

Figure 2.34 VARCHAR-to-VARCHAR2 data type conversion.

Number

NUMBER fields only accept numeric data. A NUMBER column can accept positive and negative numbers and floating-point numbers between 1.0×10^{-130} and $9.9...9 \times 10^{125}$. These are really small and really big numbers. If no length is specified, Oracle can store up to 38 digits of precision. It will, however, only use as much room as it needs to store a number.

Oracle will translate INTEGER fields to NUMBER fields, but you cannot specify a length for the integer field. Figure 2.35 illustrates the error generated when trying to specify the size of an integer field and how Oracle translates an integer into a number field. The integer has a precision of 38 and no scale value.

Oracle does support the use of the word FLOAT in specifying numeric columns.

Numeric fields can be specified with precision and scale. *Precision* is the total number of digits allowed in the column. *Scale* is the total number of digits to the right of the decimal place. If a precision is specified without a scale, the column will accept only integers. Precision in Oracle is not the number of digits to the left of the decimal place, as illustrated in Figure 2.36.

Refer to the specific Oracle programming guides if you need more information on how to handle numeric conversions such as SMALLINT or other data types that are used in different programming languages.

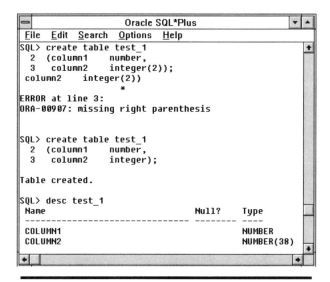

Figure 2.35 Integer-to-number data type conversions.

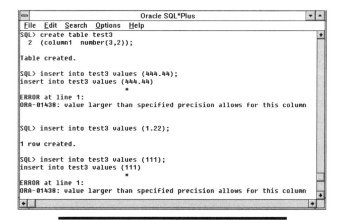

Figure 2.36 Precision and scale in Oracle.

Date

Oracle has a DATE datatype that can store and manipulate dates in a variety of ways. If specified, it will store times up to one-hundredth of a second. These is no specific time data type. There are numerous date functions to handle date conversion, display, and math.

The function SYSDATE returns the current system date and time, as illustrated in Figure 2.37. The first select shows the default date display, while the second shows the full date and time in a different format.

```
┌─────────────────── Oracle SQL*Plus ──────────────────▼│▲─┐
│ File  Edit  Search  Options  Help                          │
│ SQL> select sysdate from dual;                           ▲ │
│                                                            │
│ SYSDATE                                                    │
│ ---------                                                  │
│ 24-JUL-95                                                  │
│                                                            │
│ SQL> select to_char(sysdate, 'mm/dd/yy hh:mi:ss') from dual;│
│                                                            │
│ TO_CHAR(SYSDATE,'MM/DD/YYHH:MI:SS')                        │
│ ---------------------------------------------------------  │
│ 07/24/95 10:14:42                                        ▼ │
│ ◆│                                                      ▶  │
└────────────────────────────────────────────────────────────┘
```

Figure 2.37 SYSDATE function.

NOTE

Figure 2.37 illustrates an interesting little table in Oracle, DUAL. DUAL is a table that has one column and one row. It is created whenever a database is created, and it is owned by users SYS but is accessible to all users.

Certain functions like SYSDATE, USER, and LENGTH, are used to show certain data or perform certain calculations or conversions. (See the *SQL Language Reference Manual* for full details.) But using these functions on a table with more than one row will return multiple results, as illustrated in Figure 2.38. Note how the select from DUAL returned one row, while the select from JOB returned multiple rows. DUAL guarantees that only one row is returned.

DUAL can even be used to perform math calculations, as illustrated in Figure 2.39. Note how performing the same calculations on a regular table returns multiple rows.

DUAL is often used by programmers to gather certain system information or other functions. We will see more practical applications for DUAL when we cover security in Chapter 5.

Oracle SQL*Plus
File Edit Search Options Help
SQL> select user from dual;
USER

SCOTT
SQL> select user from job;
USER

SCOTT
SCOTT
SCOTT
SCOTT
SCOTT
SCOTT
6 rows selected.

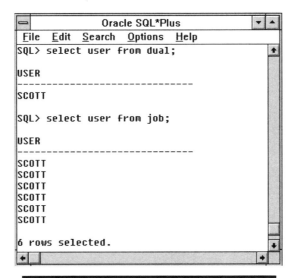

Figure 2.38 Selects using functions and DUAL.

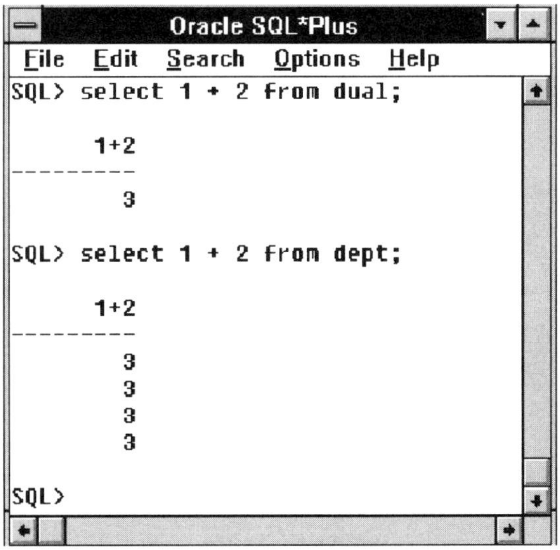

Oracle SQL*Plus
File Edit Search Options Help
SQL> select 1 + 2 from dual;
1+2

3
SQL> select 1 + 2 from dept;
1+2

3
3
3
3
SQL>

Figure 2.39 DUAL used for calculations.

Long

LONG columns can store up to 2 gigabytes of character data. There can be only one long column per table, and there are numerous other restrictions about how a long column is accessed and used with queries, constraints, indexes, and more.

Details for accessing/using LONG columns in applications is provided in the *Programmer's Guide to the Oracle Call Interface*.

Raw and Long Raw

RAW columns can store up to 255 bytes of binary data. LONG RAW columns can store up to 2 gigabytes of binary data. These types of columns can store graphics, scanned images, video, and sound.

LONG RAW columns have the same restrictions as LONG columns.

Pseudo Columns

Pseudo columns are columns that can be included in a SELECT (or other type of) statement but the values are not actually stored in the database. The value of the pseudo column are calculated or derived during statement processing.

As discussed with data blocks, the ROWID is a combination of the row's data block, the row number within the block, and the data files that contain the block.

WARNING

You cannot use ROWIDs for primary keys because Oracle will change the values without you knowing it. The ROWID can, nay, will change with table reorganizations, deletes, and inserts. I made this mistake during my first "experience" with Oracle.

The ROWNUM is a value that is calculated as rows are returned from a query. The first row returned from the database has a ROWNUM of 1, the next row returned has a ROWNUM of 2, and so on.

Figure 2.40 shows the ROWNUM, and ROWID returned from a select on the JOB table.

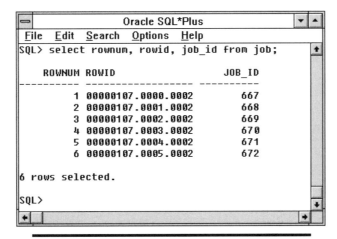

Figure 2.40 SELECT with ROWNUM and ROWID.

You can use ROWNUMs to limit the number of rows returned from a query. This limit is extremely helpful in testing queries or when you just want to see a sample of the data. You can use the ROWNUM to select, say, just the first three rows that would be returned from a query. You cannot use the ROWNUM to select a specific range of rows greater than a given number. These two scenarios are illustrated in Figure 2.41. The first query returns only the first three rows from the JOB table. The second does not return any rows because the ROWNUM always starts with 1, and in the example, Oracle never gets to 1, so it cannot return the rows greater than 2.

Two other pseudo columns are NEXTVAL and CURRVAL. These columns are used in conjunction with sequences. NEXTVAL is used to get the next number from a sequence. CURRVAL is used to show the current sequence value in use.

Both NEXTVAL and CURRVAL must be qualified by a sequence name. The SCOTT/TIGER database has three sequences that are used to generate primary key values for various tables. Figure 2.42 shows the sequences that are part of the SCOTT/TIGER database and then performs an insert using the PRODID sequence into the product table.

CURRVAL is used to support inserts into multiple table as in master detail relationships like an order table with its associated order line items. NEXTVAL could be used to create the order number, the CURRVAL would be used to insert the same order number into all the line items that are added for the order. Figure 2.43 shows how CURRVAL is picked up after the NEXTVAL.

```
┌─────────────────────────────────────────────────────┐
│ ─    │           Oracle SQL*Plus           │  ▼ │ ▲ │
├─────────────────────────────────────────────────────┤
│ File   Edit   Search   Options   Help               │
├─────────────────────────────────────────────────────┤
│SQL> select * from job                             │▲│
│  2   where rownum <= 3;                            │ │
│                                                     │ │
│     JOB_ID FUNCTION                                 │ │
│ ---------- ------------------------------           │ │
│        667 CLERK                                    │ │
│        668 STAFF                                    │ │
│        669 ANALYST                                  │ │
│                                                     │ │
│SQL> select * from job                             │ │
│  2   where rownum > 2;                             │ │
│                                                     │ │
│no rows selected                                     │ │
│                                                     │ │
│SQL>                                               │▼│
├─────────────────────────────────────────────────────┤
│ ◄ │                                             │ ► │
└─────────────────────────────────────────────────────┘
```

Figure 2.41 ROWNUM used to limit query results.

Figure 2.42 INSERT using NEXTVAL.

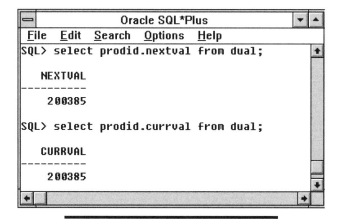

Figure 2.43 NEXTVAL and CURRVAL.

Constraints

For every table in a database, you can define constraints. *Constraints* can limit certain actions that can be performed and control the data that is inserted, updated, or deleted form the database. There are constraints to enforce referential and entity integrity as described in the section on the relational model, as well as several additional constraints to enforce business rules or edit criteria.

Constraints can be defined for individual columns in a table; these are called *column constraints*. Constraints that cover several columns must be defined at the table level and are called *table constraints*. You will see examples of both types. Constraints can be included as part of a CREATE TABLE statement, or they can be created and added to a table later with an ALTER TABLE command.

Refer to the section on naming standards in Chapter 9 for guidelines for naming constraints.

Primary Key

Just as in the relational model, primary key constraints enforce entity integrity. This rule states that all the columns in a primary key must be unique, and they cannot contain any nulls. You can only create one primary key per table.

Oracle primary keys create special indexes to enforce the uniqueness and not null requirements. Therefore, it is not necessary to declare a primary key column as not null because the primary key will make sure that all columns have values in them.

I prefer to create separate scripts for the primary and foreign key constraints. This eliminates any problems with indexes existing while trying to do data loads because loading a table with indexes on it can take longer than loading a table without indexes. Separate scripts also eliminate problems associated with the order in which table have to be created because a primary key must exist before a foreign key can reference it. Rather than add the constraints as part of the CREATE TABLE DDL, I use the ALTER TABLE command to add the constraints after the tables are created.

Figure 2.44 shows a primary key created for the SALES_ORDER table using an **ALTER TABLE** command. This example also shows use of the USING INDEX clause. With this clause, you can specify the tablespace for the index and add a storage clause for the index. (Storage clauses are covered in detail in Chapter 5.) The index name for this primary key is the same as the constraint name, SALES_ORDER_PK.

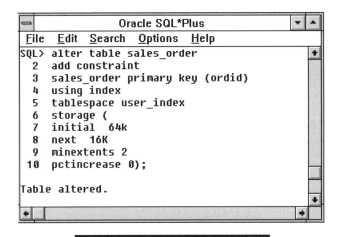

```
Oracle SQL*Plus
File  Edit  Search  Options  Help
SQL> alter table sales_order
  2  add constraint
  3  sales_order primary key (ordid)
  4  using index
  5  tablespace user_index
  6  storage (
  7  initial  64k
  8  next  16K
  9  minextents 2
 10  pctincrease 0);

Table altered.
```

Figure 2.44 Primary key constraint.

Foreign Key

Again, as in the relational model, foreign key constraints enforce referential integrity. This rule states that a foreign key value in a table must reference a primary key value in the table referenced by the foreign key. The SALES_ORDER table includes a column for the customer identifier. This CUSTID is a foreign key that points to the customer table. Figure 2.45 shows an ALTER TABLE constraint that adds the foreign key in SALES_ORDER that references the primary key of the CUST table.

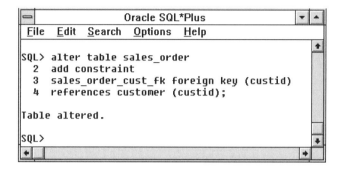

Figure 2.45 Foreign key constraint.

Oracle supports cascade and restrict delete integrity with the ON DELETE clause of the CONSTRAINT statement. These two types of delete integrity prevent "orphan" records in the database. An *orphan* record is a row in the database that has a foreign key that no longer references a valid primary key value. The child or children remain (the foreign key rows) but the parent is gone (the primary key row). Using delete constraints can prevent situations where SALES_ORDERS appear in the database (orphans) but there are no matching CUSTOMER records that indicate who the CUSTOMER is.

A restrict delete means that when a user wishes to delete a row in a table, Oracle will check to see if there are any foreign key references to that record. If references are found, Oracle will not allow the delete of the row. Oracle defaults to a restrict delete unless otherwise specified. In the preceding example, there was no ON DELETE CASCADE clause added to the foreign key. If a user tried to delete a CUSTOMER, Oracle would check the SALES_ORDER table for any orders for that CUSTOMER. If any SALES_ORDERS were found, Oracle would not allow the delete of the CUSTOMER.

Similar to a restrict delete, Oracle will not allow updates to primary key values if there are any foreign key rows for that value. You cannot cascade an update for a primary key to any of its foreign keys. A primary/foreign key update must be handled programmatically. Oracle will allow you to change a primary key if there are no foreign key values. Again using the preceding example, if a user tried to update a customer identifier, Oracle would check the SALES_ORDER table to see if any orders exist for that customer. If the customer had orders Oracle would not allow the update. If there were no orders for the customer, Oracle would allow a change to the customer identifier.

A *cascade delete* means that when a row is deleted in a table that is referenced by a foreign key, then all the rows that contain the foreign key will be deleted as well. For example, if a SALES_ORDER row is deleted then all of the ITEM records associated with the SALES_ORDER should be deleted. A cascade deleted is explicitly enforced by the constraint clause ON DELETE CASCADE. Figure 2.46 show a foreign key for the ITEM table that would perform such a cascade delete.

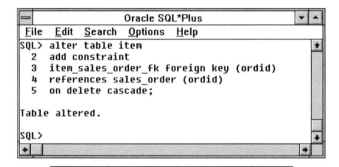

Figure 2.46 Foreign key with cascade delete.

Check

Check constraints are a powerful feature that is used to make sure that certain values are used when adding or updating data in a particular column of a table.

Figure 2.47 illustrates two check constraints. The check constraint on EMP_NAME prevents anyone from entering a name that is not entirely in uppercase letters. The second check constraint on the gender column shows how to validate values during inserts and updates.

The second check constraint shows how values for a specific column can be checked and validated during data entry. These kinds of check constraints are especially useful in eliminating the need for foreign key table lookups. Normally, a lookup table would be created for GENDER to validate the values M and F. A foreign key in the EMPLOYEE table would reference the GENDER table. Every time a value is added or changed for the GENDER column in the EMPLOYEE table, the foreign key would cause I/O to the GENDER table to validate the values entered for the GENDER of the employee. For systems that perform a lot of inserts and updates, these kinds of check constraints can potentially reduce a significant amount of I/O and thus increase performance.

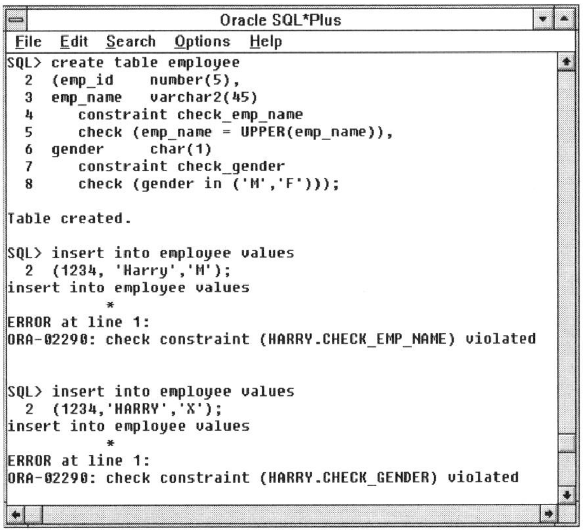

```
┌──────────────────────────────────────────────────────┐
│  ─               Oracle SQL*Plus              ▼ ▲ │
├──────────────────────────────────────────────────────┤
│ File   Edit   Search   Options   Help                │
│ SQL> create table employee                         ▲ │
│   2  (emp_id    number(5),                           │
│   3  emp_name   varchar2(45)                         │
│   4     constraint check_emp_name                    │
│   5     check (emp_name = UPPER(emp_name)),          │
│   6  gender     char(1)                              │
│   7     constraint check_gender                      │
│   8     check (gender in ('M','F')));                │
│                                                      │
│ Table created.                                       │
│                                                      │
│ SQL> insert into employee values                     │
│   2  (1234, 'Harry','M');                            │
│ insert into employee values                          │
│             *                                        │
│ ERROR at line 1:                                     │
│ ORA-02290: check constraint (HARRY.CHECK_EMP_NAME) violated │
│                                                      │
│                                                      │
│ SQL> insert into employee values                     │
│   2  (1234,'HARRY','X');                             │
│ insert into employee values                          │
│             *                                        │
│ ERROR at line 1:                                     │
│ ORA-02290: check constraint (HARRY.CHECK_GENDER) violated │
│                                                    ▼ │
│ ◀                                                  ▶ │
└──────────────────────────────────────────────────────┘
```

Figure 2.47 Check constraints.

Eliminating the foreign key lookups can cause a problem, however. If you eliminate the lookup table entirely and use only a check constraint, the user would not be able to tell what the valid values are for the column with the check constraint. You cannot directly perform any kind of lookup to show what the values are for the column with the check constraints. There are several work arounds for this problem.

One way to solve the problem is to create the lookup table but not to reference it with a foreign key. If a user needs to find out what the valid values are for a certain column, the application would simply perform a read on the lookup table to show a list of valid values. The issue here is keeping the values in the lookup table in sync with the values in the check constraints. This can be done either manually or programmatically. A manual method means a procedure must be in place to make sure that the values in both places are updated simultaneously. A safer method would be to add a routine to the table maintenance program that would generate a new/updated constraint whenever values are changed or added to the lookup table.

Another way to solve the problem is to use the Oracle column comment table in the data dictionary to store a list of valid values. As with the preceding example, when a user needs to see a list of valid values, the application would read the USER_COL_COMMENTS or ALL_COL_COMMENTS table to display the list of values. Again, the issue is keeping that data in the comment table in sync with the check constraint. As with the preceding example, the solutions are similar. Either keep the values in sync manually or create a routine to update both values simultaneously.

Check constraints can reference several columns in a single table but they cannot reference columns outside the table that has the constraints. A trigger or procedure must be used to reference a value in another table.

Not Null

NOT NULL constants are used to make sure that a column has a value in it when data is added to or updated in a column. While not null constraints can be added as a named constraint as on the gender column in Figure 2. 48, they are usually just placed at the column level.

```
                          Oracle SQL*Plus
 File  Edit  Search  Options  Help
SQL> create table employee
  2  (emp_id    number(5) not null,
  3   emp_name  varchar2(45) not null,
  4   gender    char(1)
  5      constraint gender_not_null not null);

Table created.

SQL> insert into employee values
  2  (1234,'','M');
insert into employee values
               *
ERROR at line 1:
ORA-01400: mandatory (NOT NULL) column is missing or NULL during insert


SQL> insert into employee values
  2  (1234,'HARRY','');
insert into employee values
               *
ERROR at line 1:
ORA-01400: mandatory (NOT NULL) column is missing or NULL during insert


SQL> insert into employee
  2  values(1234,' ',' ');
1 row created.
```

Figure 2.48 NOT NULL constraints.

The above screen illustrates two points. The first is that, unlike primary and foreign key constraints, a named not null constraint will not display the name of the constraint that was violated, so why bother with a name? The second point is more important. In the first two insert statements the null value was represented with two single quote marks with no spaces in between them as ' '. The last insert however, actually inserts blanks into the not null columns. This was done by putting spaces between the single quote marks as ' '. This, again, illustrates the point discussed in Chapter 1 that blanks are not the same as nulls.

Unique

A *unique constraint* is similar to a primary key constraint in that it will not allow duplicate values for a column or set of columns in a table. The difference between the two are that there can be more than one unique constraint on a table, and unique constraints will allow nulls while preventing duplicate values. Unique constraints should never be used to enforce entity integrity; that's why we have primary keys.

Default

A *default value* specification is not technically a constraint, but it performs in much the same way. Figure 2.49 shows the column DATE_ADDED that has a default value of SYSDATE. When a row is added to the EMPLOYEE table, the current date is automatically supplied for the DATE_ADDED column. Defaults cannot reference other columns or pseudo columns.

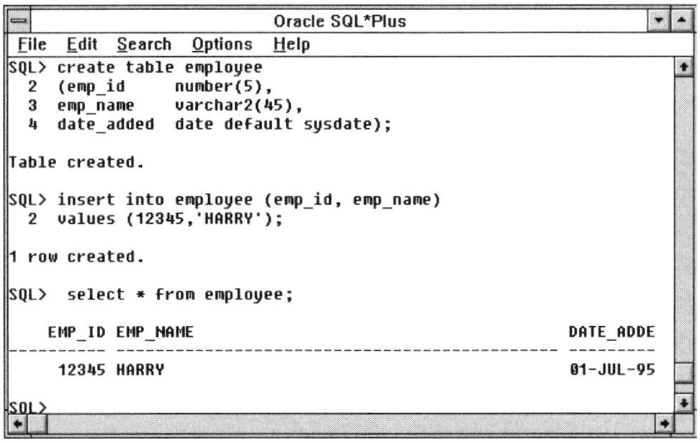

```
Oracle SQL*Plus
 File   Edit   Search   Options   Help
SQL> create table employee
  2  (emp_id      number(5),
  3   emp_name    varchar2(45),
  4   date_added  date default sysdate);

Table created.

SQL> insert into employee (emp_id, emp_name)
  2  values (12345,'HARRY');

1 row created.

SQL> select * from employee;

    EMP_ID EMP_NAME                                    DATE_ADDE
---------- ------------------------------------------- ---------
     12345 HARRY                                       01-JUL-95

SQL>
```

Figure 2.49 DEFAULT values.

Users

Users in an Oracle database are similar to an account or set of authorizations that allow someone to log on to Oracle and perform, or not perform, certain actions against certain objects in the database. Users can also be granted or denied access to Oracle resources such as CPU time, elapsed time, or I/O. A user account can be shared but many people, and a single person can actually log on to a database as the same user multiple times.

Users are covered in detail in Chapter 5 as part of system security.

Data Dictionary

The *data dictionary* is the Oracle database that contains information about your database. The information in the dictionary is called *meta data*, which means data about data. Within the data dictionary you can find the definitions of every object in the database.

Most users access the data dictionary through views. The actual tables for the data dictionary are created by the SQL.BSQ script that is run when a database is created. The script CATALOG.SQL creates the views that most people use to look at the information in the data dictionary. If you really want to see how Oracle's data dictionary is structured print out the SQL.BSQ and CATALOG.SQL scripts to see how the views are written. Prepare to be intimidated by the complexity of some of the views. I will cover the data dictionary views but not the actual data dictionary tables. All the data dictionary tables and views are owned by the user SYS.

WARNING

While you can select information from the data dictionary views, under no circumstance should you attempt to insert, update, or delete any data or alter any structures. This wouldn't be a database without an exception. You can and should add data to the two comment tables, which are covered shortly. If you do intend to reference the data dictionary tables in an application, you should reference the public synonyms rather than the tables themselves, in case Oracle changes the dictionary in future releases.

In addition to the permanent tables and views in the data dictionary, a number of *dynamic performance tables* are created whenever an instance is started. These tables collect statistics as the database is running and are used primarily for performance tuning. Run the script UTLMONTR.SQL as user SYS to grant access to all of these tables to DBA users.

For most objects there are three sets of views that allow different types of users to see objects based on ownership. Each set of views is prefixed with one of the following:

```
USER_
ALL_
DBA_
```

The USER_ views allow the user to only see those objects that he or she owns. The ALL_ views let a user see objects that he or she can access, that is objects to which they have been granted access. The DBA_ views show information on all the objects regardless of the owner but, these views can only be accessed by users that are granted DBA authority. The USER_ and ALL_ views provide information on most of the schema objects, while the DBA_ views include all the schema objects as well as additional information about other database objects, such as redo logs and data files.

Appendix A includes a series of data models that illustrate different portions of Oracle's data dictionary. The following physical data model is an example that shows the dictionary views that describe users/owners, tablespaces, tables, clusters, indexes, and the relationships between the objects (Figure 2.50). These objects must be prefixed by USE_, ALL_, or DBA_ as in

```
SELECT * FROM USER_TABLES
SELECT * FROM ALL_TABLES
SELECT * FROM DBA_TABLES
```

The Oracle data dictionary contains several views that are worth special note. These are the table and column comment views. Comments about every table and every column can be added directly to the data dictionary. These tables provide an excellent method to document your system and provide a foundation for a help system. These are the only two tables to which users should add data.

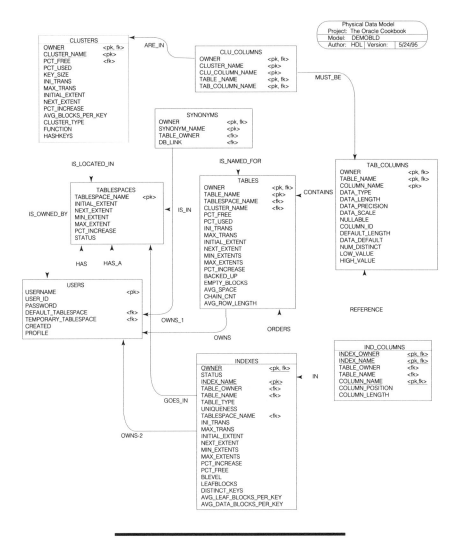

Figure 2.50 Oracle data dictionary model.

Oracle includes comments on most of the views in the data dictionary. The comments can be up to 2000 characters long. You can add and view comments as illustrated in Figure 2.51.

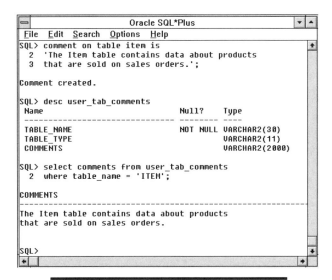

```
       =                    Oracle SQL*Plus              ▼ ▲
      File  Edit  Search  Options  Help
      SQL> comment on table item is                              ↑
        2  'The Item table contains data about products
        3  that are sold on sales orders.';

      Comment created.

      SQL> desc user_tab_comments
       Name                          Null?    Type
       ----------------------------- -------- ----
       TABLE_NAME                    NOT NULL VARCHAR2(30)
       TABLE_TYPE                             VARCHAR2(11)
       COMMENTS                               VARCHAR2(2000)

      SQL> select comments from user_tab_comments
        2  where table_name = 'ITEM';

      COMMENTS
      ------------------------------------------------------------
      The Item table contains data about products
      that are sold on sales orders.

      SQL>                                                        ↓
       ←                                                          →
```

Figure 2.51 Adding and viewing comments.

There are two characteristics about the COMMENT views that also make them special. One characteristic is that the COMMENTS column stores the data exactly as it is keyed in, including carriage returns. This formatting is really a function of the VARCHAR2 data type of the column, but it helps to be aware of it. It may be best to key your comments in as one long string without carriage returns. Your application/help system could then format the data as necessary. Figure 2.52 illustrates the difference in format for the same comment.

Another characteristic is the fact that the COMMENT views do not follow normal DML syntax. You do not Insert, Update, or Delete from any of the COMMENT views as you would a normal table. Also, COMMENT rows are automatically added to the data dictionary when any table is created. A row is added for a table comment, and rows are added for each column in the table for column comments. Since the rows are automatically created you do not need to Insert them. Regardless of your privileges, you cannot Delete or Update any rows from the COMMENT views. To remove or change a comment, simply issue a COMMENT ON TABLE, or COMMENT ON COLUMN command and either change the text, or use quotation marks without text to remove the comment text as illustrated in Figure 2.53.

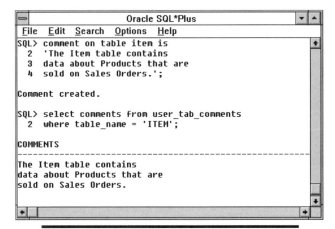

Figure 2.52 Comments with a different format.

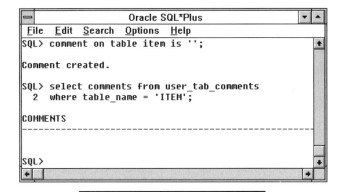

Figure 2.53 Removing comments,

Figure 2.54 illustrates adding and displaying a comment to the COLUMN_COMMENT table for the column COL1 in the COMMENT_TEST table.

A practical use for these comment tables is to support help systems. If a user needs help with what to type into a field on the screen, a help system could retrieve the comment for the column stored in the data dictionary to use it as a prompt or hint.

Some CASE tools will generate these comments for you from definitions stored in the CASE tool. This is one of the best ways to document any system because it is in the system.

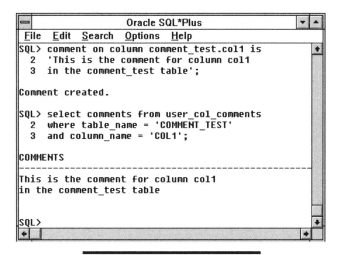

Figure 2.54 Column comments.

The Optimizer

When a user or application submits a query to Oracle, Oracle must decide how to access the data requested in the query. The choice is made by the *optimizer*. Each query must be *optimized*, whether the SQL command is **SELECT**, **INSERT**, **UPDATE**, **DELETE**, **ALTER**, or **DROP**. The output of the optimizer is an *execution plan*, which is a set of instructions detailing how Oracle should access the data. This execution plan is stored in the shared SQL area.

Oracle has two methods, or optimizer modes, for determining the best execution plan. One method uses a fixed set of rules to determine how to access the data and is called the *rule-based optimizer*. The other method, the *cost-based optimizer*, uses statistics stored in the data dictionary with certain rules to determine how to best access the data.

The *Oracle7 Server Tunning, Release 7.2* manual makes the following statement, "... you should eventually migrate you listing applications to use rhe cost-based approach, because the rule-based approach will not be available in future versions of Oracle.

NOTE

The optimizers examine, or parse, the query to see which columns are required from which tables. Once the query knows what data it is after, it looks in the data dictionary to see what kinds of structures are available for access. In trying to determine how to access the data, the optimizer looks at things like available indexes or hash clusters to see if there are ways of getting the data besides a full table scan. The optimizer also looks at table joins, columns in the WHERE clause, and other operators or functions that might affect the results set.

You can see the execution plan for any query using the EXPLAIN PLAN facility. Details on EXPLAIN PLAN and viewing the execution plan the optimizer chooses are covered in Chapter 8, "Tuning." The *SQL Application's Developers Guide* and the *Oracle7 Server Tunning Release 7.2* manual detail how to program and write SQL to effectively use the optimizer. I also recommend that programmers attend classes geared to applications development with Oracle SQL and tuning SQL statements (these topics are beyond the scope of this book).

The rule-based optimizer uses a fixed ranking of the access paths or methods to determine how best to access the data. While this ranking may vary with different releases of Oracle, the top and bottom of the lists are always the same. The top of the ranking, which is the most efficient access path, is to access data by the ROWID. The bottom ranking is a full table scan.

The rule-based optimizer determines which access paths are available and then chooses which to use based on the rank of the available paths.

One of the limitations of the rule-based optimizer is that it has no knowledge about the number of rows in a table or the distribution of data. Even though the full table scan is at the bottom of the rule-based optimizer's ranking, it is not always the slowest way to access data. For small tables, say less than eight blocks in size, it is probably faster to read the entire table into memory with a full table scan than to access an index and then read the table. If there were an index on one of these small tables, the rule-based optimizer would choose it first because it has a higher ranking than a full table scan, even though it would probably be slower.

The cost-based optimizer may create several possible execution plans for a given query. It then examines various rules and statistics to determine the cost to perform each execution plan in terms of total resources. The optimizer then chooses the execution plan that has the lowest cost. Rather than using just rules, the cost-based optimizer uses statistics gathered about the tables and indexes to help make its choice. (The overhead of all this analysis is another good reason to try and get consistency for equivalent SQL statements. Once a statement is parsed the execution plan is placed in the shared pool and can be reused.)

In order to run effectivly, the cost-based optimizer requires statistics for at least one of the tables it is evaluating. The statistics are gathered with the ANALYZE command. The statistics are collected for tables, indexes, columns, and clusters, and these statistics can be viewed in the data dictionary. If there are no statistics, Oracle will currently use the rule-based optimizer.

Figure 2.55 shows some of the statistics for the CUSTOMER table before and after running the ANALYZE command. Similar statistics are gathered for indexes and clusters.

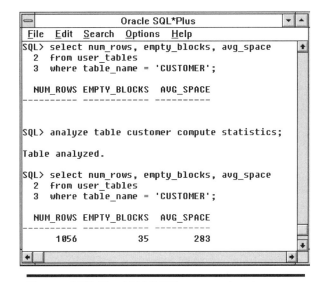

Figure 2.55 The ANALYZE command and statistics.

The cost-based optimizer needs statistics before it will run, but—and this is critical— in order to run effectively, the statistics must be kept up to date.

I had a client that used Oracle to run point-of-sales systems in its stores. Every night the statistics were updated by running the ANALYZE command against all the tables and indexes. By the end of the day, however, the systems slowed down because the numerous inserts that occurred during the day altered the distribution of data enough so that the cost-based optimizer was no longer making good decisions because it was working with old information. The solution was to simply switch to the rule-based optimizer and spend a little more effort tuning the queries. It was impractical to run the ANALYZE command during business hours.

The optimizer mode can be set in several ways and even changed on the fly. In fact, the cost-based optimizer and individual SQL statements can be adjusted to create execution plans that support different processing requirements.

The optimizer mode for an entire instance can be set by the **init.ora** parameter OPTIMIZER_MODE. The default is COST for the cost-based optimizer; but, again, unless there are statistics Oracle will use the rule-based optimizer. The optimizer mode can be set for a users session using the ALTER SESSION SET OPTIMIZER GOAL command. Hints can also be embedded into individual SQL statements to determine the optimizer mode for an individual SQL statement.

In addition to choosing the optimizer mode, the cost-based optimizer allows two additional methods for retrieving data based on processing needs. One method attempts to increase system throughput by figuring out the best way to return all the rows requested by a query. This is best for queries that will return a lot of rows or certain kinds of batch processing or reporting. The goal of this type of optimization is to reduce the total elapsed time to complete, or return, all the rows for the query. This mode is set for a session by the command ALTER SESSION SET OPTIMIZER_GOAL ALL_ROWS. You can also specify all rows for an individual query by using a hint of ALL_ROWS as illustrated in Figure 2.56.

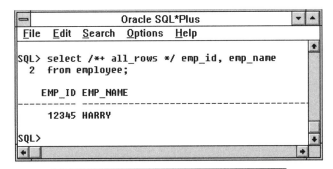

Figure 2.56 Select ALL_ROWS using hints.

The other cost-based optimizer mode will optimize queries that return just a few rows. The goal of this mode is to reduce the total elapsed time to return the first row or rows to the query. This mode is good for data queries, or data entry screens that view data one row at a time. It is also excellent for decision support systems, where a user may want to see just a few rows of sample data before deciding whether to get all the rows. For this kind of query, the optimizer goal or hint is set to FIRST_ROW.

The default method of access for the cost-based optimizer is to return all rows.

If you intend to use the cost-based optimizer, consider these issues:

- You should run the ANALYZE command whenever there are a significant number of changes to the indexes and the rows in the tables.

- For large tables and indexes ANALYZE can take a while and be a resource hog. You may run out of temporary tablespace when trying to analyze a table with more than a million rows.

- The cost-based optimizer requires planning which GOAL to use and planning for time to run the ANALYZE command.

- Use COMPUTE STATISTICS instead of ESTIMATE STATISTICS. Estimating statistics produces "unpredictable" results.

- **No matter how good the cost-based optimizer may be it is not a substitute for learning how to write good SQL queries!**

So, what should you do? Start by using the rule-based optimizer and learn how to write good queries. Set up benchmarks to see which of the many options gives you the best results.

Startup and Shutdown

Oracle instances and databases can be started and shut down in several different modes. The different modes allow different levels of access to commands and files in the database.

Oracle is providing new tools to monitor and manage its databases. One of the tools is the Oracle Database Manager, which can be used to start and shut down a database. Figure 2.57 shows the graphical nature of this tool. Other tools are similar in nature as more and more computers have monitors or clients that support graphical user interfaces, or GUIs. Besides being very obvious as to what they do (and in most cases how to do it), the help systems are superb.

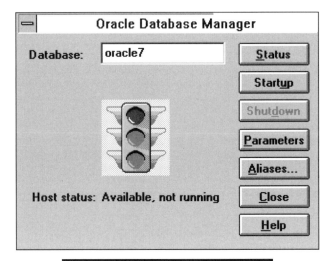

Figure 2.57 Oracle Database Manager.

While these tools will make the lives of many DBAs a lot simpler (do you think you can tell how to start the database by looking at the database manager?), they do not always tell the whole story. The following section, and others later, do tell the rest of the story.

Startup

While the second button on the Oracle Database Manager screen, **Startup**, will start the database, it actually starts and opens the database. Startup and shutdown have several options, which are described here. All the options are available in the Oracle tool SQL*DBA.

You must CONNECT INTERNAL to start an instance from within SQL*DBA. INTERNAL is a special user account that is permitted to perform certain commands and functions. In order to connect as INTERNAL, your user account must belong to the DBA group.

You can also specify which **init.ora** file, and therefore which database to use by specifying a PFILE = parameter, as in:

```
SQLDBA> STARTUP PFILE=initday.ora
SQLDBA> STARTUP PFILE=initnite.ora
```

If you have multiple databases, it is a good idea to get in the habit of always specifying the pfile when performing a startup to be sure you are starting the correct database. If a PFILE or database is not specified, Oracle starts the database listed as the instance identifier in the users ORACLE_SID.

When starting a database, Oracle reads the **init.ora** file to determine how the database will be initialized. This includes the parameters that determine the size of the SGA. After reading the **init.ora**, Oracle creates the SGA and starts the background processes.

The following options determine how the database may or may not be accessed when an instance is started.

Nomount

When started with the NOMOUNT option, the database is not accessible in any way. Oracle does not read the control files does not open any data or redo log files. This option is used to create a new database.

Mount

This option reads the control files and checks for the existence all the files listed in the control file. The data and redo log files, however, are not opened. The database, therefore, is not available for normal SQL operations or any kind of data access.

With the database mounted, you can perform certain maintenance functions on different types of files, such as adding, dropping, or renaming redo log files; renaming data files; changing archiving options; or performing full database recovery.

Open

This option mounts the database and opens the data and redo log files. This makes the database available for normal operations and prepares the data files for transactions. Any tablespaces that were off-line before the database is opened will remain off-line.

If the **STARTUP** command is issued without any qualifiers the instance will start and the database will be opened.

Restricted Mode

You may want to startup and open a database but still not have it available to end users. The RESTRICTED mode makes the database accessible to only those users with CREATE SESSION and RESTRICTED SESSION permission. This permission should only be granted to DBAs.

RESTRICTED mode is good for performing such tasks as data loads, exports or imports, or executing DDL.

Exclusive or Parallel mode

These two modes are used with the OPS. In exclusive mode only one instance can start up and mount the database. The exclusive mode is used to perform certain maintenance functions such as switching to ARCHIVELOG mode. PARALLEL is required to allow multiple instances to access the database.

Shutdown

An Oracle database can be shut down in three ways. Unlike STARTUP, which can separately control the instance and the database, SHUTDOWN stops the database and the instance.

Normal

A SHUTDOWN NORMAL, which is the default, waits for all users to disconnect from the database before shutting it down. No new connections are allowed. Once all user are disconnected, a checkpoint occurs and the current log sequence number is synchronized among all necessary files. The database will not require recovery when next started.

Immediate

If you need to shut down the database, but users are still logged on and connected, you can issue a SHUTDOWN IMMEDIATE. In this case, all uncommitted transactions are terminated and rolled back. After the rollbacks, all users are disconnected. Once all the users are disconnected, a checkpoint occurs and the current log sequence number is synchronized among all necessary files. The database may require a recovery when next started, which Oracle will perform automatically.

This is not a user-friendly way to get users off the system, and despite its name it may take awhile if there are many users performing transactions.

If, for some reason, you cannot shut down the database with the immediate option, try to kill the offending user sessions manually. Try the **ALTER SYSTEM KILL SESSION** command or kill the sessions from the operating system. After the user processes are killed, try shutting down again before moving on to the next option.

Abort

A SHUTDOWN ABORT should only be used when you cannot shut down the database using any other option. Using the abort option means that all transactions are terminated but not rolled back. No checkpoint is performed. Because operations are aborted, the current log sequence number is not synchronized across all files, and the database will require recovery when next started.

This kind of shutdown will be instantaneous, but nothing will be saved.

STARTUP FORCE

Using the FORCE option actually performs a SHUTDOWN ABORT and then restarts the database. This will cause Oracle to perform a recovery because of the abort. This should be used with extreme caution, but it can be useful in a development or test environment if you want to try different memory parameters or processes are hung and you cannot shut down the database using NORMAL or IMMEDIATE.

Oracle Architectures

Oracle can operate is several different configurations.

- Single instance—A single instance can run on a single machine
- Multiple instances—A single machine can run more than one instance at a time. Each instance is connected to its own database.
- Distributed Processing—Different instances on different machines can communicate with each other using database links and the distributed option. Oracle supports full two-phase commits which means that inserts,

updates, and deletes can occur on remote database via a network running SQL*Net.

- Parallel Processing—The Oracle Parallel Server allows multiple instance to share a single database on a shared disk system. The instances can run on a parallel computer, or on different computers in a cluster.

Figure 2.58 illustrates the different configurations.

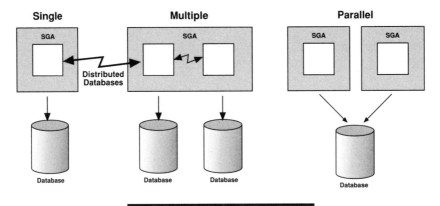

Figure 2.58 Oracle configurations.

CHAPTER 3

Installation

The focus of this chapter is just on installing Oracle on your machine. Before you can build any databases you have to get Oracle installed. The results of theis installation step are used later when you build a disk map in preparation for database design.

The first thing to say about installing Oracle is that it is getting much, much easier. The new CD_ROMs practically install themselves. Because installing Oracle will affect, and is affected by different machine variables, such as directory structures and user profiles, a systems administrator should work closely with the database administrator (DBA) during the installation. Sometimes the systems administrators perform the actual Oracle installation and the DBAs take over after Oracle is installed.

Before beginning the Oracle installation make sure the machine is fully configured. Make sure all of the peripherals are configured, swap space is allocated, and file systems are set up.

If you are new to Oracle, and performing your first installation, when the software asks if you want to create a default database - say yes. Seeing how Oracle sets up and installs itself should be very educational.

Oracle provides special documentation for the installation of their products on each platform. And because UNIX is different from VMS, which is different from Windows NT, which is different from... well, you get the idea—because of all of the different platforms on which Oracle will run, it is impossible to provide guidelines on exactly how all installations should be performed. With each set of software Oracle provides an *Installation and User's Guide* (IUG) and/or *Installation and Configuration Guide* (ICG).

In lieu of a single standard installation guide, Gary Milsap of Oracle developed the Oracle Flexible Architecture as a guide for setting up and installing the Oracle directory structures and files. This guide will prove invaluable in setting up your directory structures.

Most installations will need to address the following points:

- Environment variables
- Users, groups, and owners
- Directory structures

There are several THINGS called environment variables that need to be set for most Oracle installations. The number and names of these variables varies from platform to platform, and operating system to operating system. There are however, several environment variables that are, if not standard, at least common. And if these variables are not explicitly stated as in a .login, .profile, or .ini file, they are referenced or implied through other means such as defaults set in the database. The environment variables are:

```
ORACLE_HOME
ORACLE_SID
ORACLE_PATH
```

ORACLE_HOME specifies the home directory for Oracle, and is used to specify the location of the executables, and data files that should be run for a particular session with a particular Oracle database. As long as there is only one version, or copy of the Oracle software on a particular machine, all of the users will use the same ORACLE_HOME directory.

If there are several version of the software, such as different release levels, or versions, of Oracle, then each version must have its own ORACLE_HOME directory. For example, if you had a copy of Oracle Version 7.1.4 and a copy of Oracle

Version 7.2 on the same machine, you would have two ORACLE_HOME directories, one for each version of the software. You specify which version of the software you wish to use by the ORACLE_HOME directory you choose. For most operating systems you must specify the a default ORACLE_HOME directory for each user. Refer to your IUG to see how to set the ORACLE_HOME directory.

A particular machine can have multiple Oracle instances. Each instance needs a system identifier, or SID. The ORACLE_SID identifies a particular Oracle instance on a machine.

A common practice is to make the SID four characters or less, although it can be from one to thirty two characters depending on the operating system. Making the SID short makes it easier to type and makes it transportable across operating systems. The SID is usually included in or appended to a number of files used or written by Oracle, like the init.ora file and the trace files. Keeping the SID short makes it less likely that an operating system file name limit is exceeded.

With some operating systems a user is assigned a default ORACLE_SID. This SID determines which instance a user accesses when logging on to Oracle. Changing their SID will change the instance and the databases that a user is logging on to.

The ORACLE_PATH specifies the location of the executables for various Oracle tools, such as SQL*Plus, or SQL*Forms. In addition the path tells Oracle where to go when either looking for files to read, or the location to write files. As with ORACLE_HOME there will be different paths if there are different versions of Oracle on the same machine.

Users, Groups, and Owners

Some operating systems, such as UNIX require special operating system accounts as well as groups or types of users. Before you can successfully install Oracle these account must be set up on the machine.

The two accounts that are generally required are oracle and root. Root is an operating system "super user, and is needed to run the installation routines. The oracle user owns the RDBMS and performs maintenance on the Oracle database. On smaller systems these two accounts are often combined.

Some operating systems require a special dba group. Members of this dba group are the only ones that can perform certain functions within Oracle.

Directory Structures

A directory path needs to be specified to install the Oracle software. This path is called the home directory and Oracle will create additional directories below it during the installation.

Most installations for Oracle will create some or all of the following subdirectories in ORACLE_HOME directory:

```
ORACLE_HOME
          /bin-contains the binary files for all of the products
          /dbs-a default location for database files
          /rdbms-the location for more directories and scripts
               /admin-contains Oracle scripts
               /log
               /doc
```

Figure 3-1 shows the directories created by the installer for a Windows installation. In this case the ORACLE_HOME directory is orawin.

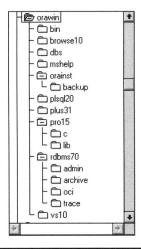

Figure 3.1 Directory structure for a Windows installation

Install

Once the environment variables are set, the proper owners and users created, and a home directory created, you can run the installation program. As I said earlier in this chapter, installation is getting easier and easier, and more automated. You may find that your particular set of Oracle software may perform all of the tasks as part of the installation routine.

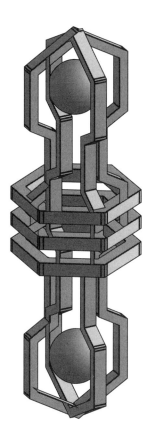

PART TWO

BUILDING A PHYSICAL DATABASE

Chapter 4: Backups, Archiving, and Recovery

Chapter 5: Getting Down to Business

Chapter 6: Data Loads and Conversions

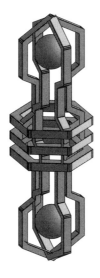

CHAPTER 4

Backups, Archiving, and Recovery

There are two types of people in this world: those who have lost data and those who will. Rick Jones of BLUware, Inc., in Houston has provided a slightly different perspective: "What the mean time between failure (MTBF) claims from your disk vendor really mean is that given sufficient time all disks will fail." These two points of view provide an appropriate frame of reference within which to discuss database safety.

One of my criteria for judging database quality is a database protected from machine and other failures that can be recovered quickly and completely in the event a failure or crash does occur. Oracle provides many outstanding features that allow you to keep a database running 24 hours a day, 7 days a week while backing it up on a regular basis and to have it recoverable in relatively short order.

Because it runs on so many different operating systems and machines, Oracle does not perform database backups directly. Instead, it provides several different methods to allow you to perform operating system backups of your database. One method is to perform a *cold backup*, where the database is shut down and all the files are backed up at one time. Another method is to perform *hot*, or *on-line*, backups where the database is backed up while it is still operating. There is a utility, Export that can be used to "backup" your database in certain situations.

There are several issues you need to explore when developing a backup strategy:

1. Do your processing requirements require backups?
2. Can you afford to lose **any** data?
3. How long can you be out of business if you have a crash and must recover your systems?

The first question relates to your type of processing and is addressed mainly to those working with decision support systems that perform few or no updates. If the DSS is used mostly for read-only transactions and the data doesn't change, why back it up? What this means, however, is that the source data used to load the DSS is available to **rebuild** the DSS should it crash. Since most DSSe are not used for mission-critical systems, that is, your business can still operate if the DSS is down, rebuilding it may be a viable strategy. In addition, many DSSes are too big to back up in any reasonable time frame, so there must be a rebuild strategy.

In addressing the second and third questions, it is important to distinguish between media failure and instance failure. *Media failure* relates to hardware and is usually associated with a disk crash. An *instance failure* is where something has occurred, such as an operating system crash, that creates certain types of errors, or in extreme cases, shuts down or locks up the database.

Instance failures seldom pose a problem for Oracle because SMON automatically performs recovery whenever a database is started. (With the Oracle Parallel Server, an instance failure is recovered by another instance.) SMON uses the on-line redo logs to restore the database to the last committed transaction. This "instant" recovery is possible because of the checkpoints that are performed, usually at every log switch. During a checkpoint, DBWR writes all changes in the database buffers to the database files, and all the file headers and control files are synchronized with the appropriate log sequence numbers. Therefore, when a checkpoint completes, the data in the database files are up to date. The changes since the last checkpoint are written to the current on-line redo log file.

The second and third questions can be addressed in terms of hardware and software. If you have mission critical systems that must be up all the time and you cannot afford to lose any data, you should consider several hardware options. The most expensive is fault-tolerant computers that have built-in redundancy of all components. While not completely fault-tolerant, Oracle provides a high availability option with the Oracle Parallel Server (OPS). With OPS, multiple machines running multiple Oracle instances can be used to access a single Oracle database. This hardware configuration is commonly referred to as a *cluster*. If one machine should fail, the other(s) could continue to operate and can recover the failed instance when the machine is returned to operations.

The other hardware consideration is the disk drives. Most hardware vendors sell disks that can be mirrored, and Redundant Array of Independent Disk (RAID) devices. (Oracle cannot mirror the database files, just the on-line redo log files.) Mirrored disks are pairs of disks that contain the same information; they are mirror images of each other. Data is often read from a single disk but is always written to both disks. If one disk should fail, the other continues to operate while the bad one is fixed or replaced. When the repaired or replaced disk is returned to service, the machine will automatically synchronize the drives so that they are again mirror images of each other. Mirroring basically doubles the cost of your storage, but disks are relatively cheap—and getting cheaper.

RAID devices take a slightly different approach. They combine hardware and software to protect data. RAID devices offer different levels of protection. RAID Level 3 is basically a mirrored system, while RAID Level 5 performs parity checks of data to make sure that things are working as they should. While the details of how they work are not important, the basic effect is that a Level 3 to 5 RAID device can lose a disk and continue to operate. There are several drawbacks to RAID devices, however. They are not Redundant Arrays of *Inexpensive* Disks, and you do not have as much control over where to place your database objects. Most RAID devices stripe all the data across all the drives, essentially creating one big logical drive. (Placing objects and tuning I/O are covered in detail later in the book.) The final drawback to RAID devices is that they can be much slower, especially at RAID Level 5, than plain mirrored drives. Parity checking is the major culprit in the slowdown.

If you have a mission-critical application and you cannot afford to be without your disk drives, you should mirror the disks. If you need further safety at the machine level, consider OPS or fault-tolerant computers.

The second question related to whether you must operate in `ARCHIVELOG` mode and whether the on-line redo logs are mirrored. When the database is in

ARCHIVELOG mode, the ARCH process copies the on-line redo log files to archive log files after each log switch. If a database is in ARCHIVELOG mode, it can be recovered to the last committed transaction that was performed. The database could also be recovered to a specific point in time or a specific transaction if there is a data corruption problem. If you mirror the on-line redo logs, you are spared potential loss of data if one of the disks containing an on-line redo log file should crash.

All production systems (except some DSSes) should operate in ARCHIVELOG mode and mirror the redo logs.

The last question relates to how often you perform backups and the size of the on-line redo log files. While the database is in ARCHIVELOG mode, you perform on-line backups while the database is running. The amount of time it takes to recover will depend on the time since the last backup and the size and number of the archive redo logs.

To recover a database that is in ARCHIVELOG mode, you apply, or restore, the last good backup and then apply the archive redo logs that were written since that backup was made. Basically, you are rolling forward all the changes (which were recorded in the redo logs) made since the last backup. The time it takes to recover depends on the time of the last backup and the number of transactions that have occurred since then. The older the backup and the more transactions there were, i.e., more archive redo logs, the longer it will take to recover.

When recovering from an instance failure, Oracle usually only needs to go to the on-line redo logs and apply all the changes since the last checkpoint. The time it takes to recover from an instance failure is more dependent on the size of the on-line redo logs. (All redo logs should be the same size.) The bigger the redo log files and the more transactions they contain, the longer it will take to recover.

The V$LOG_HISTORY view shows all of the archive log files and the times of the log file was first used. You can use this view to see how often the log files are switching and gage the amount of time needed for recovery by the amount of time between log switches and the size of the log files.

There are some subtle trade-offs to consider when sizing the redo log files. The trade-offs relate to the overhead associated with checkpoints and the time it takes to recover. Checkpoints automatically occur at every log switch, but the interval can be reduced so that they occur more often. Checkpoints synchronize the data/changes in memory with the data on the disk. At each checkpoint, all the dirty buffers are written to disk, and this may momentarily degrade performance slightly. Keeping the redo logs small should eliminate the need to perform additional checkpoints and reduce the amount of time it takes to recover your database.

One good thing about on-line backups is that you can perform backups several times a day if recover time is important. You can also be selective about your backups and just concentrate on, or back up, those tables that have the highest transaction volume.

One thing Oracle cannot do is develop and test your backup **and** recovery procedures for you. Before you move to a production environment, be sure to test your backup procedures and try to recover the test database from an induced crash. Simulating a crash is as easy as disconnecting some critical cables, pulling out the plug on the machine, or removing one or more database files. You should try this before it's too late.

TIP

You should perform a backup before and after you make changes to the database structures of a production system, especially if you add, change, or delete any data files.

Cold or Off-Line Backups

Cold backups are performed when the database is **SHUT DOWN**, not just quiet; even if all the users are logged off, the Oracle background processes may still or quiescent active and performing work. Performing a full operating system backup while the database is up can lead to unpredictable results, the most likely of which is that you will not be able to restore your database when the need arises, because the data will be inconsistent.

If you perform only cold or off-line backups you can only restore your database to the last backup; any data entered or changed since the last backup will be lost.

For an off-line backup, you back up the data files, the control files, and the on-line redo log files. Figure 4.1 shows queries you can use to find the names of all of the files that should be included in a cold backup.

Figure 4.1 Files for an off-line backup.

A full or cold database backup is performed with the following steps:

1. Shut down the database in normal mode. If you had to shutdown using IMMEDIATE or ABORT, then restart the database and shut it down normally.

2. Perform an operating system backup of all the files produced by the preceding queries. You may also wish to backup your **init.ora** files.

3. Restart the database.

Archiving and Hot/On-Line Backups

If you want to be able run your database around the clock, your system must operate in ARCHIVELOG mode. This means that the archiver process, ARCH, is turned on and the on-line redo log files are being copied to the ARCHIVE_LOG_DESTination whenever there is a log switch. The **init.ora** parameter ARCHIVE_LOG_DEST determines where all the archive log files are written. (If you are running multiple Oracle instances, not in parallel, on the same machine, the archive log destinations should be in different directories.)

Make sure there is enough room on the disk that will hold all of the archive log files. If Oracle runs out of room in the ARCHIVE_LOG_DEST the database will stop. At that point you must make room on the disk and archive the online redo logs manually before you can begin operations again.

Figure 4.2 shows how to place the database in ARCHIVELOG mode. In addition to running these commands, set the init.ora parameter LOG_ARCHIVE_START to TRUE.

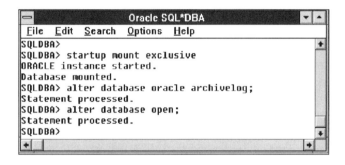

Figure 4.2 Starting archiving

Unlike the cold backup, where you just perform an operating system backup of the entire machine or at least of the directories that contain Oracle data, an on-line backup requires knowledge of all the tablespaces and data files in the database.

The following steps are required for an on-line backup:

1. Back up all the data files for each tablespace. Each tablespace must be backed up separately. Again, you can query the data dictionary (use the DBA_DATA_FILES view) to find the names of all the tablespaces and their associated data files.

2. Perform an **ALTER SYSTEM SWITCH LOGFILE**. This is necessary because Oracle continues to write transactions to the on-line redo logs during the backup.

3. Back up the archive log files. You do not need to back up the on-line redo log files when doing a hot backup.

4. Back up the control files.

This entire process can be scripted, and with the proper devices, it can run unattended. One of the device considerations for both cold and hot backups is whether to back up to disk or to tape. Backing up to disk will usually be faster in term of the amount of time it takes to back up the database, but there is the extra step of copying the backup files to tape or a WORM drive (an optical Write-Once, Read-Many times device), or whatever. If you will backup to disk be sure to reserve space for the backup files. (see Figure 4.3).

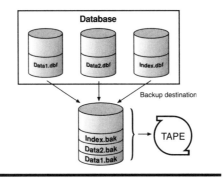

Figure 4.3 Backing up to disk, then to tape.

The following is a non–operating system–specific script to illustrate the hot backup process. Where words or commands appear in italics, you should substitute the appropriate operating system backup commands:

```
sqldba
connect internal
alter tablespace tbs_1 begin backup;
exit

copy tbs_1 datafiles to destination

sqldba
connect internal
alter tablespace tbs_1 end backup;
alter tablespace tbs_2 begin backup;
exit
```

```
copy tbs_2 datafiles to destination

sqldba
connect internal
alter tablespace tbs_2 end backup;
exit
```

Oracle Backup Manager

Oracle has developed several GUI tools to help with backups, recovery, and Export and Import. The following two screens show the Oracle Backup Manager. The Backup Manger detects whether the database is in ARCHIVELOG mode, then presents the appropriate screen. Notice the difference in Database Status on Figures 4.4 and 4.5.

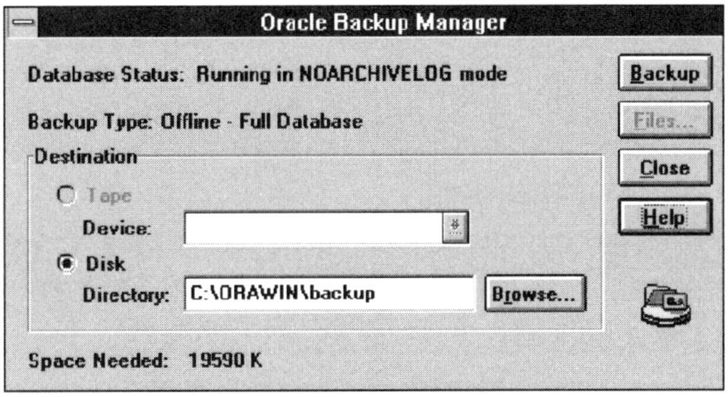

Figure 4.4 Oracle Backup Manager

When in NOARCHIVELOG mode the Backup Manager displays the total space needed to backup the entire database.

When in ARCHIVELOG mode the Database Manager displays the space needed to backup each tablespace.

Figure 4.5 Oracle Backup Manager for ARCHIVELOG mode

Recovery

In the event of a database failure or crash, data in the redo logs is *rolled forward* to the last committed transaction. Depending on the severity of the failure backups may have to be applied and the archive logs used to roll forward the database transactions. The actual steps necessary to perform a recovery depend on the type of failure. Fortunately, the new Oracle Recovery Manager can, in most circumstances, detect the type of failure and the screen highlights the type of recovery that should be performed (Figure 4.6).

Once you determine the type of recovery necessary, the next screen of the Recovery Manager suggests which files should be used for the backup.

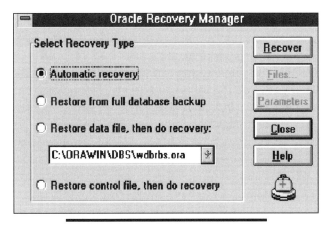

Figure 4.6 Oracle Recovery Manager

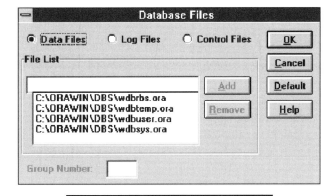

Figure 4.7 Database files for recovery.

Export and Import

Export is an Oracle utility that writes data and database information from an Oracle database to an operating system file. *Import* reads the data from the export files back into an Oracle database.

Many sites use Exports as their only means of database backup, even for their production systems. This has several pitfalls, especially for large databases. One problem is the same as for cold backups: the database cannot be recovered to the last committed transaction in the event of media failure. Just as with cold backups, where you can only recover to the last backup, with exports, you can only recover to the last export. Another problem is that exports do not take the index data with them, only the index definitions. The indexes must be rebuilt after the data is imported, and with large systems, this may take a very long time. Production databases should be run in ARCHIVELOG mode.

Oracle has also developed several GUI tools to help with Export and Import. Figure 4.8 shows the Database Exporter and the options that are available for an Export. Note that in addition to specifying which tables to export, you can specify the Export of Grants, Rows, Constraints, or Indexes. The Rows options indicates whether to actually take the data in the tables during an Export. If the Rows option is not selected, the Export will only take the table definitions, and not the data.

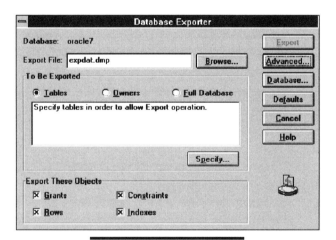

Figure 4.8 Database Exporter

You can specify whether to Export specific tables, all of the objects for one or more users, or the entire database. Figure 4.9 illustrates exporting specific tables.

In addition to specifying which objects to export there are several other options available during an export. Refer to the excellent on-line Help facilities for details of each option. Of note, however, is the Compress option which is described in detail in Figure 4.10.

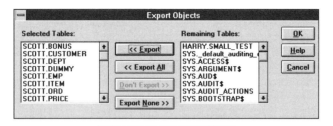

Figure 4.9 Export Objects

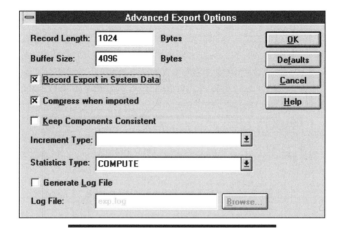

Figure 4.10 Advanced Export Options

Exports can also be used to resize and defragment tables or indexes. Oracle will normally compress data on an export. The COMPRESS parameter will cause all data for an object to be compressed into a single extent. (The default is **Y** for compress.) While the data is in a single extent, that single extent is the size of all the extents of the previous structure.

As an example, let's look at a table that was created with the Oracle defaults for the initial and next extent, and a PCTINCREASE of 50%. (Details on sizing and storage parameters are covered in Chapter 5.) Figure 4.11 shows the size of each extent and the total size the table would be if it had grown to 20 extents.

Number of extents	Initial Extent	Next Extent	PCTINCREASE	Size of next extent	Total size of object
1	10240	10240	50	10,240	10,240
2	10240	10240	50	10,240	20,480
3	10240	10240	50	15,361	35,841
4	10240	10240	50	23,043	58,884
5	10240	10240	50	34,565	93,448
6	10240	10240	50	51,848	145,296
7	10240	10240	50	77,773	223,070
8	10240	10240	50	116,661	339,730
9	10240	10240	50	174,992	514,723
10	10240	10240	50	262,489	777,212
11	10240	10240	50	393,735	1,170,947
12	10240	10240	50	590,603	1,761,550
13	10240	10240	50	885,906	2,647,456
14	10240	10240	50	1,328,860	3,976,316
15	10240	10240	50	1,993,291	5,969,607
16	10240	10240	50	2,989,937	8,959,544
17	10240	10240	50	4,484,907	13,444,452
18	10240	10240	50	6,727,362	20,171,814
19	10240	10240	50	10,091,044	30,262,857
20	10240	10240	50	15,136,567	45,399,424

Figure 4.11 Multiple extents.

The purpose of using COMPRESS is to put all the data into a single extent. You might also think that COMPRESS would reclaim empty space. An Export and Import using compress will create just one extent for the newly imported object, but it will not make the total size of any table or index smaller. So, while COMPRESS will create a single extent, that extent will be the size of all the extents of the prior structure. If you had 20 extents that took up 45,339,424 bytes, after the import, there would only be one extent, but it would still take up 45,339,424 bytes.

What COMPRESS does is defragment objects. It takes the data from multiple extents and puts it all into a single extent. It will not reduce the amount of space used by the table. If you want to reclaim space, you must drop the table and re-create it using proper storage parameters.

Once a database or specific tables are Exported, they can be Imported back into the original database or into a new database. Moving objects or entire databases is one of the most important uses for Export and Import. Export and Import are used to help migrate from one version of Oracle to another, or move data from one environment to another.

Figure 4.12 shows the Database Importer tool.

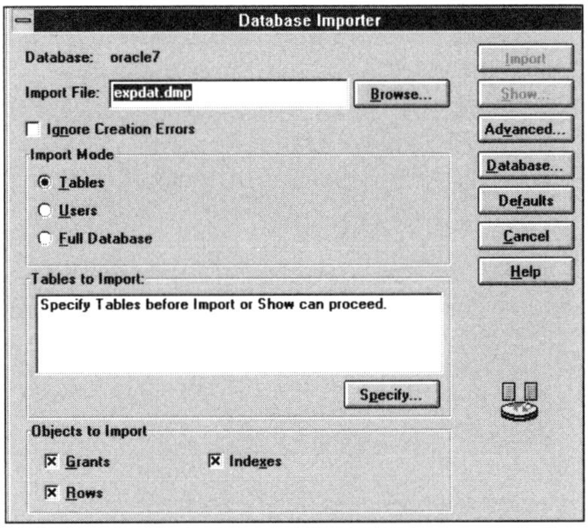

Figure 4.12 Database Importer

An important feature on the Advanced Import Options screen illustrated in Figure 4.13 is the Write Index-Creation Commands to File. What this option actually does is create a script that includes all of the DDL for all of the objects that are imported. This is an excellent way to get documentation for undocumented systems.

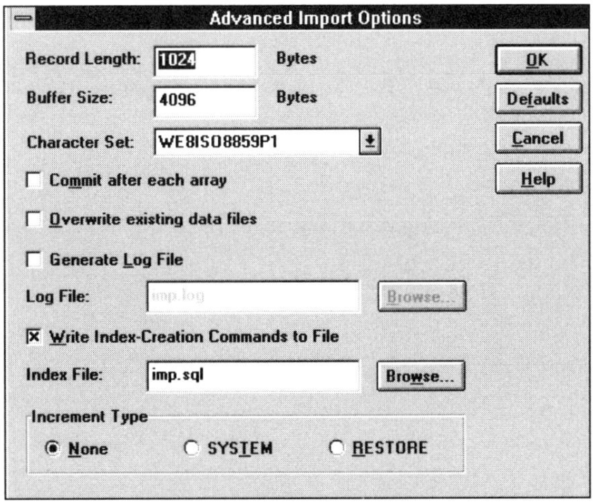

Figure 4.13 The Write Index-Creation Commands to File.

While Export and Import should not be used to backup production systems, they do have several excellent capabilities. They work well in the development, test, and production environments to quickly restore, or clean up an environment. After a class is completed, the tables in the training database could be dropped and the environment restored with an import. If someone should trash the development environment (Oops! I dropped a table by mistake.), use Import to restore either the whole environment or just selected tables.

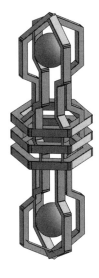

CHAPTER 5

Getting Down to Business

If you are one of those individuals contemplating building a database without the help of CASE tools (or at least diagrams, documentation, and table listings of some sort), you are doing yourself a great disservice. How hard is a little documentation? Plans are good.

This chapter assumes that the system being designed is a single Oracle database for a single production environment on a single machine. The reality is more like several environments (development, test, production, etc.) running on several machines, in fact, there may be several databases/environments running on a single machine.

System Goals or Purpose

Before trying to figure out where everything will go and how big things will be, it is wise to understand how the system will be used, the number and types of environments that must be supported, and the architecture(s) that will be supported. It is also important to know the number and type of users expected on the system.

Purpose

When faced with physical data modeling and database design, it is first important to know the type or types of processing the system is expected to handle. That is, what is the new system intended for? Will it be primarily an on-line transaction processing system (OLTP), or a decision support system (DSS), or some combination? A database without an application is an empty shell.

For OLTP systems, you will usually have to concentrate on being able to support large numbers of users performing many short, well-defined transactions. This might be the case for a customer order-entry system where operators take orders over the phone and key them directly into the system. In this case, most of the transactions are the same, and just a few rows are added or updated per transaction. The transactions are well-defined and can be well-tuned. The challenge will be to support the large number of users and possible rapid growth of the database. You will also want to be sure that the database can be quickly recovered with the least possible loss of data.

A DSS, on the other hand, often starts out large. It may have relatively few users who submit queries that request, or act on, large amounts of data. Unlike the OLTP environment, where the transactions are well-defined, short, and well-tuned, the DSS queries are often random and ad hoc. In this case, the challenge will be to process large numbers of rows during a single query. For many DSSs, backup and recovery may not be an issue because the system is not needed to run the business in an up-to-the-minute fashion. Also, the DSS could be rebuilt from the OLTP systems. If the DSS system is down for several days, or perhaps even weeks, the business can continue to operate.

Sometimes a single database is used for several purposes. During the day, the system may be tuned to support the OLTP operations, then at night shifted to batch processing, reporting, or DSS. With larger (much larger) machines [clusters, or MPP machines (massively parallel processing computers)], you may even be able to support multiple kinds of processing simultaneously.

In addition to understanding the mix of applications, be sure to ask yourself and the customer, "how perfect is perfect?" That is how much effort should be spent, wringing out the last ounce of performance from the system. How good is good enough? Is subsecond response truly necessary, or is a few seconds OK? One of the trade-offs you will face here is the cost of labor versus the cost of hardware. Many times, a little more hardware can go a long way to improve performance.

Environments

How many environments or databases do you plan to create and support? Will there be separate development, test, production, and training environments? How much machine, and/or how many machines, will be available for all the environments? Coordinating all the environments can require substantial time and resources.

Architecture

As described earlier, Oracle provides several architectures, or methods of operations. The choice you make will affect a number of components and options.

Concurrent Users

How many users will be on the system? There are really two types of users on any system: those that are logged onto the system and those that are executing transactions against the system. Those users performing transactions are referred to as *concurrent users*, and this is the number that will most affect system performance. The number of concurrent users is usually a shifting subset of the total number of users.

System Inventory and Sizing

In order to build any system, you have to know what you have to work with. If you are reading this book to determine what kind of system you need for Oracle, this section will help you understand your options.

There are three major areas you have to examine. One is the hardware components that are available or planned. Another is the software and applications that will run on the machine besides the database itself. The final piece of the puzzle is the architecture for the environment, such as client/server, multiuser, parallel server, and so on.

Once you know what you have to work with, you can go about the business of deciding where all your Oracle structures will go.

Hardware Components

How big is this machine, or machines, anyway? One of the really nice trends in the computer industry is the downward trend in hardware costs. I seldom have to work on machines where you need a shoehorn to get the database to fit.

The two things that will most affect your system's performance are the amount of memory and the number of disks. If you are using the Parallel Query Option (PQO), or the Oracle Parallel Server (OPS), the number of CPUs and the number of machines will also have a significant impact. Tape drives may affect your database design because they can affect your backup strategy.

With regards to memory, the basic question is, how much memory is in the machine. Do you have 64MB, 128MB, 256MB, or more of RAM? Depending on budgets and types of processing, you will probably also want to know how much memory can go into the machine.

The number of CPUs in the machine is generally not very important in relation to database design unless you plan on using the PQO.

With the PQO, you can design the database and the queries to take advantage of multiple CPUs. A query using the PQO is split, or parallelized, across multiple CPUs with each CPU retrieving a portion of the data. Once all of the CPUs retrieve the requested data, the data is processed for return to the user submitting the query. These parallel queries are most effective when the data is spread across multiple drives. Regardless of the number of CPUs in a machine, if there are not enough disks, and controllers, the CPUs will have to wait.

Your disk drive configuration will be one of the most important components affecting the performance of your Oracle installation. This is a little more complex than counting the number of drives in the machine, because performance is also affected by the number of disk controllers and whether those controllers can have multiple channels. This is referred to as a bandwidth issue, that is, the more disks, controllers, and channels, the broader the I/O bandwidth and thus the higher the throughput capabilities. The broader the I/O bandwidth, the more data Oracle and your operating system can generally read and write from and to the disks.

The first questions to answer about your disk drives are:

- How many drives are there?
- How big is each drive?
- Are there any differences in speed among the drives?
- What currently resides on each disk?

This information is used to build a diskmap, which we'll eventually use to lay out your Oracle database. If you are working with an existing machine, it may not be critical to know what every single file in every single directory on the machine is. It will be more helpful to know the *types* of files in the various directories and how much space they use.

In the UNIX environment, there are several types of disk configurations. One way to set up disks is as UNIX file systems, another is as raw devices, and or can be configured into logical volumes. An important point about the UNIX file systems is that the operating system block size can sometimes be set when they are created.

I have seen raw devices referred to as a theological issue rather than a technical one. Raw devices are supposed to increase performance by allowing a process to read from and write directly to a disk without going through the UNIX buffer cache in memory. For Oracle, this means that data goes directly from the SGA to disk, and vice versa, without buffering by the UNIX kernel. This is supposed to be faster than systems that use UNIX file systems. But while raw devices reduce system overhead, they can create considerable additional administrative overhead. Technical merits aside, do not consider using raw devices unless you have very qualified staff that can build and administer them. This is not a job for amateurs. If your system administration staff is high quality, let them decide what to use, and have them do the work. If you decide to use raw devices, make all the raw partitions the same size so it is easier to move objects.

Logical volumes are disks, or sections of disks created to look like a single disk drive. Sometimes a single disk is partitioned to look like multiple disks.

Disk mirroring was covered as part of the discussion on backup and recovery and has little design impact except on the on-line redo logs. If high system availability is important, strongly consider disk mirroring. The decision may be easier if you discover that you have no manual or paper-based processes to continue operating with if the computer does go down. All those paper records that you may have will have to be keyed into the system when it does come up. How will you clear the backlog? This point has not been lost on the disk drive manufactures. An ad in *Forbes* magazine from disk drive manufacturer EMC2 reads:

How Important Is Data Storage To Your Company?

We'll rephrase that:

How Important Is Revenue To Your Company?

Tape drives play a more significant role as databases get bigger. The drives come in various configurations and capacities. Some vendors now provide tape drives that can read from or write to several disks in parallel. One of the most important consideration for Oracle is whether you can archive directly to tape. The other considerations include how big the tape drive is; that is, how much data it can hold and how fast it is. Again, the more data you have, the more critical the drives become.

Don't forget to include items that are on order in your inventory list.

Software Components

List all the software you intend to run on the target platform. The list should include your operating system, the Oracle executables, compilers, and any other software that will take up space and cause I/O. Calculate the space requirements and I/O characteristics for each. This list does not need to be measured to the exact byte; ballpark estimates of the sizes can work fine.

You may find it helpful to create a disk map that shows each drive, as well as the controllers and channels for each disk. The software inventory is used to develop an initial disk map. Figure 5.1 will help in this inventory. (There are several variations on this map later in the chapter, where they are used to help lay out the database.Do not include your Oracle database files yet unless you are putting your database on a machine with an existing Oracle database or adding to a database. For now, just collect information about everything except the database files. The database information comes later.

	Controller								
	Disk	0	1	2	3	4	5	6	7
Object	**Size**	2000000	2000000	2000000	2000000	2000000	2000000	2000000	2000000

Figure 5.1 New diskmap.

Note the size and location of the operating system files. In addition, most operating systems use swap space, or swap files, to extend the real memory of the machine. These areas act as virtual memory, and the buffers are paged, or swapped from real memory to the swap space. The size and location of these swap files is important, because they can have a very high amount of I/O to them.

The OFA manual suggests the way to create the directory structures to support the Oracle database and other Oracle products, such as SQL*Forms and the CASE tools. In addition, Oracle provides numerous scripts that are needed to use certain tools, utilities, and options. This is actually accomplished during the installation process. Note the size and location of the Oracle applications and scripts. The Oracle Installation Guide will tell you how much space is need for each Oracle component, or you can install the products and see for yourself.

Note the location and size of the application files and any compilers or interpreters, they may need. Also note whether the applications will need access to or create any other files. These may be text files to create documents or documents created by the applications.

Many shops have tools, or utilities, that help manage the computer and applications. Some are machine and operating system utilities; others monitor and/or tune the database.

You may need to reserve room for various files needed to support the system. These could include flat files used to transfer data into or out of the system. You may want to back up the database to disk before copying it out to tape.

Once all of the files referenced above are inventoried, fill in the disk map showing the size and location of the files. The space that is left over will be the area available for your Oracle database files.

Database Design

Design for performance, safety, security, and ease of maintenance begin with documentation and ends with a lack of documentation. It is extremely important to know what, why, how, and where something was done.

The actual database design process begins with the logical data model (LDM). Before you can build a good database, you must have a good LDM. So, unless you created the LDM yourself, you should check it to make sure you can implement it.

Once the LDM is validated, you need to decide what will be implemented and how. After you have decided what you will implement, you must size the objects and decide where to place them on the target machine. When you know where everything will go, you can create the DDL that will actually create the database and all the objects in it.

Validate Logical Data Model

This book is about physical database design, not logical data modeling, but a good database begins with a good LDM. The point here is not to teach data modeling, rather, how to check a data model to see if it is suitable for database design and implementation.

Most of what occurs during this stage is applying the rules of the relational model to the data model. The next section will cover the types of processing and transactions for the new system.

Check for the following items in the LDM:

- Are all of the relations in third normal form?
- Do the indicated foreign keys point to the entire primary key of the target or referenced table?
- Are there any columns that are not part of the primary key that are marked as unique?
- Do the data types specified in the LDM match Oracle's data types?
- What is the number of rows for each table?

There are several common mistakes I see in data models that involve foreign keys and the resulting referential integrity or the lack thereof. One common error (although this error is less common because many of today's CASE tool actually "propagate," or build, the foreign keys) is where fields appear in several tables, and they are called *foreign keys* even though they do not point to the correct, or any primary key. Another error is where a foreign key does not point to the **entire** primary key of the target table.

Figure 5.2 illustrates a PURCHASE_ORDER that has PO_LINE_ITEMs. Each line item is for one product. The dashed line from PO_LINE_ITEM to PRODUCT is the foreign key between the two entities/tables. The problem with this model is that we cannot be sure that the products listed on the purchase order are products that are actually supplied by the supplier, to whom we are sending the purchase order. While there is a foreign key from PO_LINE_ITEM to PRODUCT, it points to the wrong table.

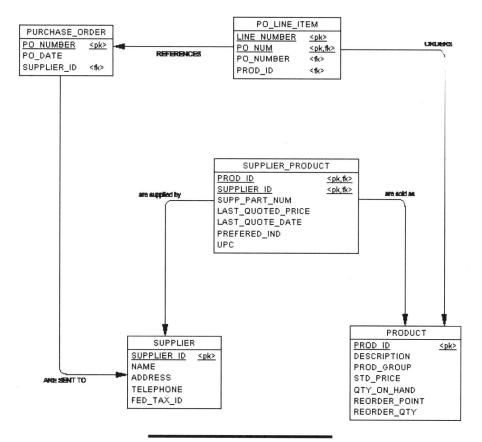

Figure 5.2 The wrong foreign key.

Figure 5.3 shows a common problem when people use drawing tools to produce their ERDs, or they just use their CASE tools to draw pictures rather than any rigorous engineering.

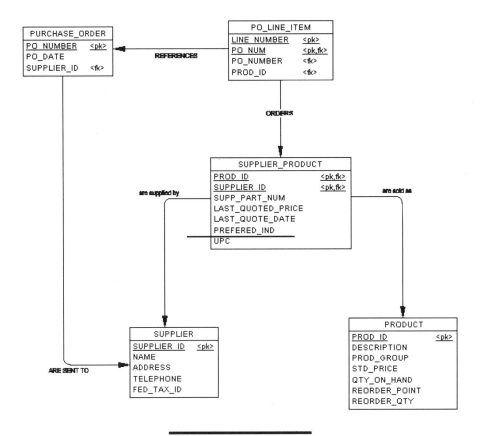

Figure 5.3 No foreign key.

Figure 5.3 shows a relationship/foreign key from PO_LINE_ITEM to SUPPLIER_PRODUCT. This should solve the problem described in the previous illustration. The problem here, however, is that the relationship is not really a foreign key. As before, we cannot be sure, through the use of foreign keys, that the product we are ordering is sold by the supplier to whom we are sending the purchase order. What should be the foreign key in the table PO_LINE_ITEM does not point to the entire primary key of SUPPLIER_PRODUCT table; it only points to the PROD_ID. The column PROD_ID in PO_LINE_ITEM is only part of the entire primary key of SUPPLIER_PRODUCT.

The reality is that there is no foreign keys from PO_LINE_ITEM to SUPPLIER_PRODUCT, just a line. The standard workaround is to code a routine in the purchasing applications to match the supplier in the PURCHASE_ORDER with the supplier in the SUPPLIER_PRODUCT. How we may choose to implement the system is not the issue here. The issue here is to get the LDM right.

To solve the problem, the LDM should look like Figure 5.4.

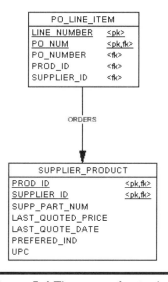

Figure 5.4 The proper foreign key.

In the PO_LINE_ITEM table, SUPPLIER_ID was added to complete the foreign key. Now, whenever a line is added to a purchase order, the foreign key can check to make sure that the product ordered is, indeed, a product sold by that supplier.

If you follow the methodologies and steps that come with most CASE tools, these kinds of errors are prevented. Most CASE tools actually build the foreign key relations for you. In the S-Designor tool I used to produce these examples, it took me a while to figure out how to produce the errors illustrated here, because the CASE tool kept telling me there were errors. As you can see, I finally did figure out how to produce the errors, but the tool, to its credit, made a valiant effort to prevent me from doing so.

Evaluate Processing and Transactions

The data model tells you about the structures that a system will need, but to build a high performance database we also need to know about how those structures will be used. What kind of applications will run against the database? Will the system be used for online transaction processing (OLTP), or decision support (DSS), or some combination? These might seem like easy questions to answer because of what's implied by the different types of processing. For instance, say DSS and most people say read-only processing. Well, maybe.

Many DSSs perform different kinds of rollup or summary transactions that are stored in summary tables or columns. Rather than read through all of the invoices for every month, a summary table could carry monthly totals which are generated by batch jobs at the end of every month. In this case the DSS is not read-only.

OLTP implies lots of insert, update, and delete transactions. The questions are: What is the mix and what is the volume of each type? These types of questions should be answered to help in the design process.

The types of transactions are often more difficult to answer in the early stages of development. Over time (and especially when performing prototyping) patterns will appear that show the following:

- Which tables are accessed most often?
- What kinds of transactions are usually applied to each table: SELECT, INSERT, UPDATE, or DELETE?
- What are the transaction volumes for each table within a specified time frame: daily, monthly, weekly, etc.?
- Which columns are used to access data in each table?
- Which tables are often or usually accessed or joined together, and which columns are used for the joins?
- Which of the tables are lookup tables?
- Is there data that needs to be ordered or grouped?

This information is important because it helps to determine where tables should be located, how they should be structured (are they candidates for clusters?), and which tables and columns should have indexes.

Stored Procedures, Triggers, Functions, and Packages

Oracle7 gives us greatly expanded capabilities for controlling database access and manipulation at the database level rather than at the application level.

Lookup tables that have time constraints provide an example of a problem that cannot be solved with just foreign keys. Suppose you had a set of codes that were only valid between certain periods. These values should only be added as foreign keys between certain dates, but they need to be available for lookups year round. For example, a retailer has a set of codes used to indicate the type of sale under which an item was discounted. The codes may look like Figure 5.5.

SALES CODE

SALE_CODE	SALE_NAME
IC	Inventory clearance
CH	Christmas
MD	Mother's Day
MC	Match competition
FJ	Fourth of July

Figure 5.5 SALES_CODE table.

Two of these codes, IC and MC, could apply any time of the year. That is, items could be discounted at any time to clear excess inventory or match the competition. The remaining three codes, CH, MD, and FJ, should obviously be used only during certain times of the year. This means we need to put some kind of time constraint on when they can be added to a record, but they need to always be available for lookups of the SALE_NAME. So, we add two columns to the table for begin and end dates that show the month and dates that sales are valid (Figure 5.6).

Now, let's look at the ERD that shows how these sales codes actually relate to the purchase of a product (Figure 5.7).

SALES CODE

SALE_CODE	SALE_NAME	BEGIN_DATE	END_DATE
IC	Inventory clearance		
CH	Christmas	12/15	1/5
MD	Mother's Day	5/10	5/30
MC	Match competition		
FJ	Fourth of July	6/30	7/10

Figure 5.6 SALES_CODE with date ranges.

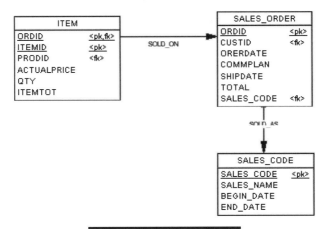

Figure 5.7 Sales order ERD.

There is a problem here. We do not want to carry the SALES_CODE begin and end dates with every order line item, and SALES_CODE is the only column necessary to uniquely identify a row in the SALES_CODE table. Thus the foreign key from LINE_ITEM points only to the SALES_CODE column or primary key. So, how do we control when we can use a certain sales code?

Foreign keys will not do the job for us here. What we need is some programming. In the good old days, the controls and logic necessary to control this process would be added to every application that dealt with lookups to the SALES_CODE table. Besides the code in the application, there were calls to the database issued by the application to check the business rules. In order for the application to know whether a particular sales code can be used, the application would have to perform a SELECT on the SALES_CODE table to check on valid dates (Figure 5.8). These calls also increase network traffic.

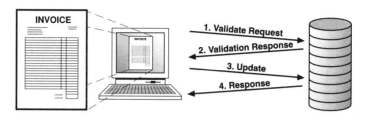

Figure 5.8 Multiple calls to the database.

A better solution to this problem is provided by using Oracle database triggers that execute PL/SQL code. A *trigger* is a program stored in the database that is *activated*, or fired, when a certain action is requested for the table associated with the trigger. Triggers are event-driven; they are written to fire either before or after one of the following statements: INSERT, UPDATE, or DELETE.

In our sales example, a foreign key would only tell us that a certain SALES_CODE exists, not whether it is valid for a certain date. Instead of a foreign key, we can use a trigger to both check the foreign key reference and determine whether we are within a valid date range. One trigger would be created and fire during inserts, and a similar trigger should be created for updates.

Transform Logical to Physical

The LDM you are working with may or may not be in a shape or form that is directly convertible or usable by an Oracle database. For example, Oracle has a data type called VARCHAR2. This particular data type is not included with every CASE tool. Some data modelers do not even believe the LDM should contain anything besides tables, columns, and relationships. They think that data type and field length are physical considerations, not part of data modeling.

As you go from the LDM to the physical model, you will use the information about your processing environment and the types of transactions to build a database that has a sound theoretical foundation (the relational model) but performs well. Oracle provides numerous design options that, when applied to an LDM, produce a high-performance database.

Specify All Objects

List all the logical structures that will be created as schema objects for the new database. This includes tables, indexes, clusters, constraints, and sequences.

There is no law that states that every single entity and every single attribute in an LDM must be implemented in a physical database. Some of the factors that will determine which entities and attributes you implement include:

- **Budget**—How much money, time, and resources are available for the project or for phases of the project?
- **Priorities and dependencies**—Which objects have to be in place before other development can proceed?

Tables

The easiest thing to do when creating the physical database is to have a one-to-one mapping between the logical entities and the physical tables. In a perfect world, where there are no performance problems, this mapping would certainly be the recommended choice. There are, however, several issues that may require changes to table structures.

Tables with columns that are very long require special attention. The data type VARCHAR2 can contain up to 2000 bytes, and a LONG column can store up to 2GB. A table can only have one LONG column, but you can add many long VARCHAR2 columns to a table. Some tables may have several comment fields, where users can add various kinds of notes. The problem you will likely encounter when a lot of text can be added to a record is row chaining. Row chaining occurs when all the data for a row cannot fit into a single block, and the data must be "chained" to one or more additional blocks. This is especially prevalent with small block sizes, like 2K. Row chaining is one of the worst things that can happen to a table; it should be avoided whenever possible.

Here are a few basic guidelines for comment columns and LONG columns:

- Put LONG and LONGRAW columns into a separate table.
- If there are long VARCHAR2 columns, and especially if the table has several of them, consider placing them in a separate table.
- If these long columns will be updated after the record is inserted, consider using a high PCTFREE value, so the data can fit into a single block. (PCTFREE will be covered soon.)

- Consider a larger Oracle block size.

You can almost guarantee that the problems just described will create chaining problems. Figure 5.9 illustrates this point by analyzing the customer table, then expanding the column CITY from 30 to 100 characters. Because CITY is a CHARACTER type column, it will take up 100 characters whether there is any data in it or not. (Figure 5.9). This example also illustrates what can happen if existing VARCHAR2 columns in a table are updated in a manner that adds additional data to the existing row.

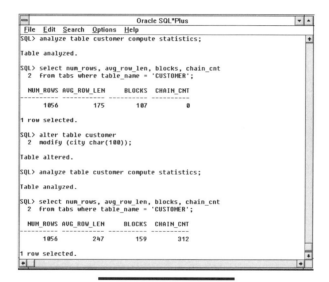

Figure 5.9 Row chaining.

Note that the table started with 1056 rows contained in 107 blocks, and there are 0 chained rows. After the CITY column is modified to 100 characters from 30, there are 159 blocks and 312 chained rows in the table. The increase in the CITY column initially filled the unused portion of each data block. When each block was filled, the rows had to chain to compensate for the new space. Any updates to the existing records that increase the record length, would cause those rows to chain as well.

The results of this example would change depending on the block size, the value of PCTFREE, the data type, and the actual increase in the size of the column(s). The question you have to ask whenever anyone wants to increase the length of any column is, do you want to risk chaining rows. If you modify one or more columns by making them longer, you should check the results with the **ANALYZE** command.

Clusters

Identify candidates for clusters. You may want to hold off on clusters until you determine you have performance problems. Chapter 7 covers tuning and shows how, using EXPLAIN PLAN, Oracle will execute SQL statements. If you are experiencing performance problems, you might consider clusters to solve certain problems. As noted in Chapter 2, clusters have several limitations and will require extra effort to build. Why exert the effort if there isn't a problem?

Indexes

Indexes have three functions in Oracle. They are used to ensure uniqueness, speed access to rows in table, and/or order or sort the rows in a table. Choosing indexes is not as obvious as it might seem. With Oracle's declarative integrity, it is no longer necessary to explicitly create unique indexes to enforce primary key uniqueness or entity integrity. An index is automatically created when a primary key or unique constraint is declared or enabled. Details of these primary keys and unique indexes were covered in Chapter 2 in the section on constraints.

Once the unique and primary keys are chosen, the task turns to creating indexes for better performance and sorting/ordering. There are several factors that influence the choice of columns for indexes.

- How are accesses requested from the table(s)? For example, if you know that the employee table will usually be accessed by the employee Social Security number, then create an index on that column.

- The type of transactions. Indexes generally help during reads, but they can severely, and adversely, affect insert, update, and delete transactions. During these write transactions, the table is updated, but every index must also be updated.

- The size of the table. Many people are surprised to fine that they have more space allocated to indexes than tables. Big tables, tables with many rows will usually have big indexes. There are often several indexes for a single table. This translates into more space, and longer times to load and/or build the indexes.

- The distribution of data—the uniqueness factor. While indexes generally help with reads, they don't help all reads. An index should be used when the data retrieved for the column, or columns, indexes returns a small subset of data. For the employee table, the Social Security number would be a good index candidate because there is a high "uniqueness" factor, that is, there will seldom be more than one row for each Social Security number value. However, if a column contains just a few values (as in, say, gender or department) relative to the total number of rows in the table, then it has a low uniqueness factor, and an index may actually be counterproductive.

- Data that must be ordered or sorted. If data is retrieved in a specified order, indexes can usually improve performance. Sorting must be balanced against other types of transactions, as noted earlier.

Some of this information comes from the same transaction information you used to help make decisions on your table structures. Other information, especially the data distributions, will only be available after real or production-quality data is loaded. Some final decisions may not be made until testing is done on specific queries and applications using EXPLAIN PLAN or SQLTRACE and TKPROF. As with clusters, indexes can be added later when you discover performance problems You are generally better off starting with fewer indexes and adding them as you find you need them.

Many CASE tools will automatically generate indexes for foreign keys. For any foreign key that points to a lookup table, this is probably a bad idea because the uniqueness factor of the index may be very low, especially if there are relatively few values in the target lookup table.

Constraints

Most of your constraints, especially all of the primary and foreign keys, should be generated by your CASE tool. Many CASE tools will even generate check constraints, triggers, and defaults. If the power is there, use it.

Sequences

Oracle provides a tool for generating numbers called *sequences*. These sequences are intended to generate primary key values when inserting new rows into a table. A sequence can place a predefined number of these sequence values, or blind keys, in memory from which any application can draw.

People often create a sequence generator for each table that needs primary key values. If the primary key values are truly blind keys that have no meaning associated with them, you need not have more than one sequence.

There are, however, two situations for which you may need multiple sequences. One case is where the number of digits in the primary keys varies between tables. This would be where one table has a primary key that is a NUMBER(7) and another table has a primary key of NUMBER(9). The other case is where gaps in the numbers is an issue. If you want to limit the number of gaps between numbers, set the INCREMENT BY parameter to 1, and use the NOCACHE and ORDER options when creating the sequence and only use the sequence for a single table.

For design purposes, you need not worry about sizing or placing sequences because their definitions and values are stored in the data dictionary. If sequences are not cached, Oracle will have to perform I/O to the data dictionary to get the next value.

Size Objects

Sizing should occur twice. The first is a rough guess or first-cut estimate, which uses the total row length of the table multiplied by the total number of rows for the table to give you the total size of the table or index. Some CASE tools will even calculate these values for you if you specify the number of rows in each table. Figure 5.10 shows an example from S-Designor.

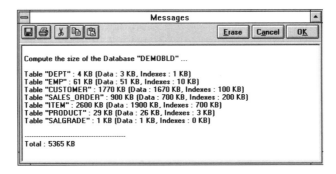

Figure 5.10 Calculating object sizes.

All the tables and indexes should be resized using the **ANALYZE** command after the tables have been full or partially loaded with production data. Production-quality data is very important for accurate sizing. Most of the columns in most databases are VARCHAR2, or variable-length fields. Most of these columns will not be completely full, so it is not uncommon to find many tables 70% full. If there were a number of comment columns in the table, these tables may not even be 50% full.

Figures 5.11 and 5.12 contain spreadsheets that perform several functions. One section calculates the size of each table and index. The section on the right helps in placing objects and sizing tablespaces.

TABLE NAME	PCTFREE	Space available	Max len	Avg len	% filled	Rows per block	Total rows	Blocks required	Space required	% growth	Initial extent	Lookup tables	Data_1	Data_2
Database block size:	4096													
Approx space per block:		3996												
TABLE NAME														
CUSTOMER	20%	3,197	357	200	56%	15.98	10,000	625.63	2,562,563	50%	3,843,844		4,000,000	
DEPARTMENT	5%	3,796	29	20	69%	189.81	100	0.53	2,158	10%	2,374	8,192		
EMPLOYEE	10%	3,596	50	38	76%	94.64	1,000	10.57	43,279	10%	47,607			48,000
ITEM	20%	3,197	38	30	79%	106.56	60,000	563.06	2,306,306	50%	3,459,459		4,000,000	
JOB	5%	3,796	25	20	80%	189.81	10	0.05	216	10%	237	8,192		
LOCATION	5%	3,796	30	25	83%	151.85	10	0.07	270	10%	297	8,192		
PRICE	5%	3,796	26	20	77%	189.81	500	2.63	10,790	10%	11,869	16,384		
PRODUCT	5%	3,796	52	40	77%	94.91	500	5.27	21,579	10%	23,737		32,000	
SALARY_GRADE	5%	3,796	30	25	83%	151.85	5	0.03	135	10%	148	8,192		
SALES_ORDER	20%	3,197	35	30	86%	106.56	20,000	187.69	768,769	50%	1,153,153			2,000,000
									5,716,064		8,542,725	49,152	8,032,000	2,048,000

Figure 5.11 Sizing table spreadsheets.

For tables, you initially need to specify the Oracle block size, then fill in the values for the following columns: PCTFREE, Max len, Avg len, Total rows, and % growth. The PCTFREE (covered in detail soon) indicates how much space you want to leave in each block for updates. The maximum length is the sum of the lengths of all the columns in the table. The average length column is an estimate of how much data each row will have in it. The total rows is how many rows you expect the table to start with, that is, how many rows you plan to load into the table. The % growth column is used to indicate how much growth you anticipate for a certain time frame. If, for example, you expect the customer table to grow by 50% a year and you want the initial extent to hold one year's worth of data, the % growth figure should be 50.

For indexes you need to gather the block size, PCTFREE, the number of rows in the table, a % growth number, and the number and size of the columns in each index (Figure 5.12).

Table	Index	PK	PCT REE	Rows	Num of cols	Total Index Length	Blocks Required	Estimated Size	% growth	Estimated Initial Extent	Dinstinct values	Leaf blocks	Actual Space Used	Ioindex	Index 1	Index 2
Database block size:	4096															
Approx space per block:	4096															
CUSTOMER	customer_pk	Y	5	10,000	1	5	37.94	155,415	50%	233,122	9,211	46	188,416			256,000
DEPARTMENT	department_pk	Y	5	100	1	2	0.31	1,263	10%	1,389	100	1	4,096	8,192		
EMPLOYEE	employee_pk	Y	5	1,000	1	2	3.08	12,627	10%	13,890	923	3	12,288	16,000		
ITEM	otem_pk	N	5	60,000	2	10	313.03	1,282,173	10%	1,923,259	58,243	309	1,265,664		2,000,000	
JOB	job_pk	Y	5	10	1	2	0.03	126	10%	139	10	1	4,096	8,192		
LOCATION	location_pk	Y	5	10	1	2	0.03	126	10%	139	10	1	4,096	8,192		
PRICE	pnce_pk	N	5	500	1	5	1.90	7,771	10%	8,548	485	3	12,288	16,000		
PRODUCT	product_pk	Y	5	500	1	5	1.90	7,771	10%	8,548	485	3	12,288	16,000		
SALARY_GRADE	sal_grade_pk	Y	5	5	1	2	0.02	63	50%	95	5	1	4,096	8,192		
SALES_ORDER	sales_ord_pk	N	5	20,000	1	5	75.89	310,830	50%	466,245	21,632	83	339,968			512,000
	so_cust	N	5	20,000	1	5	75.89	310,830	50%	466,245	8,723	43	176,128		256,000	
								2,088,995		3,121,618		494	2,023,424	80,768	2,256,000	768,000

Figure 5.12 Sizing index spreadsheet.

The **ANALYZE** command will show the actual number of rows in the tables and indexes, the actual average row length of each table, and the actual number of blocks used for each index. These numbers should be entered later to get better estimates.

The columns on the right of each spreadsheet are for the tablespaces you expect to create. The columns help you visualize the location and spread of data and calculate the size of each tablespace. Note that the sizes of most objects is rounded upward, and the lookup tables and indexes have at least the Oracle minimum of two blocks for their size.

In placing each object in a tablespace, your goal is to try and separate objects that are accessed together. In the case of the table spreadsheet, the ITEM table and the SALES_ORDER table will usually be accessed together by the applications, so they go into different tablespaces.

You need not labor over every single object (note that all the lookup tables and indexes were just placed into a single tablespace). Concentrate your efforts on those objects that will have the most activity and put the remaining objects in a more or less random fashion. (There is usually a diminishing rate of return associated with too much attention to detail. With Oracle, getting it close is usually as good as getting it perfect.)

Oracle Block Size

The Oracle block size will affect how much room each object will use and may also affect performance. Larger blocks can store more data; smaller blocks are good for OLTP where applications perform reads and writes that affect single rows at a time. You can get more blocks in the SGA. Larger blocks are good for applications that perform mostly reads, like DSSes.

Storage Parameters

In addition to the structure of a table or index, which includes the columns, data types, and lengths, there are other Oracle-specific parameters that affect the size of the object, where it is located, and performance. Collectively, these additional parameters are referred to as *storage parameters*. You should specify the storage parameters for any and all objects that will take more than several blocks of space. A CREATE TABLE statement looks like Figure 5.13.

```
─                    Oracle SQL*Plus                ▼ ▲
 File   Edit   Search   Options   Help
SQL> create table dept (                                ↑
   2   deptno  number(2),
   3   dname   varchar2(14),
   4   loc     varchar(13))
   5   PCTFREE     10
   6   PCTUSED     40
   7   INITRANS    1
   8   MAXTRANS    255
   9   TABLESPACE USER_DATA
  10   STORAGE (
  11   INITIAL     8k
  12   NEXT        8K
  13   MINEXTENTS 1
  14   MAXEXTENTS 20
  15   PCTINCREASE 0
  16   FREELISTS    1);

Table created.

SQL>                                                    ↓
◄  ◄                                                 ►  ►
```

Figure 5.13 CREATE TABLE statement.

Each of these parameters has a default value. If you do not specify a value, the object will take the default.

PCTFREE and PCTUSED

These two parameters perform several functions. They determine which data blocks have room for adding new rows, and therefore which data blocks are on the freelists. They represent high- and low-water marks for each data block. When adding new rows to an empty block, no new rows should be added above the high-water mark. When data is deleted from a block, no new rows should be added to the block until it hits the low-water mark. These parameters are expressed as percentages, and the defaults are 10% for PCTFREE and 40% for PCTUSED (see Figure 5.14).

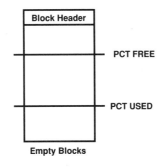

Figure 5.14 PCTFREE and PCTUSE.

When a block has more than the specified PCTFREE space available, new rows can be added to the data block. Once rows are added to the PCTFREE level, the block is removed from the freelist, and the remaining space in the block is reserved for updates to existing records. If the PCTFREE value is 10, then 10% of the data block is reserved for adding data to the existing rows in the block. No new rows can be added once the block is 90% full (Figure 5.15).

When a block is full, it is not returned to the freelist until data is deleted from the block to a point below the PCTUSED level. The deleted data can be entire records or data from within existing records. When enough data is removed from the block to drop below the PCTUSED, or low-water mark, then the block is returned to the top of the freelist. Oracle tries to keep blocks with data in them full, rather than add data to an empty block.

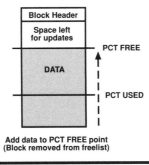

Figure 5.15 Data block removed from freelist.

If the value of PCTUSED is 40, then no new records can be added to the block (the block cannot go back on the freelist) until 40% of the data is removed. The block would go back on the freelist when it reaches 60% full (Figure 5.16).

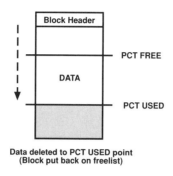

Figure 5.16 Data block returned to the freelist.

Tables that are mostly read-only should have a low PCTFREE, 5% or less, but not 0. Tables that have high insert or update activity should have a higher PCTFREE, 10 to 20%. In cases where substantial amounts data are added to existing rows in a table, even higher PCTFREE values may be needed. This maybe the case where data is added to a record over the life of the record rather than when the record is first created. For instance, data and comments may be added to a customer record as the customer does more business with a company. When the customer is first added to the database there may only be several columns in the customer table filled in with data. As more information is learned about the customer, their record may grow from 40 bytes to 200 bytes in length. In this case a PCTFREE of 50 or 60% may not be unreasonable if most of the customer records have substantial amounts of data added during their life on the system.

For most tables, the default PCTUSED value of 40% is quite sufficient. If there are high numbers of delete transactions, a higher value may be in order.

INITRANS and MAXTRANS

These two parameters affect the amount of space that is, and can be, allocated in the data block header to hold transaction information. Any time a row in a data block is accessed, space (approximately 23 bytes, but it is operating system–dependent) is allocated to hold transaction and lock information. If space for the transaction entries is not allocated, Oracle will allocate space for each new concurrent transaction. The space is freed when the transaction completes.

If a data block is completely full, no new transactions can access the block, because they cannot allocate space for the transaction information. INITRANS is the number of sections allocated for transaction entries. What the value is for INITRANS is the number of concurrent transactions guaranteed access to the data block, because space is already allocated for the transaction information. The minimum and default values for INITRANS are one for a table and two for a cluster or index.

Consider increasing the value for INITRANS if the table or index will be updated heavily. This may be more important for large blocks that contain many rows. Remember that you reduce the space available for data by increasing the value for INITRANS.

MAXTRANS limits the number of concurrent transactions that can simultaneously access a data block. The default for MAXTRANS is 255 and need not be changed.

TABLESPACE

The TABLESPACE is the location for the object. If no TABLESPACE is specified, the object is placed in the DEFAULT TABLESPACE for the user that created it. Users are covered later in this chapter. If there is no DEFAULT TABLESPACE specified, the object will go into the system tablespace. Every object should have a tablespace specified for it.

The following parameters make up the STORAGE clause for an object and directly affect its size.

INITIAL Extent

The initial extent is the amount of space allocated when an object is created. Extents are made up of contiguous blocks. The initial extent must be at least two blocks. The initial extent should be large enough to hold all the data for the table, cluster, or index for a specified time. This decision often varies significantly, depending on the type of processing. OLTP systems usually hold a finite set of data (two months', three months', maybe even six months', or a year's worth of data), while a DSS may accumulate data for many years.

Some on-line systems only hold a certain number of days' worth of data. After perhaps 60, 90, or 120 days, the data in the on-line system is moved from the on-line system to a historical or DSS system. In these types of systems, the size of most tables and indexes is fairly stable. The only growth you need to plan for is an increase in the number of transaction for a given time frame. For example, we expect to process 2% more orders per month given current sales projections.

Systems that continuously grow over time, like DSSes, are sometimes harder to size. The basic question you need to answer is how many days, months, or years of data you want to store in the table. This decision will also affect the size of any indexes for the table.

Again, regardless of the number of rows in a table or how small you specify the initial extent, the initial extent actually requires two blocks. If you have a data block size of 4K or 8K, and you are creating a small lookup table that may have only 20 rows that are 50 characters long (for a total of 1000 bytes), your initial extent will be two blocks large, even if you specify it at 2K.

If you are curious about how multiple extents can affect performance, try the following against a table that has many extents. This script will show how long the scan takes by listing the time before and after the query. The function UPPER in the WHERE will force a full table scan even if there is an index on the field.

```
SELECT TO_CHAR(SYSDATA, 'HH:MI:SS') FROM DUAL;


SELECT *
FROM table_name
WHERE UPPER(field_name) = 'anything';
SELECT TO_CHAR(SYSDATA, 'HH:MI:SS') FROM DUAL;
```

After running the query, Export and Import the table compressing the number of extents. Run the query again. The time for the second query should be substantially shorter.

One additional note on extent sizes. An extent is a set of contiguous data blocks. This means that an extent cannot span datafiles. If any of your objects are larger than your disks, you must create multiple extents to hold all of the data. Placing multiple extents on different disk is called *table striping*, and an example of this is provided in Very Large Databases section of Chapter 9.

NEXT Extent

The NEXT extent is the size of the extent allocated after the INITIAL extent. If the PCTINCREASE is zero, every additional extent will be the same size.

MINEXTENTS

All objects that can be created with a storage clause require at least one extent, and it will be at least two data blocks in size. The default is one extent. Rollback segments require a minimum of two extents.

When Oracle fills an extent, it must add any new data to another extent. If that extent is not already allocated, Oracle must create one. When Oracle creates another extent to add data, it is called *dynamic allocation of extents*. In order to dynamically allocate an extent, Oracle must perform multiple queries against the data dictionary to find space for the new extent. Then it must actually allocate the space for the new extent. If there is not enough room left in the data file(s) to allocate the new extent, you get the very unfriendly error message:

```
Failed to Allocate Extent
```

When this message occurs, users can no longer insert new data into the object in question. This error can occur for indexes, tables, roolback segments, and clusters. It is referred to as a *show stopper*.

As part of your database design, you want to prevent dynamic allocation of extents, and you should never see the preceding error message. To prevent dynamic allocation, I suggest you create your objects with at least two extents. The first should be sized to hold the predetermined amount of data for the given time frames discussed earlier. The next extent is smaller and is used to monitor growth. When data begins to appear in the second extent, you know it is time to reorganize the object, that is, to make it larger. The size of the second extent will depend on how often you can bring the database down for maintenance. If the database is shut down regularly, such as on weekends or monthly, then the second extent may not have to be too large because you will be able to reorganize or resize the object fairly quickly.

MAXEXTENTS

The maximum number of extents is determined by the Oracle block size. I have had several calls from clients who have received the Failed To Allocate Extent error message. They swore that they had set the MAXEXTENTS parameter to 999; therefore, they could not be out of extents. Figure 5.17 illustrates the problem. Even if you set MAXEXTENTS to a million, with a block size of, say, 2K you will never get more than 121 extents.

Oracle block size	Number of extents
512 bytes	25
1K	57
2K	121
4K	249
8K	505
16K	1017

Figure 5.17 MAXEXTENTS by block size.

If you follow the design principles outlined in this section, these limits should not be a problem. If your database and your maintenance are planned, you should never run out of extents.

PCTINCREASE (Percent Increase)

The PCTINCREASE parameter determines how much larger the next extent will be when it is allocated. The next extent is equal to the last extent plus the PCTINCREASE amount. Figure 5.18 illustrates this point with the Oracle default of a 50% increase.

You should always set the PCTINCREASE to zero (0). As the preceding figure illustrates, Oracle tries to create bigger and bigger extents as new ones are created. The problem with this is that as the database grows, there is usually less and less space left in each datafile from which to create new extents. As the free space becomes smaller and the extents get larger, there is less chance of finding room for the larger extents. The result in this scenario is the Failed to Allocate Extent error.

Number of extents	Initial Extent	Next Extent	PCTINCREASE	Size of next extent	Total size of object
1	10240	10240	50	10,240	10,240
2	10240	10240	50	10,240	20,480
3	10240	10240	50	15,361	35,841
4	10240	10240	50	23,043	58,884
5	10240	10240	50	34,565	93,448
6	10240	10240	50	51,848	145,296
7	10240	10240	50	77,773	223,070
8	10240	10240	50	116,661	339,730
9	10240	10240	50	174,992	514,723
10	10240	10240	50	262,489	777,212
11	10240	10240	50	393,735	1,170,947
12	10240	10240	50	590,603	1,761,550
13	10240	10240	50	885,906	2,647,456
14	10240	10240	50	1,328,860	3,976,316
15	10240	10240	50	1,993,291	5,969,607
16	10240	10240	50	2,989,937	8,959,544
17	10240	10240	50	4,484,907	13,444,452
18	10240	10240	50	6,727,362	20,171,814
19	10240	10240	50	10,091,044	30,262,857
20	10240	10240	50	15,136,567	45,399,424
21	10240	10240	50	22,704,851	68,104,275
22	10240	10240	50	34,057,277	102,161,552
23	10240	10240	50	51,085,917	153,247,469
24	10240	10240	50	76,628,877	229,876,346
25	10240	10240	50	114,943,316	344,819,662
26	10240	10240	50	172,414,975	517,234,637
27	10240	10240	50	258,622,464	775,857,101

Figure 5.18 PCTINCREASE increases.

FREELISTS

Every table, index, and cluster has a freelist, which contains a list of all the data blocks that have space available in them to add new rows, that is, blocks that have not yet reached the PCTFREE high-water mark. The default number of freelists is one, which is sufficient for most applications.

Where an application has a large number of users inserting data into a small number of tables, performance may suffer due to contention for access to the objects' freelist. For example, an order-entry system that is primarily adding new order header records and order line records may slow down as processes have to wait to get a block address from a single freelist. Increasing the number of freelists for tables and indexes with heavy inserts may increase performance. See the section in Chapter 7 on tuning contention for more details.

Freelist Groups

Freelist groups are used exclusively in the Oracle Parallel Server environment. They are used to reduce "pinging."

OPS allows multiple instances to access a common database. These instances can be on the same machine, as in a massively parallel processor (MPP), or on different machines, as in a cluster. Remember that before a user can get access to data, an instance must read the data block that contains the row or rows into the SGA. For a single instance, this works fine. However, what happens when another instance needs the same row or the same data blocks? How does the requesting instance know that the block is already in another SGA? More importantly, how does the requesting instance know whether any data was changed by the other instance?

This interinstance contention for data blocks is called *pinging*. For Oracle to fulfill the request of the second instance, the first instance is forced to write the requested block back to disk—*ping*.

To reduce pinging, you can create separate extents for each instance by manually allocating extents. Each extent has its own freelist or freelist groups. Refer to the *Oracle Parallel Server Administrator's Guide* for more details.

CACHE

This parameter specifies whether an entire table should be cached in memory. When a table that was created with the CACHE parameter is accessed with a full table scan the data blocks are placed at the top of the LRU list in memory. (The cache parameter can also be specified as part of a hint in an individual query.) This can be especially effective for certain lookup tables which are accessed frequently. If there is enough memory in the machine (many 32-bit machines can access two gigabytes of RAM, while 64 bit machine can access up to **fourteen gigabytes** of RAM - that's memory, not disk.), you can consider caching larger tables that are accessed very frequently. This is especially true for tables that are not updated, since there will be no need to write them out to disk for changes.

Group objects by tablespace

Tablespaces and their associated datafiles are the means by which tables and indexes can be grouped to improve I/O performance. In general, it is best to control the placement of objects in an Oracle database. An oft-quoted recommendation is to group all of the tables in a single application into a single tablespace. While this may appear convenient, it makes it almost impossible to control I/O.

Controlling I/O is the same reason that I do not recommend tuning logical volumes to create large virtual disks. While it may be convenient to place all of your tablespaces on a single large virtual disk, you cannot tune the I/O as well since you lose much of the ability to place files on particular disks.

Design objectives

With the individual tables and indexes sized, it's time to decide where to place them. Each table and index should be assigned to a specific tablespace. The right-hand columns of the index and table sizing spreadsheets contained columns to help locate each object in a tablespace. At the bottom of each column was a total for the space required for each tablespace. The size of each tablespace is based on the combined size of all the objects it contains. Each tablespace is made up of one or more datafiles. In designing your tablespaces and data files there are three basic objectives:

- Get it to fit.
- Spread the I/O.
- Make it maintainable.

Get it to fit. Your first objective is to get everything to fit on the machine. A lot more goes into an Oracle database than data and indexes. Besides the database objects, there are all the applications, including but not limited to the operating system (which usually wants swap space equal to twice the size of the machine memory), Oracle executables, and whatever other applications and utilities may be floating around on the machine. In addition, you will probably need space to load and back up your database. And don't forget logging and recovery.

Fortunately, most machines have plenty of disk space, and new disks are relatively inexpensive. The table and index sizing spreadsheets should give you a good picture of how much room you will need. If the initial calculations point to a space problem, load data into the tables and indexes to get accurate size information using the **ANALYZE** command.

If the real data shows that you still have a space problem, you may need to examine the scope of the project. You can look at the number of rows in the tables to see if six months' worth of data is really necessary or if you get by with just three or four months' worth. You may have to scale back the number of tables. The easiest thing to do is usually call a hardware salesperson, but for very large systems this is not always an option and the system gets scaled back.

Spread I/O. This is where the rubber hits the road in terms of physical database design. Up to this point, we have covered the various types of objects and files that will make up the database. Now you need to decide where everything will go on the disks.

The goal of this stage is to spread the I/O across all the disks available on the machine. You want to avoid bottlenecks, or hot spots. These are disks that have a high percentage of the system's I/O, and as a result they slow performance. Only so much data can be read from and written to a single disk a one time. If many users need data from a certain disk, there can be contention problems and poor performance as processes have to wait for access to the disk.

Designing the database layout is a two-step process that can be repeated after testing to improve performance. The first step uses the table and index sizing spreadsheets to place the tables and indexes into their respective tablespaces. The next step is to place the tablespaces onto the diskmap that was developed as part of the initial machine inventory.

In addition to the tablespaces for tables and indexes, you should create one or more tablespaces for the rollback segments. The number of rollback segments depends on the number of concurrent users and write transactions. Create one rollback for every four concurrent users. If you have the disk capacity (in terms of the number of disks rather than the disk space), create multiple tablespaces for the rollback segments and place them on different drives. The rollback segments can be very active, so they should be separated from other active tablespaces.

Performance is not the only issue when laying out the database. The other concern is safety. Remember the redo logs? Because the on-line redo log files and the archived redo log files contain data that is needed to recover a database, they should not go on any disks that contain tablespaces that have tables in them.

The redo logs can go on disks with indexes because the indexes can always be rebuilt from the data in the tables. You cannot fully recover the database if you lose both the redo logs and the tables.

Maintenance issues. In addition to getting it all to fit into one place so that it performs well, the database will need maintenance. The following are areas that will also affect the layout of the database:

- backups/archiving
- loads and data transfers
- the ability to move data files

The following spreadsheets in Figure 5.19 are diskmaps that show various sample configurations for OLPT- and DSS-type systems. Each type of processing has two spreadsheets/examples. One example has four disk drives, the other six drives. These spreadsheet are included ont he disk that accompanies this book.

Space is in megabytes	Controller	Internal SCSI		
Disk	0	1	2	3
Space available	2,000	2,000	2,000	2,000
Operating system	100			
Swap space		256	256	
Applications	500			
Staging & backups				1,500
Oracle objects — **Datafile**				
Control file 1 — control.ctl	1			
Control file 2 — control.ctl		1		
Control file 3 — control.ctl			1	
System tablespace — system.dbf	50			
Redo log group 1 — redo_1a.log		5		
Redo log group 1 — redo_1b.log				5
Redo log group 2 — redo_2a.log		5		
Redo log group 2 — redo_2b.log				5
Archive log destination	100			
Rollback tablespace — rbs.dbf				100
Lookup table tablespace — lookup.dbf	100			
Data_1 tablespace — data_1.dbf			1,000	
Temporary tablespace — temp.dbf		200		
Default tablespace — default.dbf				100
Lookup index tablespace — loindex.dbf				50
Index_1 tablespace — index_1.dbf		1,000		
Total file sizes	851	1,467	1,257	1,760
Space remaining	1,150	533	743	240

Figure 5.19 OLTP diskmap with four disk drives.

This first example (Figure 15.9) is for an OLTP system with four disks. The rows near the top of the sheet show the space allocated for the software and swap space, as well as space used for staging (data loads) and backups. Under the **Oracle objects** section are all the files that make up the database.

The important thing to note about this example is there is only one disk where the data can safely go because of the limits placed by the locations of the redo log groupss. With the redo logs and data tablespaces separate, the entire database can be recovered if any one disk should fail. In this case, the safety factor may limit performance.

The lookup table tablespace is located with the archive log files, because they should be relatively stable, and you should be able to restore or rebuild them a lot easier than trying to reconstruct your major tables.

The second example (Figure 5.20) shows a machine with six drives. Note the additional tablespaces for data and indexes. The extra tablespaces give you more flexibility to separate objects and protect the database from failure. You would ideally need to have at least eight disk drives to be able to completely separate all the objects that should be separated. The point that many people miss is that more smaller disk drives is better than fewer larger drives. Given equal access time, eight 1GB drives are better than four 2GB drives.

Space is in megabytes	Controller		Internal SCSI				External SCSI	
	Disk	0	1	2	3	4	5
	Space available	2,000	2,000	2,000	2,000	2,000	2,000
Operating system		100					
Swap space			256	256			
Applications		500					
Staging & backups					1,500		
Oracle objects	**Datafile**						
Control file 1	control.ctl	1					
Control file 2	control.ctl		1				
Control file 3	control.ctl						1
System tablespace	system.dbf	50					
Redo log group 1	redo_1a.log		5				
Redo log group 1	redo_1b.log				5		
Redo log group 2	redo_2a.log		5				
Redo log group 2	redo_2b.log				5		
Archive log destination		100					
Rollback tablespace	rbs_1.dbf				100		
	rbs_2.dbf	50					
Lookup table tablespace	lookup.dbf	100					
Data_1 tablespace	data_1.dbf			500			
Data_2 tablespace	data_2.dbf					500	
Temporary tablespace	temp.dbf					200	
Default tablespace	default.dbf				100		
Lookup index tablespace	loindex.dbf				100		
Index_1 tablespace	index_1.dbf		500				500
Index_2 tablespace	index_2.dbf						
	Total file sizes	901	767	756	1,810	700	501
	Space remaining	1,100	1,233	1,244	190	1,300	1,499

Figure 5.20 OLTP diskmap with six disk drives.

The following two spread sheets in Figure 5.21 (a) and (b) illustrate similar problems for a DSS. Note, however, that the online redo logs are not mirrored and there are no archived redo logs. Every Oracle database requires at least two online redo log files which are used to recover in case of an instance failure. So while we have gained some space and flexibility in terms of placing the data and index tablespaces, this database might not be able to recover from a media failure because the database is not in ARCHIVELOG mode.

Space is in megabytes	Controller	Internal SCSI			
	Disk	0	1	2	3
	Space available	2,000	2,000	2,000	2,000
Operating system		100			
Swap space			256	256	
Applications		500			
Staging & backups					1,000
Oracle objects	**Datafile**				
Control file 1	control.ctl	1			
Control file 2	control.ctl		1		
Control file 3	control.ctl			1	
System tablespace	system.dbf	50			
Redo log 1	redo_1.log		20		
Redo log 2	redo_2.log		20		
Rollback tablespace	rbs.dbf	100			
Lookup table tablespace	lookup.dbf	500			
Data_1 tablespace	data_1.dbf			500	
Data_2 tablespace	data_2.dbf				500
Data_3 tablespace	data_3.dbf	500			
Temporary tablespace	temp.dbf		500		
Default tablespace	default.dbf				200
Lookup index tablespace	loindex.dbf				200
Index_1 tablespace	index_1.dbf			500	
Index_2 tablespace	index_2.dbf		500		
	Total file sizes	1,751	1,297	1,257	1,900
	Space remaining	250	703	743	100

Figure 5.21a DSS diskmap with four disk drives;

With six disk drives, the DSS has even more options to spread the I/O across more drives.

Space is in megabytes	Controller		Internal SCSI			External SCSI	
Disk		0	1	2	3	4	5
Space available		2,000	2,000	2,000	2,000	2,000	2,000
Operating system		100					
Swap space			256	256			
Applications		500					
Staging & backups					1,000		
Oracle objects	**Datafile**						
Control file 1	control.ctl	1					
Control file 2	control.ctl		1				
Control file 3	control.ctl				1		
System tablespace	system.dbf	50					
Redo log 1	redo_1.log		20				
Redo log 2	redo_2.log		20				
Rollback tablespace	rbs.dbf						100
Lookup table tablespace	lookup.dbf	500					
Data_1 tablespace	data_1.dbf			500			
Data_2 tablespace	data_2.dbf				500		
Data_3 tablespace	data_3.dbf					500	
Temporary tablespace	temp.dbf						500
Default tablespace	default.dbf				200		
Lookup index tablespace	loindex.dbf					500	
Index_1 tablespace	index_1.dbf			500			
Index_2 tablespace	index_2.dbf		500				
Total file sizes		1,151	797	1,256	1,701	1,000	600
Space remaining		850	1,203	744	299	1,000	1,400

Figure 5.21b DSS diskmap with six disk drives.

With the release of Oracle7 Server, Release 7.2, there is an important new feature that affects tablespaces.

Most operating systems and machines have a fixed limit on the number of files that can be accessed while a machine is running. You set a limit on the maximum number of files that can be created for a single database with the init.ora parameter DB_FILES and the MAXDATAFILES parameter of the CREATE DATABASE command. The datafiles in an Oracle database are grouped by tablespaces and each tablespace has one or more datafiles.

Prior to Oracle7 Server, Release 7.2, all tablespaces were made up of datafiles that were a fixed size and the size of the files could not be changed once they were created. In order to add more room to a database you either had to create a new tablespace with one or more new datafiles, or add one or more datafiles to an existing tablespace. Either way, prior to Release 7.2, it was common to run out of datafiles as the database grew. The only solutions were to create a new database with fewer datafiles, or reorganize an existing database using Export and Import.

With Release 7.2, the datafiles in a tablespace can now be expanded or shrunk manually, or they can be set up to extend automatically. This means that you can add (or remove) space to existing datafiles, rather than having to add additional datafiles to allocate more room.

A datafile is expanded or shrunk manually with the new command:

```
ALTER DATABASE DATAFILE 'filename' RESIZE 100M;
```

A tablespace is automatically extended with the new parameter AUTOEXTEND. This parameter can be used in the CREATE TABLESPACE statement, or with the ALTER TABLESPACE command. With the AUTOEXTEND parameter you specify the size of the NEXT increment, and a MAXSIZE for the file. It is important to set the MAXSIZE to a point where the datafile will not exceed the disk capacity or interfere with the expansion of other datafiles.

Develop DDL

Once you have decided where everything will go, you are ready to create the DDL to build the database. This is where a good CASE tool will make your life easier. If you don't have one, try and get one that will generate all the Oracle-specific objects and parameters such as tablespaces and storage parameters.

Plan to develop and run several DDL scripts to create the database and all the objects. You could actually create a single script to build the entire database and all the objects at once, but if you are doing any data loads you will want to build your indexes and constraints after the data is loaded. I think you will find it easiest to develop separate scripts and then write a script that calls all the other scripts.

The following is a list of scripts that should be created:

- a script to create the database
- a script to clusters (optional)
- a script for all the CREATE TABLE statements
- a script to build the sequences
- a script to add/enable all the primary keys
- a script to add/enable the foreign keys
- a script to create the remaining indexes
- scripts for adding roles, users, and profiles

- one or more scripts to add triggers, procedures, or other constraints

There are two main reasons for developing and running separate scripts. The first is that tables should be loaded before any indexes are created. It usually takes significantly longer to load a table that has enabled indexes than to build the indexes after the table is loaded.

The other reason for creating separate scripts is to support the declarative referential integrity. A foreign key must reference a valid primary key. The easiest way to do this is to create all the tablesand primary keys and then add the foreign key constraints. What often happens when the primary and foreign key constraints are included with the CREATE TABLE statements are numerous errors that say there are invalid references, because a foreign key constraint was created before the target table with the referenced primary key was created. One way to prevent the errors is to disable all the constraints within the CREATE TABLE statement. If you do that, you will still need another set of commands to enable the constraints later (Figure 5.22). If you need multiple scripts anyway, why not just separate the constraints from the tables to begin with? So, separate the three kinds of statements into three scripts, and this is not a problem.

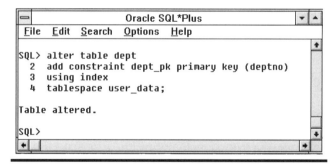

Figure 5.22 ALTER TABLE command to add a constraint.

Another way to prevent constraint errors is to use the CREATE SCHEMA command to combine all of your create table DDL. When you use CREATE SCHEMA, Oracle processes all of the statements as a group so that improper foreign key reference errors are eliminated. In this way you can embed your primary and foreign keys constraints with each CREATE TABLE statement. However, if you do use CREATE SCHEMA, remember that the primary keys will create indexes and this could slow down your data loads.

While the focus of this book is designing and building a database from scratch, a caveat is in order regarding the inevitable database changes, specifically adding columns to tables. If you need to add a column to a table *do not use the* ALTER TABLE ADD COLUMN command if there is already data in the table. Adding a column to an existing table will cause row chaining of the existing rows in the table.

Rather than alter the table, plan to re-create it. Either export the table and import it back to a new table or copy the data to a temporary table and then copy it back to a new table.

Develop init.ora File

When an instance is started, Oracle reads the **init.ora** file to determine how to configure the instance. Before you can create your database you must create an **init.ora** file. Oracle provides a sample with the installation media, which you can use, or you can create your own.

You should have most of the information you need to create your **init.ora** files, in terms of SVGA size, control file locations, and dump file definitions. You will need one to create the database and a different one to operate the database.

Be sure to include at least three control files in the **init.ora** parameter CONTROL_FILES, each on a different disk, in the **init.ora** file that you use to create the database.

Database Environments

Plan on creating multiple environments at various stages of the development life cycle. Most organizations actually have multiple databases to support various stages of the systems development life cycle. In fact, there are often numerous projects under development and perhaps several production systems.

There should be four different environments: one for development, one for testing, one for production, and one for training. Whether these various environments exist as separate databases and whether they exist on different machines are often budgetary decisions.

Development

The development environment is used for developing the applications or programs that will eventually support the business. Whether using prototyping, CASE tool generators, or some other method for developing programs, the programmers need a functioning database at some point.

Sometimes programmers share a common set of tables; sometimes each programmer has his or her own set of tables. Sometimes there are actually multiple Oracle databases to support different development efforts. Regardless of the makeup or breakup, there should be a single set of master tables that is strictly controlled in terms of structure and changes.

Database control is a term that often raises the hackles of programmers. Programmers develop the applications; therefore, they feel they are the ones that best know how the database should be structured. Any time they have to go to someone else to request an addition or change to the database, they feel this will slow them down. Since programming traditionally drives development efforts, developers usually get their way, and they end up driving the database development as well. Unless there are very few developers (fewer than two, one of which is the DBA) and the database will never be used with any other system, you should not let the developers have their way. (You might consider using dBASE, FoxPro, Access, or some other database that is good for small stand-alone applications.)

Remember the three-schema architecture? Most programmers never seem to have learned it, so they can be forgiven for not applying its lessons. The point of the three-schema architecture is to share, yet control, data. To share data, you must have common data structures. These common data structures and the rules that apply to them are defined in the conceptual schema. The conceptual schema must, of course, support the various external schemas. This subtle (in terms of cost of development and maintenance of systems, it is about as subtle as a ton of bricks) yet important point usually determines the long-term success or failure of relational technology for a particular organization.

The problem with having programmers drive database development is that by definition they are developing the external schema(s)—not the conceptual schema. In this scenario you end up with redundant and/or incompatible data structures. Too often, programmers say, "here are the database structures I need to support my application," but they do not know about—or care about—anyone else because they have deadlines to meet.

The fact that the programmers are developing just a portion of an entire system and that they have deadlines makes their desire to control their own structures understandable. However, systems are seldom developed in a vacuum; other systems may need to share data from those "stand-alone" systems. As soon as someone in an organization goes to the trouble and expense of developing a system that collects data, someone else in the organization usually wants to look at or use that data in another system. Almost all points of data collection have a value that needs to be shared.

The database for the development environment (indeed all environments) needs to be defined by data administration and implemented and maintained by the database administrators.

Test

A test environment is usually associated with testing application programs before they are moved into production. There may actually be several test environments for testing applications at various stages. One environment may be for module, or program, testing. This environment is used to test the individual components of a system. The other type of test environment is used for system, or integration, testing. This is where the entire set of applications and the entire system as a whole is tested.

When building Oracle databases, you need to consider testing in a different light. Rather than think of testing solely to support testing of the applications, you also need to test the design, construction, and maintenance of the database.

There are many factors that go into building a production database. Some of these factors are the physical database design, the DDL used to create the database, and load routines used to add data. Other factors are ongoing jobs or functions that still need to be developed and tested at an early stage. These include database backups, database replication, external interfaces, and disaster recovery.

To build your database(s) you will need the hardware, software, and personnel resources to develop and test the preceding items before any applications can be tested against the database.

An important consideration in testing the database is whether the test database environment, mainly the hardware components, is equivalent to the actual production hardware platform. Where the database is designed and tested on the platform on which it will ultimately reside, factors like timing the database builds and data loads should reflect what you can expect when you actually begin building and loading the production system. Often, however, a new production database will go on to an existing production machine that has limited time frames during which the system can be down. This window of opportunity is usually limited to evenings and/or weekends. Many mission-critical systems operate 24 hours a day, 7 days a week. For these high-availability systems, maintenance time is even more limited—to perhaps once a month or once a quarter.

What I am leading to is *risk*. Unless a database build is tested on a duplicate of the production machine, you may not be able to precisely predict how long certain events, such as the CREATE DATABASE or data loads, may take. This means that you should have an alternate plan ready in case the build or load fails.

Production

Ultimately, a database is used to support some business function via application programs. These are your production environments. While you can run multiple instances and databases on a single machine, each instance requires its own SGA and other resources. The more memory you can give to Oracle, the better the performance. Don't forget that each instance will have its own set of background processes like DBWR and LGWR, which will all be competing for CPU and I/O resources. The fewer database processes that are running, the more machine resources there are available for the applications.

Rather than create multiple databases on the production machine, consider creating a single database and use separate directories and/or tablespaces to separate applications. Using on-line backups, the separate systems can even be backed up independently.

Training

The training environment may or may not be a separate Oracle instance or database. Training environments usually get placed wherever there is space left for them. I have seen clients add special training tables to production databases. Other organizations put training on the same machine as the test and development environments.

Security

Security for individuals or groups of individuals can be controlled at various points in most computer environments. Some form or level of security can be provided at one or more of the following points:

- machine/operating system
- network
- application
- database

Some operating systems control access to the machine through user logons and passwords. Users can also be limited to certain resources at the machine level, such as which directories they may read from or write to. Networks can control which machine a user can access across a network. Applications can control who can see what menus and screens, what actions they are allowed to perform, and what data they may access from the database. Oracle also provides numerous ways to protect the data in your database. For our purposes, I will limit the discussion to a review of the options available at the database and application levels. Machine and network security are more of a systems administration issue and therefore are beyond the scope of this book.

At the database level, users can be given or denied access to specific objects in the database, as well as specific commands that may be executed against those objects. The access is given by granting system or object privileges to users. Privileges can also be revoked.

Rather than specifying every desired privilege for every user on the system, Oracle provides *roles* to which you can assign multiple users. Oracle also provides *profiles* to control the consumption of resources for a user. With a profile, you can limit the amount of time a user can work on the system, as well as the amount of CPU time and I/O resources he or she can consume.

Security is extended to the applications primarily through the use of views. Views are used to further restrict the columns and/or rows that a user or role can access.

In addition to granting access, Oracle can track different types of access by *auditing* system usage. The audit feature creates records of statements that were executed or objects that were accessed and who performed or accessed them.

All of these security options require planning. They can easily become hideously complex, and some can place a significant administrative and performance burden on the system. Especially for new users of Oracle, the key words here are *keep it simple*. It's not that the security does not work or is flaky— it works beautifully. You need a plan, and the plan needs to start *simply*. You can add complexity as the need arises.

Grants

Users and roles (covered in detail later) are *granted* or given privileges to perform certain actions on certain objects. The privileges can be granted to PUBLIC, meaning all users. Privileges can also be revoked. Once a user or role is created, it is granted privileges, as illustrated in Figure 5.23. This example creates the role CLERK and then issues several grants on several tables to that role. It also shows the role being granted to several users.

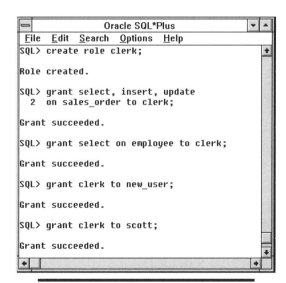

Figure 5.23a Granting access to a table.

While Figure 5.23 (a) shows grants on tables, the following example shows grants at the column level for a table. The SQL commands INSERT and UPDATE can be limited to specific columns in specific tables or views. However, you cannot limit column access for the SELECT or DELETE commands. A view should be used to limit SELECT and DELETE. Figure 5.23 (b) shows how certain access to specific columns can and cannot be controlled. The first statement attempts to limit **SELECT** to just the EMP_NAME name column but fails. The second command limits **UPDATE** to the EMP_NAME column and succeeds.

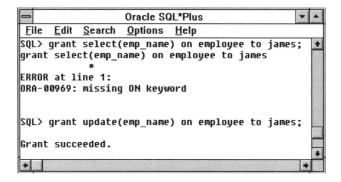

Figure 5.23b Grants at the column level.

In addition to granting access to specific objects, a view can be created with limited access, and then access to the view is granted to users or roles.

The following example shows how to limit access to certain rows in a table by a user using a view. In order to use this scheme, the Oracle user name should be part of the employee table, as illustrated in Figure 5.24.

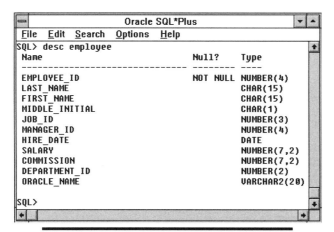

Figure 5.24 Description of an employee table.

The query in Figure 5.25 shows how to use the Oracle function USER to select the EMPLOYEE_ID of the user currently logged onto Oracle. This user name is then used to limit access in the view, as shown in the next screen. The first query shows how to get the user name, and the second shows how to get the EMPLOYEE_ID based on the Oracle USER.

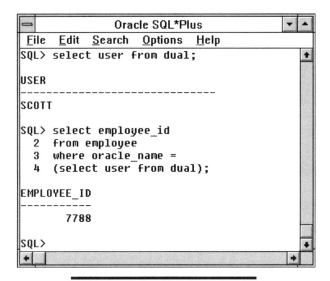

```
Oracle SQL*Plus

File   Edit   Search   Options   Help
SQL> select user from dual;

USER
------------------------------
SCOTT

SQL> select employee_id
  2    from employee
  3    where oracle_name =
  4    (select user from dual);

EMPLOYEE_ID
-----------
       7788

SQL>
```

Figure 5.25 Select user from dual.

User SCOTT, who owns the CUSTOMER table, can now create a view that limits the rows viewed to only those customers of the user currently logged onto the system. SCOTT creates a view that has a nested SELECT statement in the WHERE clause of the view. This nested SELECT statement from Figure 5.25 limits access to the customer table to those customers of the user currently accessing the table. In the example in Figure 5.26, the user SCOTT does not have any customers; he is not a salesperson. Even though SCOTT owns the table and there are 1056 rows in the table, the view prevents him from seeing any rows, because he is not a salesperson.

Figure 5.26 also shows the need for planning. In this case, the planning must go all the way back to the table design to include the ORACLE_NAME in the EMPLOYEE table.

Figure 5.26 Limiting table access with views.

Roles

Roles can greatly simplify the entire grant procedure. Rather than grant every user the appropriate privileges to every table and view, the privileges are first granted to sets of roles, then the roles are granted to users. A user can belong to one or more roles. In effect, roles help consolidate the grant effort to a few roles rather than to every user. Roles, in essence, group similar types of users.

Consider a situation where a table must be dropped and readded to a production database in order to reorganize the data or change the table structure. Without roles, **every** user that needs access to the table must be regranted that access before they can access the new table. With roles, the access need only be granted to the role or roles instead of all the users.

Oracle provides several predefined roles. Figures 5.27 and 5.28 show the privileges associated with the predefined roles of CONNECT and RESOURCE. The DBA role can perform almost all commands. In addition, there are two roles, EXP_FULL_DATABASE and IMP_FULL_DATABASE, that allow for full database Exports and Imports. Grant these predefined roles to users who need these privileges. Be sure to limit your use of the DBA role; very few people have any need for DBA authority.

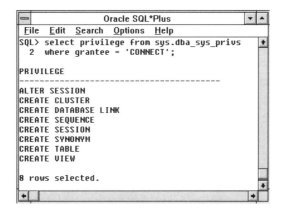

Figure 5.27 Connect privileges.

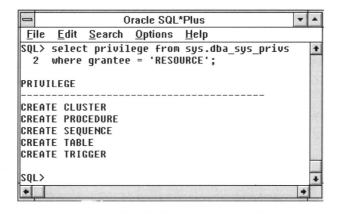

Figure 5.28 Resource privileges.

The strategy for creating roles is to identify classes of users that generally relate to the functional requirements of a system. Such roles might include order entry, purchasing, inventory control, and accounting. Sometimes roles are also defined along job classifications such as manager, database administrator, or data-entry clerk. These roles are then granted the appropriate system and object privileges. Users are then granted access to one or more roles.

Until you become familiar with all the possibilities and pitfalls of privileges with all of a new system's functional requirements and usage patterns, your production systems will be safer if you err on the side of being too restrictive. It is easier to grant a particular access, especially if you are using roles, than to rebuild a table or fix corrupt data.

I am often asked how to recover tables that are mistakenly dropped from the production environment. This issue should never come up. One of the principal design criteria is to create a database that is safe and secure.

The solution is simple. All DROP and ALTER privileges should be revoked for objects in the production environment to limit these little mistakes. When changes have to occur, then the particular DROP or ALTER privileges are granted just before the objects are changed and revoked again after the changes are made. Also the DDL for the grants, changes, and revokes should be part of a script that is written and tested, *before* it is run in the production environment. An ounce of prevention is worth a lot more than any amount of cure.

Users

Any person who wishes to access an Oracle database must first log on or connect to Oracle. This is true whether the user logs on directly through Oracle products like SQL*Plus or SQL*DBA or through an application program. As discussed earlier, most of the system and object privileges should be controlled through roles. There are, however, several additional controls that are only available at the user level.

Figure 5.29 shows most of the CREATE USER properties.

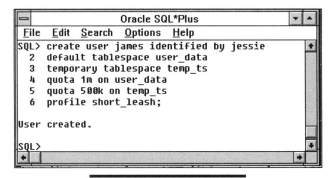

Figure 5.29 Creating a user.

The default tablespace specifies the location where tables and indexes are created if a tablespace is not specified as part of a CREATE statement. If the user does not specify a tablespace for a new object and the default tablespace was not specified for the user, the new object will go in the system tablespace. The only thing in the system tablespace should be the data dictionary and two rollback segments. Since the system tablespace is generally very small, it is easy to run out of room there. You should create a separate tablespace in which users can create objects and make that their default tablespace.

The temporary tablespace is the area where sorts and other functions are performed for certain SQL statements. These include, but are not limited to creating indexes, order by statements, and certain aggregate functions. This activity is very read-and-write intensive. If a default tablespace is not specified for the users, these sorts will occur in the system tablespace. You do not want this kind of activity going on in the system tablespace. You do not want to contend with Oracle as it tries to read and write to the data dictionary. Be sure to create a temporary tablespace and make it every user's temporary tablespace.

Quotas are used to limit the amount of space a user can allocate in any tablespace. These quotas may or may not be necessary, especially in a production environment where users do not usually create objects. In the preceding example, the user JAMES would not be allowed to allocate more than 1 MB in the USER_DATA tablespace and only 500KB in the TEMP_TS tablespace. A quota of UNLIMITED is allowed. Unless a quota is specified, there is no limit for the user.

Profiles are a handy way to limit system resources for a user. If a user exceeds any of the limits, he or she receives an error message and can no longer operate. The user is not kicked out of his or her application, just logged off of Oracle, and they must reconnect in order to perform any more transactions. If a transaction was in progress when the limit was reached, it is stopped and rolled back. Profiles must be created before they can be assigned. Figure 5.30 shows a new profile named SHORT_LEASH because a user with this profile would not be able to perform too many transactions, and their time on the system would be limited.

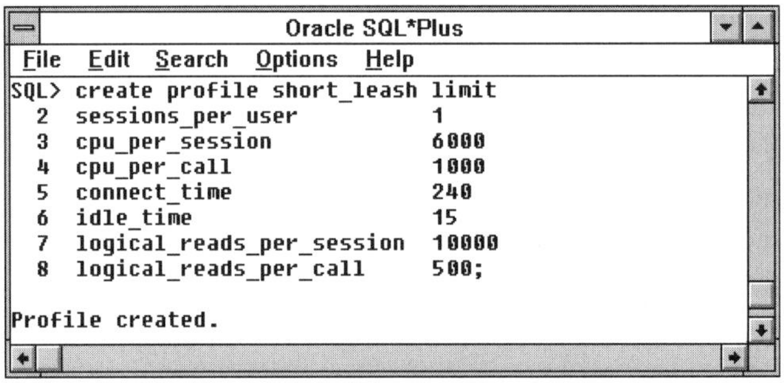

```
┌─────────────────────────────────────────────────────┐
│ ─                  Oracle SQL*Plus            ▼ ▲    │
├─────────────────────────────────────────────────────┤
│ File  Edit  Search  Options  Help                   │
├─────────────────────────────────────────────────────┤
│SQL> create profile short_leash limit             ↑ │
│   2  sessions_per_user          1                   │
│   3  cpu_per_session            6000                │
│   4  cpu_per_call               1000                │
│   5  connect_time               240                 │
│   6  idle_time                  15                  │
│   7  logical_reads_per_session  10000               │
│   8  logical_reads_per_call     500;                │
│                                                     │
│Profile created.                                  ↓ │
├─────────────────────────────────────────────────────┤
│ ←                                              →    │
└─────────────────────────────────────────────────────┘
```

Figure 5.30 Creating a profile.

This profile will limit use of the following resources:

- SESSIONS_PER_USER limits the number of times a user account can log on to the database. Setting the limit to 1 would prevent anyone from logging on more than once, but more importantly, it would prevent multiple users from sharing a single Oracle user account.

- CPU_PER_SESSION is the maximum amount of CPU time a user can consume for an entire session expressed in hundredths of a second. The SHORT_LEASH limit is 60 seconds of CPU time.

- CPU_PER_CALL is the total CPU time, also expressed in hundredths of a second, that a user can consume for a single call performing a fetch, parse, or execute. The SHORT_LEASH limit is 10 seconds.

- CONNECT_TIME is the total amount of time, expressed in minutes, that a user can stay connected to the database regardless of whether he or she is performing an activity or not. This limit is especially useful for users who forget to log off the system at night, thus making it hard to shut down your database when performing maintenance or backups. It's also useful if a system is constrained because there are too many users logged on and memory is in short supply. The SHORT_LEASH limit would log a user off the system after 4 hours.

- IDLE_TIME is the total time, expressed in minutes, that a user can remain *idle*, that is, not performing any activity against the database, before being kicked off. This limit is useful where systems are short of memory. The SHORT_LEASH limit is 15 minutes.

- LOGICAL_READS_PER_SESSION is a limit expressed as the number of data blocks that can be read from either disk or memory during an entire session. The SHORT_LEASH limit is 10,000 data blocks. This limit is also affected by the Oracle block size. With a 2K block size, the amount of data that could be read would be 20 MB while an 8K block size would allow 80 MB of data for reads.

- LOGICAL_READS_PER_CALL SESSION limit expressed as the number of data blocks that can be read either from disk or memory during a single call. This limit is useful in preventing poorly written and runaway queries from hogging the machine. The SHORT_LEASH limit of 500 would limit a single call to 500 data blocks. This would be 1 MB for a 2K block size or 4 MB for an 8K block size.

There are two other profile limits. One is PRIVATE_SGA that can limit the amount of memory used with the multithreaded server. The other is COMPOSIT_LIMIT which can be used to express limits for several parameters in a single value. By the time you figure it out and do the math, you can just as easily specify each parameter.

Note that the SHORT_LEASH example is intended to show just how limiting or restrictive you can be. I am not suggesting that you need to do this for any of your users, but you should know the power is there. If you do have to put tight limits on the resources for your users because of hardware constraints, you should buy more hardware; these limits can really irritate people.

When limiting resources, Oracle does not perform any calculations to see whether a particular activity might exceed the limits set in the user profiles. For example, a user will not know that the query just executed may exceed CPU or read privileges or both. They will get an error message that the privileges were exceeded when they hit the limit. They will also be logged off the database. Profiles are not very user friendly in the way they handle limits.

If more user friendly limits are needed, you may want to build some routines that perform calculations to show the users how many rows will be returned and some sample data for a given query in case they run into a CALLS limit. These kind of routines and limits would be more appropriate in a DSS environment where very long running queries are common.

Before a user can log onto Oracle, they must be granted the CREATE SESSION privilege. Figure 5.31 shows user JAMES trying to log on without the CREATE SESSION privilege and then JAMES logging on after the privilege is granted.

Figure 5.31 Create session.

When you create an Oracle database, Oracle creates two users - SYS and SYSTEM, so you can access the database. These user accounts are essentially superusers and should not be used on a day-to-day basis. You should also plan to change their passwords since these passwords are common on all Oracle installations. Figure 5.32 shows how to change passwords, as well as assigning the user SYSTEM to default and temporary tablespaces.

Figure 5.32 Changing passwords

You can create new users any time after the database is created. Another one of the new Oracle tools is the Oracle User Manager (Figure 5.33). While this tool may be impractical for creating users for large systems with hundreds or even thousands of users, it could be quite useful for smaller systems and individual user maintenance.

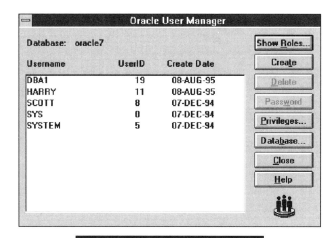

Figure 5.33 Oracle User Manager

Audit

Auditing is a feature included with Oracle that will let you collect data about who is accessing what objects, issuing what statements, and/or using what privileges.

When auditing is turned on, information is recorded in the table SYS.AUD$ files. Before you can audit, you must build an audit table by running the Oracle provided script, CATAUDIT.SQL. The table is deleted by running the script CATNOAUD.SQL. The init.ora parameter AUDIT_TRAIL must also be set to enable auditing.

Auditing is usually performed for security reasons, but it can be used to collect transaction information, such as the number of times a particular table was accessed and the commands that were used during the access. Auditing can record successful and unsuccessful actions. The latter is useful when users complain that they can never get access to a particular object or they cannot get on the system. The command **AUDIT SESSION WHENEVER NOT SUCCESSFUL** would tell you exactly who it was that could not get on the system and when. This kind of information is invaluable when trying to put performance, problems, into a proper perspective.

Like users, roles, and grants, auditing can get very complex quickly. It is easy to create a situation in which you cannot extract the information you need from all the data produced because you cast too large a net.

In developing an audit strategy, consider what, who, and why you want to audit. By focusing on these issues, you can develop a plan that will allow you to go from the general to the specific. Rather than try and audit all DELETE statements in the database, concentrate on a group of tables to try and isolate suspicious activity, then audit a specific table in detail.

Refer to the *Oracle7 Server Administrator's Guide*, the *Oracle7 Server Concepts Manual*, and the *Oracle7 Server SQL Language Reference Manual* for complete details on auditing.

Create Database

Creating a database is a multistep process that requires significant planning and coordination. The actual CREATE DATABASE statement may be the easiest step in the process.

In addition to the CREATE DATABASE command, you will run a DDL that creates all your database objects. You will also need to load data into the tables, even if it's just the lookup tables. What all these activities imply is a test database—not in terms of testing application code, but in terms of testing all your DDL scripts, load scripts, and operating procedures. Don't even bother trying to create a full-sized production system until you have the bugs worked out. Conversely, because Oracle is so portable, all your DDL and load scripts can be tested on a small test machine. To move to the production environment, you would need to change object sizes, the path names and sizes for the data files and the necessary **init.ora** file parameters to reflect the larger machine

Execute Initial DDL

In each environment where you plan to create an Oracle database, you need to perform the following tasks. Whether the tasks are carried out as discrete steps or combined into fewer jobs or scripts is not important. If you are new to Oracle, you may want to perform a task and check the system to see what has happened. More experienced users will usually combine several of these tasks into a single script.

Run CREATE DATABASE Script

The **CREATE DATABASE** command performs the following

- creates the data files specified in the CREATE DATABASE script
- creates the control file(s)
- creates the redo logs
- creates the SYSTEM tablespace
- creates one rollback segment in the SYSTEM tablespace
- creates the data dictionary
- creates users SYS and SYSTEM
- mounts and opens the database

The actual CREATE DATABASE command is not very long. Most of the CREATE DATABASE scripts that I have seen, including the following example, create additional objects, including the rollback segments and tablespaces and add users as well.

To create the database. you need an **init.ora** file written to support the database creation. There are several parameters that are especially important during the create. (See Appendix B for more details on **init.ora** parameters.) These include:

- DB_BLOCK_SIZE determines the Oracle data block size. Once set, this value cannot be changed.
- DB_FILES specifies the maximum number of data files that can be opened by the database.
- CONTROL_FILES specifies the number and location of all the control files that should be created for the new database. Create at least three control files and place them on different disks.
- DB_NAME is the name of the new database.
- LOG_ARCHIVE_START should be set to FALSE when creating the database. Although I have suggested that you operate your databases in ARCHIVELOG mode, you should not do this while creating them.
- ROLLBACK_SEGMENTS are added after the database is created. Since this is a new database there are no rollback segments, other than the one created by Oracle.

- INIT_SQL_FILES is used to list scripts that should be run when creating a new database. (A copy is included on the disk with this book.)

The following script can be used as a template to create new databases. The script performs the following tasks:

- creates mirrored redo log files by creating multiple log groups.
- creates a separate tablespace for the rollback segments and adds rollback segments.
- creates these tablespaces for tables and two tablespaces for indexes.
- creates default and temporary tablespaces for the users.
- creates two users, one as a DBA and the other as the one intended to run the rest of the DDL necessary to create all the remaining schema objects.

```
REM File name = CREATE.SQL
REM Sample script to create an Oracle7 database.
REM developed by Harry Liebschutz.

REM All paths for every file must be changed to
REM reflect the locations of directories on each machine.

set echo on

spool create.log

connect internal

startup nomount pfile=path\initDBNM.ora

create database DBNM
controlfile reuse
maxdatafiles 100
datafile 'path\system.dbf' size 50M reuse
logfile group 1 ('path\log_1a.log' ,
          'path\log_1b.log')  size 5M,
```

```
        group 2 ('path\log_2a.log' ,
                'path\log_2b.log') size 5M,
        group 3 ('path\log_3a.log' ,
                'path\log_3b.log') size 5M
        group 4 ('path\log_4a.log' ,
                'path\log_4b.log') size 5M;


REM Create additional rollback to be able to
REM add additional tablespaces.

create rollback segment rb0 tablespace system;

alter rollback segment rb0 online;


REM Create a tablespace for the rest of the
REM rollback segments.
REM Using default storage parameters precludes
REM the need to define storage for every
REM rollback segment.
REM The size of the datafile must be larger
REM than the combined size of all of the
REM rollback segments.

create tablespace rbs
datafile 'path\rolbak1.dbf' size 75M
default storage (INITIAL 100K
                NEXT 100K
                MINEXTENTS 100
                MAXEXTENTS 100)
online;


REM Create the rollback segments.
```

```
create rollback segment rb1 tablespace rbs;
create rollback segment rb2 tablespace rbs;
create rollback segment rb3 tablespace rbs;
create rollback segment rb4 tablespace rbs;
create rollback segment rb5 tablespace rbs;
create rollback segment rb6 tablespace rbs;

alter rollback segment rb1 online;
alter rollback segment rb2 online;
alter rollback segment rb3 online;
alter rollback segment rb4 online;
alter rollback segment rb5 online;
alter rollback segment rb6 online;


REM Create a tablespace for lookup tables.

create tablespace LOOKUPS
datafile 'path\lookups.dbf' size 50M
default storage (INITIAL 16K
                NEXT 16K
                MINEXTENTS 2
                MAXEXTENTS 100)
online;

REM Create tablespaces for remaining tables and
REM indexes.

create tablespace DATA_01
datafile 'path\data01.dbf' size 500M
online;

create tablespace DATA_02
datafile 'path\data02.dbf' size 500M
online;
```

```
create tablespace INDEX_01
datafile 'path\index01.dbf' size 250M
default storage (INITIAL 32K
                NEXT 32K
                MINEXTENTS 2
                MAXEXTENTS 100)
online;

create tablespace INDEX_02
datafile 'path\index02.dbf' size 250M
default storage (INITIAL 256K
                NEXT 128K
                MINEXTENTS 2
                MAXEXTENTS 100)
online;

REM Create the default and temporary
REM tablespaces.

create tablespace TEMP_TS
datafile 'path\temp.dbf' size 100M
default storage (initial 500k
                next 500k
                pctincrease 0)
online;

create tablespace DEFAULT_TS
datafile 'path\deflt.dbf' size 100M
default storage (initial 100k
                next 100k
                pctincrease 0)
online;
```

```
REM Create two users. One is a DBA, the other
REM would be the owner of the objects in the
REM new system.

create user user_dba identified by user_dba
default tablespace default_ts
temporary tablespace temp_ts;

grant connect, resource, dba to user_dba;

create user sys_owner identified by sys_owner
default tablespace default_ts
temporary tablespace temp_ts;

grant connect, resource to sys_owner;


spool off
```

The time it takes to run this script will vary with the size of all the data files and the machine's capabilities. When a tablespace is created, the data files listed for that tablespace are allocated on the disk. In the case of the tablespace DATA_01 in the previous CREATE.SQL script, the data file **data01.dbf** is 500 MB in size. When the tablespace DATA_01 is created, you will have to wait while the 500 MB file is allocated on the disk.

When the database is only a few hundred megabytes, this is not an issue. Several hundred gigabytes, on the other hand, can take a substantial amount of time that must be planned for, especially when setting up the production environment.

Run Oracle Provided Scripts

Once the database is created, there are some Oracle-provided scripts that you should run. These scripts provide access to various objects and functionality. The following scripts can be listed in the INIT_SQL_FILES parameter, run in a separate script, or executed individually from the SQL*DBA command line.

The following scripts should be run by SYS:

```
CATALOG.SQL creates data dictionary views.
CATEXP.SQL creates the roles and views necessary for the Export and
Import utilities.
CATLDR.SQL creates views for using SQL*Loader direct loads.
```

The following scripts should be run by users for their individual use:

UTLMONTR.SQL grants PUBLIC access to V$ views.

CATDBSYN.SQL creates private synonyms for DBA views. This should be run for each DBA user created.

The following scripts are required to use Oracle's procedural option. They must be run in the following order:

STANDARD.SQL

DBMSSTDX.SQL

CATPROC.SQL

Run Create Table Script

After the database is created, you can create the tables for the database.

Run Create Sequence Script

Sequences may be needed to create key values during data loading. To support key generation during the loads, sequences should be added before the data loads.

Load Tables

Data loading is covered in detail in the next chapter. In the context of this chapter, it is one of the tasks necessary to bring up an operational database.

The data loads are one of the first checkpoints of the database. The loads will point out problems with the data structures, such as incorrect datatypes and misspellings of column names. Also, when you load from other systems, you may run into problems when you try to create or enable various constraints during the next phase.

Execute Remaining DDL

After the tables are loaded, you can run the remaining DDL.

Run Create/Enable Primary Key Constraints Script

Once the data is loaded, you can start creating the primary keys. Primary keys will create unique indexes, so plan to spend time on this.

Run Create Index Scripts

After the primary keys are created, build the remaining indexes.

Run Create/Enable Remaining Constraints Script

Any other constraints that were not included as part of the CREATE TABLE statement can be run now.

Run Create Synonym Script

Once the tables are created, add synonyms to facilitate and control access by all the other users on the system.

Run Create View Script

Run the scripts that create all the views.

Run Create Role Script

After all of the schema objects are created, you can create the roles that will be needed for the system.

Run Create User Script

After the roles are created, add the users to the system and assign them to their proper roles.

Shut Down Database

Now that all the objects are created and the initial data is loaded, certain maintenance tasks should be performed.

Place Database in ARCHIVELOG Mode

Once the database is created and all the objects created and loaded, The databases should be placed in ARCHIVELOG mode. To place the database in ARCHIVELOG mode, use the ALTER DATABASE ARCHIVELOG command as illustrated in Figure 5.32. Note that the database is mounted in exclusive mode but not opened.

Figure 5.34 Starting archiving.

Shut Down Database

After the database is in ARCHIVELOG mode, shutdown the database again to prepare for a full operating system/cold backup.

Back Up Database

Perform a full operating system backup of the database.

Adjust init.ora File for Operations

Before restarting the database, adjust the **init.ora** parameters to enable archiving with the LOG_ARCHIVE_START parameter. Also, reference all the rollback segments that were created. Do not include the rollback segment that you added in the system tablespace. By leaving it out of the **init.ora** file, Oracle will reserve it for its own use in working with and updating the data dictionary.

Restart Database

After the database is backed up and the init.ora parameters are adjusted, the database is ready for operation—or at least testing.

EXPORT Database

This last step is optional. An Export of the database will give you a full image of all the structures and the data. While not useful for production backups, the Exports can be used to rebuild lookup tables.

Testing

Application programs are not the only things that need to be tested when developing databases. Network and remote connections, security, backup and recovery, and performance are some of the other items that should also be checked.

If you are developing in an iterative fashion, as in prototyping (see Chapter 9), you will have numerous opportunities to test your database and applications. In this regard, the following three sections may not represent discreet activities that occur at some point near the end of your effort. The sooner you can begin testing, the better off you will be. The point of testing is to discover problems as early as possible.

Most of your performance problems will initially come from poorly written SQL statements. Once these problems begin to get sorted out, you can go about the business of tuning your database. Realize that some of this testing and tuning may result in database changes. Denormalization may be required to reduce joins, or extra tables may be needed to carry summary data rather than try and sum columns with several million rows. If things go very smoothly, consider yourself lucky. Chapter 7 covers tuning in detail.

Database Functionality

Well, it's time to taste the cooking. Does the database work after all this effort? It's time to run your first real queries. There are two aspects to testing the database. Can the structures accommodate the information requirements? Can you turn the data into information? This depends on the other aspect, which is performance. You have to see if you can get the correct answers to your queries, but the answers have to come back in a reasonable amount of time.

It is important to ultimately test with real data and preferably lots of it. The sample set of data used for development and initial testing may have several shortcomings. The most important drawback is that small tables almost always produce fast results. Bad SQL statements, inadequate database design, and limited hardware resources are seldom discovered with a little bit of data. And a lot of data annd watch your new system come to its knees

The other shortcoming of sample data is that it is usually quite clean, and the distribution of data is limited by the sample size. Columns you once thought were good candidates for indexes no longer are because certain values skew the distribution of values, and the queries start to scan the index. (This is one of the reasons I suggested going easy on the indexes at first and adding them as you need them.) What are you going to do when you bring over the real customer data and find many customers in the tables many times because people spelled their names differently? Do you start a massive data cleanup effort or build alias tables (as I have done on several occasions).

Applications

Performing application testing was covered earlier in this chapter, when we discussed the various operating environments that are necessary to support the systems development life cycle. But every time you create a database, regardless of what kind of environment you are supporting, you will need to test the applications to see if they work or if they can connect. This can be quite a task in today's world of client/server. A partial list of some of the things to check are:

- SQL*Net
- ODBC drivers
- DLLs
- proper user setup on the server
- proper user setup in the database

The most important impact the applications will have on your database will be the SQL statements. While a lot of hardware can often cover a multitude of sins, bad SQL can make the best-tuned database look like junk. Be sure the programmers know how to write and tune SQL for Oracle. It can take a very high level of expertise to get a complex query to perform properly.

Database Object and File Sizes

After the database is loaded for the first time, you should run the ANALYZE command against all the tables and indexes. The following script will generate two SQL scripts called `anatab.sql` and `anaind.sql` to run the ANALYZE command. To actually analyze the tables and indexes, run the two scripts that this script generates.

```
set echo off
set heading off
set pagesize 100

spool anatab.sql

Select 'Analyze table ||' table_name ||' compute statistics;'
from user_tables;

spool off

spool anaind.sql

Select 'Analyze index ||' index_name ||' compute statistics;'
from user_indexes;

spool off
```

Remember, unless the **init.ora** parameter is explicitly set to rule, Oracle decides whether or not to use the cost-based optimizer by determining whether there are statistics gathered for the table or index needed in a query. This means that gathering statistics with the **ANALYZE** command can invoke the cost-based optimizer.

CHAPTER 6

Data Loads and Conversions

Some computer systems are new, some replace one or more existing systems, and others are hybrids that replace some old systems while adding new functionality. Regardless of origin, most systems need to begin with some data in the database, and this means data loads of one sort or another. For a new system, the only necessary data may be the lookup tables or validation table codes. When replacing a legacy system, all the data may need to be removed from the old system and then loaded into the new one. Some systems may require frequent updates from other production systems or outside sources.

When converting legacy systems, the data loads may be the most unpredictable factor in the entire development effort. Data loads or conversions are complicated by the following factors:

- No up-to-date documentation about legacy systems. Many systems were built before there were CASE tools, so the only documentation is the system itself. While getting record layouts may not be too difficult, knowing what all the fields in the records are intended to do can be another story. If the old system included coded records, well, then prepare to pay.

- Data quality. I worked on a conversion in which the Social Security numbers in the old system were seven digits long. Haven't social security numbers always been nine digits? I also worked on a justice system where people ("clients") routinely gave bogus Social Security numbers. The most common problems will be the various and often numerous spellings for customer and supplier names and addresses. On several occasions we have added *alias*, or also known as (AKA), tables. Rather than try to fix the problem, we attempted to capture all known spellings in the alias table. The difficult task when using aliases is creating and maintaining the links between a "master record" and all the alias records.

- Users of an old system begin to enter different types of data into the existing application. This occurs when people begin to use existing fields for different purposes. Say an `INVOICE_DATE` was originally used in an accounts payable system to record the date on the vendor's invoice. Someone in the company feels that they should not have to give up prompt payment discounts because of postal or other delivery delays and decides to use `INVOICE_DATE` as the date the invoice was entered into the system. This change may not really affect the data loads but it may have an effect on system design and the algorithm that calculates discounts taken for prompt payment. Perhaps there should be two fields in the new system, one for the `VENDOR_INVOICE_DATE` and another to record `INVOICE_RECEIVED_DATE`.

- The `INVOICE_DATE` issue illustrates another significant impact that data conversions will have. As people rummage around in the legacy systems, they will find areas that may require changes to the new system. They will find fields in the old systems that were not included in the new data model and other fields that have to change because the length or data type in the old systems does not match the new design. A data administrator on a project insisted that the address column in the new client table should be 25 characters long. Unfortunately, six months into the project we found old client addresses that actually used 29 characters in their address fields. What do you do? Either clean the old addresses (truncate them?) up to make them shorter or make the new address field longer. (Don't forget to change all the screens that use that longer field.)

- Size and logistics can also complicate data loads. Loading several million records and then building all the indexes can take a long time.

I have worked on several projects where the data conversions almost completely stopped the show. And while not completely stopped, they were overbudget and behind schedule. One such project was a data cleanup problem that took three months to fix versus the original two weeks planned for data conversion. Another project took several extra months to load all the legacy data because of size and business interruptions.

There are always several methods or options to explore when faced with data loads. I suggest you begin by developing a matrix that shows the source of data for the tables in the new database. If the data maps on a one-to-one basis, where every column in the new system maps to a single field in the old systems, then life may not be too bad. However, except for straight migrations where the new database is an exact duplicate of the old one (for example, an Oracle6 to Oracle7 Server migration) there are often many-to-many relationships between the source and target data. A single field in the legacy system may populate several fields in the new database, and vice versa.

In addition to the physical mapping, you may have to deal with data cleanup. As part of the mapping strategy you will need to decide where the cleanup should occur. Your basic options are:

- Clean the source data in the source system. The trick here is to find the "dirty" data, which usually won't happen until you actually start the loads. This issue usually causes a schedule slip, so plan on it.
- Clean the data as it is extracted form the source system.
- Clean the data after it is extracted from the source system but before it is loaded into the new system.
- Clean the data as it is loaded into the new system.
- Load the new system with the old data, then clean it.

SQL*Loader

SQL*Loader is a powerful Oracle utility used to load data into Oracle tables. (The SQL*Loader is covered in the *Oracle RDBMS Utility User's Guide*, which provides numerous helpful examples.) It can load data into empty tables, append data to existing tables, or replace all the data in a table. It can split one file into many tables or combine data from several source files into one table. SQL*Loader can also perform numerous types of data conversions and generate values, such as sequences or dates, during the load. The data can be loaded from flat files or included as part of the load script or control file.

A terrific feature of SQL*Loader is its ability to write "bad" data to a bad file or a discard file. This is the point where you begin to find dirty data. Even if records are bad, the loader will continue to load records unless you hit a predefined limit for the number of bad records. Once the load completes, the bad records can be fixed and loaded using the APPEND option.

My only problem with SQL*Loader is that the scripts are difficult to write and usually require a lot of debugging. Fortunately, there are products on the market to help build SQL*Loader control files and load scripts. Some companies, such as AT&T GIS, provide data transformation services.

With the Parallel Query option, multiple SQL*Loader scripts can be run in parallel to load large tables. A separate loader process can be started for each CPU in the machine; the more CPUs, the faster the load. Parallel loads work best if there are separate input files that are loaded into separate data files. By separating the source and target files, you reduce I/O contention by spreading it across multiple drives. Separate data files for the target table implies table striping, which is covered in Chapter 9. The parallel loads must use the DIRECT PATH option, which is described later.

Under normal conditions, SQL*Loader uses a **SQL INSERT** command to add records to the database. Inserts can have a significant amount of overhead associated with them, especially if there are foreign keys involved. Direct path loads write data directly to the database files instead of using the **INSERT** command. Direct path loads work best where the data is very clean and presorted.

Figure 6.1 illustrates parallel data loads. Note that each source or input file points to a different Oracle data file.

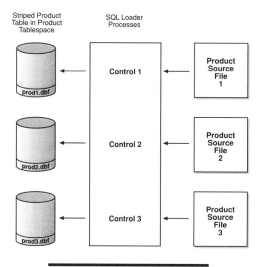

Figure 6.1 Parallel data loads.

Logistics

One of the most difficult issues you may face is that of logistics. When can all the loads be performed? Many new Oracle systems replace one or more legacy systems. Where there are two or more replacements, the system is often implemented in phases. You get one part of the system up and working, then some time later you convert the next system. Sometimes there is just a single system that is loaded in stages. When converting an existing production system, it is usually necessary to work around normal business hours to prevent interruptions to business.

The following is a list of steps you should follow when performing a conversion. (As with most of the recommendations in this book, the components of the list are more important then the precise order of the components.) The emphasis of this list is to limit risks. To insure that you can recover from any problems, be sure to perform the backups. Take an attitude that anything that can go wrong will. With this kind of skeptical attitude, you tend to take the precautions that will allow you to get your business back in operation if (when) something does go wrong and you have to revert to the old system. And with this skeptical attitude, you and everyone else will be delighted when things go as planned.

1. Shut down the database.
2. Perform a cold backup of the database(s).

If the Oracle system is being loaded for the first time, this step won't be necessary.

The legacy system may or may not require a backup.

3. Start up the database.
4. Drop indexes and/or constraints to speed up the data loads.
5. Make any necessary changes to the database tables or other schema objects, but do not change any indexes or constraints yet.
6. Sort and or clean up data.
7. Transfer data across networks or by tapes.
8. Load the data into the new system.
9. Build indexes and constraints.
10. Perform a cold backup of the new database after the loads.
11. Test the loads.
12. If the load fails, restore the old system.
13. If the loads were successful, back up the newly loaded system.
14. Switch users to the new system.

Some systems run concurrently for a time to compare the results of operations.

There are several other factors that will affect your data loads. One is indexes and constraints. Trying to load tables with constraints, especially foreign key constraints, and indexes enabled generally requires significantly more time than first loading a table and then creating the indexes. This slowdown is the reason for step 4. If the tables are large and the load is appending data to the tables, it may be faster to load the tables with the indexes and constraints rather than to drop or disable them and rebuild them after the load.

The other factor to consider is load hierarchies. If primary and foreign keys are enabled during data loads, the order in which tables are loaded will be important. Primary key values must be loaded before foreign key values.

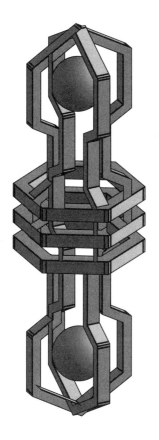

PART THREE

TUNING, MONITORING, AND MAINTENANCE

Chapter 7: Tuning, Monitoring, and Maintenance

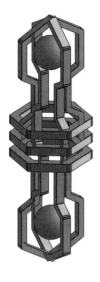

Tuning, Monitoring, and Maintenance

One major theme this book is the design of databases that do not require a lot of maintenance. If the design is good then monitoring and maintenance become proactive activities that are anticipated and planned for, versus the firefighting that so many organizations seem to tolerate.

Before you start monitoring your new database you will need to tune it. Tuning will occur in several stages, beginning when testing begins. Most of your tuning should be completed by the time you are ready to move into production, but you will need to check things and monitor the new system very closely at first.

You will also need to monitor the system over time, and no doubt, to perform some maintenance as well.

Another theme of this book is the use of software tools to help design, build, tune, and maintain your database(s). In the good old days, Oracle DBAs had to write and run all kinds of scripts to see how their database was performing. Now there are many excellent products on the market that can help you monitor and tune your database. Some tools will monitor your database for you and let you know about problems via E-mail, fax, or page. Many of the tools can even monitor remote and/or multiple databases using SQL*Net. Some of the more sophisticated tools will take corrective action when certain types of problems are detected, such as adding a data file if a tablespace runs out of room. Of special note is the ability of these tools to display information graphically and collect statistics over time.

I **highly** recommend that you purchase at least one of these tools to help tune and monitor your database. You will spend a lot more money trying to match the functionality of these tools by writing and running scripts and not do as good a job.

The following is a partial list of some of the products currently available:

- PLATINUM DBVision from PLATINUM Technology
- EcoTOOLS from Compuware
- AdHawk from Eventus Software
- DBTune from The Database Solutions Company

Applications and SQL

Most of your performance gains, will come from tuning the applications communicating with the Oracle database. In addition to tuning the SQL statements in the applications, cursors, array size, and the use of PL/SQL in the database will affect performance. Tuning the database begins after all of the SQL statements have been checked and tuned. The best tuned database in the world may still exhibit poor performance if the queries are poorly written.

To help in tuning, Oracle provides several tools and scripts that can evaluate individual components or entire systems. Besides the dynamic performance tables, which are covered later in this chapter, there are EXPLAIN PLAN, SQL TRACE and TKPROF, and UTLBSTAT and UTLESTAT. These three sets of utilities provide three different views of the application and the database. EXPLAIN PLAN is used to determine how a single query might perform, SQLTRACE and TKPROF show how a query actually performs, and UTLBSTAT and UTLESTAT show performance statistics for the entire database over a given time period.

EXPLAIN PLAN is a utility that will show how Oracle will execute a query. When running EXPLAIN PLAN, there are no calls to the database and no data is retrieved; Oracle simply tells you how the statement would be processed if it were run. The output is called the execution plan. This is your first line of defense against poorly written queries.

EXPLAIN PLAN can be run by either the programmers developing the queries or the DBAs responsible for the database. Some shops have the programmers develop the queries, run EXPLAIN PLAN, and then turn the results over to the DBAs for final testing, tuning, and approval.

SQLTRACE and TKPROF are a set of utilities that can monitor and report on database performance when one or more queries are actually run against the database. SQLTRACE is used to gather statistics when running the query, and TKPROF is a reporting tool that formats the output. In addition to producing the execution plan, SQLTRACE reports on CPU time spent on the query, physical reads needed to satisfy the query, the total number of rows processed, and several other statistics related to parsing and cache performance.

SQLTRACE and TKPROF should be run after a query is tuned using EXPLAIN PLAN. After the initial tuning, run the query with SQLTRACE enabled. TKPROF will then report what actually happened while the query was running.

Detailed use and interpretation of EXPLAIN PLAN and SQLTRACE/TKPROF are beyond the scope of this book. The following examples are intended to show how these tools work, not to teach you how to be an expert in their use.

UTLBSTAT and UTLESTAT are two scripts that gather and report statistics for the entire database over a given time period. Run UTLBSTAT to collect statistics at the beginning of the test period. UTLBSTAT takes a snapshot of various dynamic performance tables to provide a starting point. Run UTLESTAT at the end of the test period to take a snapshot and produce a report about the database performance over the test period.

EXPLAIN PLAN

The input to EXPLAIN PLAN is a single SQL query. EXPLAIN PLAN shows how Oracle will access data for a given query. No data is actually retrieved or manipulated with EXPLAIN PLAN; Oracle simply tells you how it would access the data by displaying the execution plan.

Use EXPLAIN PLAN to determine the most effective way to write queries and decide whether to index certain columns or use clusters. EXPLAIN PLAN shows:

- The type of query processed: SELECT, INSERT, UPDATE, or DELETE.
- The cost assigned by the cost-based optimizer if it is in use.
- The steps that are necessary to return the data.

- The internal operations that were performed for each step.
- The object accessed for each step.

In order to run EXPLAIN PLAN, you must run the Oracle script **UTLXPLAN.SQL**. This script creates a table called PLAN_TABLE. Figure 7.1 describes the PLAN_TABLE:

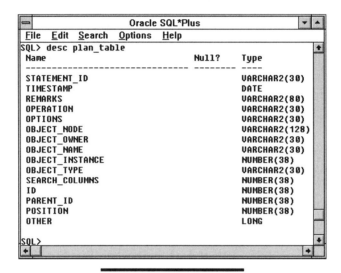

Figure 7.1 PLAN_TABLE.

To see how the optimizer will execute a query, preface the query with the words:

```
EXPLAIN PLAN
SET STATEMENT_ID = 'name'
FOR
```

The SET STATEMENT_ID = allows you to distinguish between different queries. The value for the STATEMENT_ID must be in single quotes.

Figure 7.2 shows an EXPLAIN PLAN on a query that shows the number of orders by customers in the state of New York.

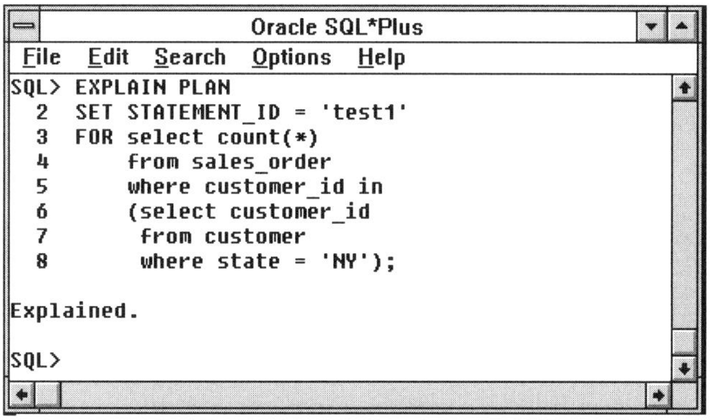

```
┌─────────────────────────────────────────────────────┐
│ ─          Oracle SQL*Plus              ▼ ▲ │
├─────────────────────────────────────────────────────┤
│ File  Edit  Search  Options  Help                   │
├─────────────────────────────────────────────────────┤
│SQL> EXPLAIN PLAN                                  ▲  │
│   2   SET STATEMENT_ID = 'test1'                     │
│   3   FOR select count(*)                            │
│   4       from sales_order                           │
│   5       where customer_id in                       │
│   6       (select customer_id                        │
│   7        from customer                             │
│   8        where state = 'NY');                      │
│                                                      │
│Explained.                                            │
│                                                      │
│SQL>                                               ▼  │
├─────────────────────────────────────────────────────┤
│ ◄ ◄                                              ► │
└─────────────────────────────────────────────────────┘
```

Figure 7.2 Submitting a query for EXPLAIN PLAN.

To see the results of the EXPLAIN PLAN, you need to run the following query:

```
select lpad(' ',2*(level-1))||operation||' '||options
||' '||object_name
||' '||decode(id, 0, 'Cost = '||position) "Query Plan"
from plan_table
start with id = 0 and statement_id = &&statement_id
connect by prior id = parent_id and statement_id = &&statement_id
```

Rather than type this query every time you want to see EXPLAIN PLAN results, type the query into a text file (I called this file **explan.sql** and it is included on the accompaning disk.) and run it to see the EXPLAIN PLAN results. The words &&statement_id in the query are substitution variables that ask for the name of the STATEMENT_ID entered in the original EXPLAIN PLAN query (Figure 7.3).

These results show that four operations were performed for the SELECT and there were two full table scans.

Figure 7.4 shows the same query after an index is created on the state column in the customer table.

```
                              Oracle SQL*Plus                    ▼ ▲
 File   Edit   Search   Options   Help
SQL> @explan                                                         ▲
Enter value for statement_id: 'test1'
old   5: start with id = 0 and statement_id = &&statement_id
new   5: start with id = 0 and statement_id = 'test1'
old   6: connect by prior id = parent_id and statement_id = &&statement_id
new   6: connect by prior id = parent_id and statement_id = 'test1'

Query Plan
-----------------------------------------------------------------
SELECT STATEMENT    Cost = 71
  SORT AGGREGATE
    MERGE JOIN
      SORT JOIN
        TABLE ACCESS FULL CUSTOMER
      SORT JOIN
        TABLE ACCESS FULL SALES_ORDER

7 rows selected.

SQL>                                                                 ▼
 ◀                                                                ▶
```

Figure 7.3 EXPLAIN PLAN results.

```
                              Oracle SQL*Plus                    ▼ ▲
 File   Edit   Search   Options   Help
SQL> create index cust_state                                         ▲
  2   on customer (state);

Index created.

SQL> EXPLAIN PLAN
  2    SET STATEMENT_ID = 'test2'
  3    FOR select count(*)
  4        from sales_order
  5        where customer_id in
  6        (select customer_id
  7         from customer
  8         where state = 'NY');

Explained.

SQL> @explan
Enter value for statement_id: 'test2'
old   5: start with id = 0 and statement_id = &&statement_id
new   5: start with id = 0 and statement_id = 'test2'
old   6: connect by prior id = parent_id and statement_id = &&statement_id
new   6: connect by prior id = parent_id and statement_id = 'test2'

Query Plan
-----------------------------------------------------------------
SELECT STATEMENT    Cost = 1
  SORT AGGREGATE
    NESTED LOOPS
      TABLE ACCESS FULL SALES_ORDER
      TABLE ACCESS BY ROWID CUSTOMER
        INDEX RANGE SCAN CUST_STATE

6 rows selected.

SQL>                                                                 ▼
 ◀                                                                ▶
```

Figure 7.4 EXPLAIN PLAN with an index added.

The results here show that there were two operations performed, but notice the difference on the table access. Rather than scan the CUSTOMER table looking for customers from New York, the optimizer used the new index to find the customers from New York. Then it uses the ROWID from the index to retrieve the CUSTOMER_ID from the CUSTOMER table.

Lets see what happens when we add an index to the CUSTOMER_ID column in the SALES_ORDER table (Figure 7.5).

```
┌─────────────────────────────────────────────────────────┐
│ ─              Oracle SQL*Plus              ▼ ▲ │
├─────────────────────────────────────────────────────────┤
│ File  Edit  Search  Options  Help                        │
│ SQL> create index so_cust                             ▲ │
│   2  on sales_order (customer_id);                       │
│                                                          │
│ Index created.                                           │
│                                                          │
│ SQL> EXPLAIN PLAN                                        │
│   2   SET STATEMENT_ID = 'test3'                         │
│   3  FOR select count(*)                                 │
│   4      from sales_order                                │
│   5      where customer_id in                            │
│   6      (select customer_id                             │
│   7       from customer                                  │
│   8       where state = 'NY');                           │
│                                                          │
│ Explained.                                               │
│                                                          │
│ SQL> @explan                                             │
│ Enter value for statement_id: 'test3'                    │
│ old   5: start with id = 0 and statement_id = &&statement_id│
│ new   5: start with id = 0 and statement_id = 'test3'    │
│ old   6: connect by prior id = parent_id and statement_id =│
│ new   6: connect by prior id = parent_id and statement_id =│
│                                                          │
│ Query Plan                                               │
│ ─────────────────────────────────────────────────────── │
│ SELECT STATEMENT    Cost =                               │
│   SORT AGGREGATE                                         │
│     NESTED LOOPS                                         │
│       TABLE ACCESS BY ROWID CUSTOMER                     │
│         INDEX RANGE SCAN CUST_STATE                      │
│       INDEX RANGE SCAN SO_CUST                           │
│                                                          │
│ 6 rows selected.                                      ▼ │
│ ◄                                                     ► │
└─────────────────────────────────────────────────────────┘
```

Figure 7.5 EXPLAIN PLAN with an additional index.

Notice that there are no more table scans. Oracle is now using both indexes to get the requested rows from the database.

Using EXPLAIN PLAN is an iterative process. To use it effectively you should have training on writing and tuning Oracle's SQL.

SQL TRACE and TKPROF

These tools go beyond telling you how Oracle would perform a query to showing you how Oracle did perform the query. The statistics collected show the number of times a step was executed, the amount of CPU time for each step, the total elapsed time for each step, and the physical and logical reads needed for each step. There are three steps analyzed for each query: the parse step that created the execution plan, the execute step that actually submits the query to the database, and the fetch step that relates to the actual data needed to answer the query.

In order to run TKPROF the **init.ora** parameter TIMED_STATISTICS must be set to TRUE. In addition, the session must be altered to collect the statistics using the following statement:

```
ALTER SESSION SET SQL_TRACE = TRUE;
```

There is an **init.ora** parameter to set SQL_TRACE, but doing so collect statistics for all the sessions and can cause performance problems.

After SQL_TRACE is set, run your query or queries. Output from the trace goes to the USER_DUMP_DEST specified in the **init.ora** file. In this example, I ran the same query that was used to illustrate EXPLAIN PLAN.

When you are ready to analyze the query or queries, you execute **tkprof.exe**. You will need to know the location of TKPROF, which is usually in the **bin** directory. The screen below shows the new GUI tool for TKPROF which is run from within Microsoft Windows using the Windows **Run** option from the File menu in Program Manger. The **Sort** option allows you to sort the output in a variety of ways. Here I am sorting on EXECPU, which lists the output for all the queries run in order of CPU usage.

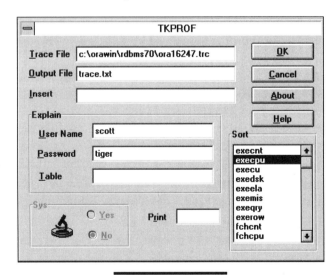

Figure 7.6 TKPROF.

The actual output from this example was several pages long because Oracle is executing many database calls even while I run my query. Each SQL statement that was executed during the session is analyzed by TKPROF.

The following listing just shows the output from TKPROF for the query about customers in New York. Note the additional statistical information that shows how the query actually performed during the parse, execution, and fetch phases of the query. (This little query did not even take one one-hundredth of a second for any of the steps, although it did fetch 162 blocks from the database to obtain the results.) The bottom portion shows the execution plan like EXPLAIN PLAN, but it also shows the number of rows that were used during each step of the actual query execution under the Rows column.

```
************************************************************************

select count(*)
from sales_order where customer_id in (select customer_id from customer
  where state in 'NY')

call        count      cpu   elapsed      disk   query current      rows
--------    -------  --------  ---------  --------  -------- -------  ----------
Parse            1     0.00      0.00         8       71       3          0
Execute          1     0.00      0.00         0        0       0          0
Fetch            1     0.00      0.00       162      162       5          1

Misses in library cache during parse: 1
Parsing user id: 8  (SCOTT)

Rows     Execution Plan
-------  -------------------------------------------------------
      0  SELECT STATEMENT
      0   SORT (AGGREGATE)
     30    MERGE JOIN
    288     SORT (JOIN)
   1056      TABLE ACCESS (FULL) OF 'CUSTOMER'
    100     SORT (JOIN)
    100      TABLE ACCESS (FULL) OF 'SALES_ORDER'

************************************************************************
```

Figure 7.7 SQLTRACE output.

As with EXPLAIN PLAN, SQLTRACE and TKPROF must be used in an iterative fashion. They help you compare one query against another to see which performs better. SQLTRACE and TKPROF are actually much harder to use and interpret than EXPLAIN PLAN, but if you must have that last ounce of performance SQLTRACE will show you down to a hundredth of a second which query is the fastest.

Memory

After properly tuned SQL queries, a well-tuned SGA will have the greatest impact on database performance. Within the three major sections of the SGA, tuning the shared pool will generally have the greatest impact on performance. Next comes the database buffers, and finally the redo buffers in order of importance. This means that a poorly tuned shared pool will generally affect performance more than poorly tuned database buffers. The word generally is important because any one of these areas can bring a system to its knees. In my experience, the biggest problems initially lie with too few database buffers, and performance can dramatically improve simply by increasing their number. However, once gross problems are addressed, it is still important to go through the exercise of checking each area to get the best overall performance.

Your goal in tuning the SGA is to achieve the highest hit ratios for the shared pool and the database buffers as possible. A *cache* hit occurs when Oracle finds requested data in memory. A *cache* miss occurs when Oracle does not find the data in memory, and it must go to disk to retrieve the data. The performance ratios are usually described as a percentage of hits, a hit ratio, or misses, a miss ratio.

While large amounts of memory usually lead to hit hit ratios, you do not want the SGA so big that it causes swapping and excessive paging of memory by the operating system. To determine where this trade off lies, you will need to work with your systems administrator to monitor memory from the operating system as well.

Shared Pool

The shared pool contains a library cache, and a dictionary cache. The library cache portion of the shared pool contains SQL statements, procedures, packages, and triggers. The triggers, procedures, and packages are stored in the data dictionary and are usually associated with the database as part of the overall conceptual schema definition. The SQL statements are submitted to the database by users directly or by applications, and they are associated with the external schema(s).

As described earlier, there is a huge amount of activity/database overhead associated with parsing and creating an execution plan. SQLTRACE can show you this explicitly. This is another reason why triggers, packages, procedures, and standards are so important in an Oracle environment. There should never be similarly written triggers that perform the same exact function in a single database. However, it is not uncommon for many different programs to request the same information with different SQL requests. It is very difficult to control how different programmers write their code. If functionality/code can be shifted from the applications to the database (using triggers, procedures, and packages) then the overall system should be much more efficient. In lieu of database programming, SQL programming standards become more important to try and ensure that similar SQL statements are written in exactly the same manner.

Oracle gives a higher priority to the library cache than the dictionary cache. If Oracle finds a query in memory, there is no need to read the data dictionary because the work has already been completed during the statement parsing. Therefore, SQL information will stay in the shared pool longer than dictionary information. If the library cache is performing well, the dictionary cache should be OK.

Performance of the library cache is affected by two factors. The first is whether equivalent SQL statements are exact matches. When similar statements do not match exactly, more space is required in the shared SQL area. Try and address this issue first.

The other factor in tuning the library cache is the amount of memory allocated to the shared pool. The miss ratio in the library cache should be close to zero. Figure 7.8 shows a query that produces the miss ratio for the library cache. The equivalent hit ratio is 73%.

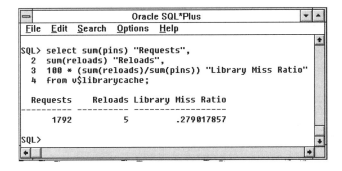

Figure 7.8 Library cache miss ratio.

The dictionary cache contains Oracle's data dictionary information. The performance of the dictionary cache is dependent on the size of the shared pool, as well as the number of objects in the data dictionary (Figure 7.9). The goal is to cache the entire data dictionary. A system with 100 tables will take up less room than a system with 1000 tables given an equivalent number of columns per table. The hit ratio for the dictionary cache should be at least 90% (a 10% miss ratio), but even higher ratios are better. For the following example, the hit ratio is only 88%, so the size of the SHARED_POOL_SIZE should be increased, even if the library cache is performing well.

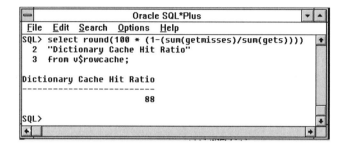

Figure 7.9 Dictionary cache hit ratio.

A small database with relatively few users may need only a few megabytes of memory for the shared pool. A database with a lot of objects and many users may need 10 megabytes of memory or more.

Database Buffers

The database buffers contain data blocks that were read on behalf of user requests. The database buffers will usually take up the largest portion of the SGA. For a large machine with a single instance of Oracle running, you may be able to use as much as 50% of the memory for the database buffers. But don't make the SGA so big that it starts to cause swapping of processes by the operating system.

Figure 7.10 shows how to get the hit ratio for the database buffers from values in the V$SYSSTAT view.

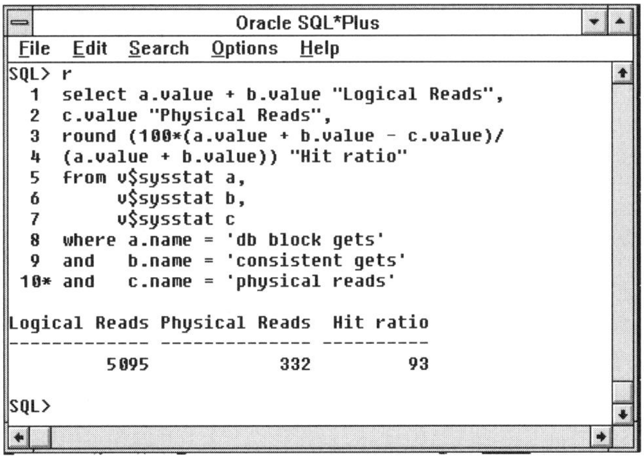

```
Oracle SQL*Plus
File  Edit  Search  Options  Help
SQL> r
  1  select a.value + b.value "Logical Reads",
  2  c.value "Physical Reads",
  3  round (100*(a.value + b.value - c.value)/
  4  (a.value + b.value)) "Hit ratio"
  5  from v$sysstat a,
  6        v$sysstat b,
  7        v$sysstat c
  8  where a.name = 'db block gets'
  9  and    b.name = 'consistent gets'
 10* and    c.name = 'physical reads'

Logical Reads Physical Reads  Hit ratio
------------- -------------- ----------
         5095            332         93

SQL>
```

Figure 7.10 Database buffer hit ratio.

For most systems, you should try to get at least a 90% hit ratio. Systems, such as division support systems, that are primarily read-only may never achieve high hit ratios because of the amount of data that is read through the database buffers. For these systems, the sort area size may be more important.

If you cannot achieve a high hit ratio and system performance is a problem, you may have to install more memory in the machine.

Redo Log Buffers

The redo log buffers contain all of the changes made to the database. These buffers are more critical for on-line tarasaction processing (OLTP) systems than DSSs because the changes made to the data require use of the log buffers. DSSs, because they don't have a lot of updates, may not have much need for the log buffers. For OLTP systems, log buffers are important especially when there are many users performing many inserts, updates, or deletes.

The concept of hit ratios does not apply to the redo buffers because the buffers are not reused like the database buffers are. The redo buffers are accessed serially by processes that need to write changes to the data that were made. The goal in tuning the redo buffers is to try and make sure that no process has to wait for space.

The following query (Figure 7.11) is used to see if there was any wait time for the redo buffers. This value should be zero. If it is not zero, increase the size of the LOG_BUFFERS in the **init.ora** file. The default for most systems is usually 32K, 64K, or 128K; most of these values can be doubled with no ill effects. If there is wait time, keep doubling the size until the problem goes away.

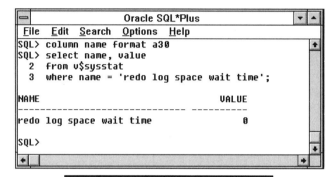

Figure 7.11 Redo log space wait time.

Sort Area

The sort area is a portion of memory outside the SGA. It is used, as its name implies, for sorting data and other things. It is a space where Oracle will store intermediate results from queries as it tries to obtain a final set of rows to satisfy a query. If the query runs out of room in the sort area, it will begin to write the data to the temporary tablespace on the disk. The goal in tuning the sort area is to try and reduce the number of times Oracle runs out of room in the sort area.

The important thing to note about the sort area is that it is allocated on a per user basis. This means that any user process can allocate as much memory as specified by the **init.ora** parameter SORT_AREA_SIZE. This, in turn, means that certain kinds of queries can quickly use a lot of memory.

The following query (Figure 7.12) shows how many times Oracle performed sorts in memory (in the sort area) and how many times sorts had to be done on disk because it ran out of sort area. Obviously, I am not performing many sorts as I prepare examples using the little SCOTT/TIGER database provided with Oracle.

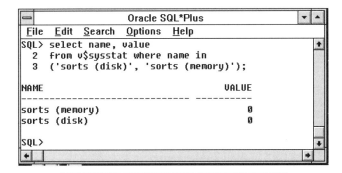

Figure 7.12 Sorts in memory and to disk.

If your system shows a total number of sorts on disk that is equal or greater than 10% of the sorts in memory, you should try two things. See if there are any queries that could be causing the problem. If the queries are well tuned, then increase the sort area to try and reduce the number of sorts on disk.

Most OLTP systems do not require much sort area, maybe a few megabytes. DSSes, on the other hand, can often make better use of sort area memory than they can of the database buffers. For a DSS, the sort area may be larger that the entire SGA.

I/O

The goal in tuning I/O is to spread, or balance the reads from and writes to the database evenly across all the machine's controllers, channels, and disks. You want to eliminate "hot spots," areas with a disproportionate amount of the I/O. This is where you test the job you did in laying out the tables, indexes, redo logs, rollback segments, and other objects in the database.

Oracle provides some facilities to monitor I/O, but they are only for the Oracle database files not all disk activity. The best way to check I/O is to use an operating system tool that will let you look at the Oracle files and every other file on the machine.

If you do find a disk with a high percentage of the total system I/O, you will generally have two remedies at hand. One is to move one or more files that are on the disk. This is one of the reasons for making more and smaller files on each disk rather than one large file. If you find a hot spot, just move some files around. Another way to fix the problem is to move objects within the database. This usually consists of moving tables and/or indexes from one tablespace to another. The question will be, which object to move? The I/O figures were at the file level, not the objects in the files.

Moving objects is one area where Export and Import do come in handy, but this may be more trouble than just moving a file or two.

Contention

Once memory is tuned the next step is to try and reduce or eliminate *contention*, which is caused by processes that compete for the same resource. Write transactions cause much more contention than read transactions. Access to most of the resources of interest is controlled through latches. A *latch* is similar to a lock. When a transaction needs to write change data to the redo buffers, for example, it must first acquire a latch. Heavy transaction volumes can often cause latch contention.

Rollback Segments

Rollback segment contention usually occurs where there are too many users and too few rollback segments. This problem should be addressed and solved as part of the design process. On systems that support many on-line users (1000 to 2000), rollback segment contention may signal a need to move to the Oracle Parallel Server. With OPS, the users would be divided among the various Oracle instances, thus reducing the number of users per instance.

The simple math for the number of rollback segments is one for every four concurrent users with a maximum of 50 rollback segments. This indicates a maximum of about 200 concurrent users. Remember that a system with 200 concurrent users may actually have more than 1000 users logged on to Oracle. The distinction is between the number of users that are logged on and the number of users that are simultaneously executing transactions.

The following queries (Figures 7.13 and 7.14) will help determine if there is rollback segment contention. The first screen shows if there are any waits for undo (rollback segment) blocks or headers.

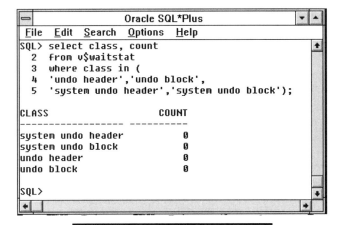

Figure 7.13 Rollback segment waits.

If the preceding values are greater than zero, perform the second query (Figure 7.14) to see how many gets were performed. If the ratio of gets to any of the undo values is greater than zero, add rollback segments.

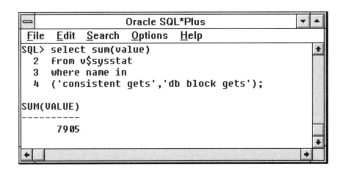

Figure 7.14 Total gets compared to rollback waits.

Redo Latches

Any changes to the database are written to the redo buffers, and from there they are written out to the redo logs. Space in the redo buffers is controlled by an allocation latch. Each transaction/change must acquire the latch before it can write to the redo buffers.

Figure 7.15 shows how to query the V$LATCH table for redo latch contention. Contention would be indicated if either of the miss columns were higher than 1% of their corresponding get columns.

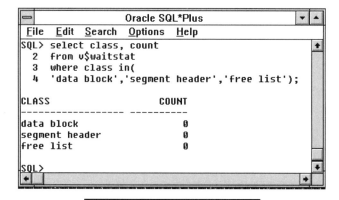

Figure 7.15 Redo latch contention.

Freelists

Check the V$WAITSTAT table for freelist contention (Figure 7/16). Contention is indicated by waits for data blocks, segment headers, or freelists. If any of theses values are above zero, consider adding additional freelists to those tables; it indexes that have the highest number of inserts. The freelists parameter can only be set when creating a table; it cannot be changed without dropping the table and re-creating it .

Figure 7.16 Freelist contention.

Also check the V$SYSSTAT table for the number of requests for data blocks (Figure 7.17).

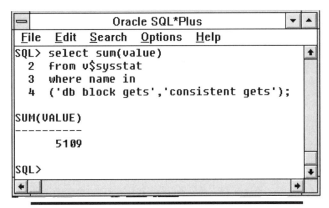

Figure 7.17 Total gets compared to freelists waits.

Compare these two results as a ratio. If there are 1% or more waits for freelists compared to the gets, consider adding additional freelists. The difficulty with this is that it does not show if a particular object, or more accurately which object, may be having problems with inserts.

If you need to add freelists, add them to the tables and indexes that have the highest proportion of inserts. Again, a freelist cannot be added to an existing object. The number of freelists is set as part of an object's CREATE statement. In order to add a freelist to a table or index, the object must be re-created. Either copy the object to a new object using a CREATE TABLE AS statement and then drop the old object and rename the new one or export the object, drop the object, recreate it with additional freelists, and then import it.

If you are designing a database that will perform a lot of inserts, consider adding additional freelists to the table(s) and index(es) that will have the most inserts during the design phase.

Finding and fixing many of these performance problems can be difficult for a production database, especially for large tables with heavy transaction volumes. In addition to having to do all the shutdowns, startups, table drops, copies, exports, imports, and so on, another problem is having to re-create synonyms and grants after any object is dropped (unless you are using Export and Import, which can take all the grants associated with the objects.) The point of good design is to avoid ever having to get to this point. If a database needs a major and unplanned reorganization, then the designer did not do a good job because the database is not easily maintained. You need to anticipate these issues as part of your design phase and try to detect them early in the build stages.

UTLBSTAT and UTLESTAT

UTLBSTAT and UTLESTAT are two scripts that gather statistics for a database over a specified time period. The statistics should only be gathered after the database has reached a steady state, meaning it has been up and running for a while.

All the tuning issues and examples earlier in this represented a point-in-time check of the system. When you use one of those queries to check this or that hit ratio, you are only checking one thing at one time. UTLBSTAT and UTLESTAT allow you to collect similar information, over a predefined period of time. However, with UTLBSTAT and UTLESTAT, you have to do all the math by hand unless you write scripts to interpret the output.

Before running these scripts, the **init.ora** parameter TIMED_STATISTICS must be set to TRUE. UTLBSTAT creates tables and begins the data collection process. There is some overhead when you run this, but not much. UTLESTAT stops the process and creates a multipage report that is a lot more detailed than what was covered earlier.

A Quick Check List

Most of this chapter has dealt with a detailed discussion of database tuning. This section is a synopsis that puts most of it together to allow you to get a quick pulse check of an existing system.

The database is only one ingredient in a larger recipe. You must also check the machine environment for potential memory, I/O, CPU, and network problems. Remember that the applications will have the biggest effect on what the users consider response time. Don't be surprised to find a database that seems to be running reasonably well, even when end users are screaming about poor response time. (There are still programmers out there who don't suspect that six-way joins or eight ORDER BY clauses might slow down an application.)

At the machine level look for:

- Paging or swapping of memory
- Overall I/O bottlenecks, not just the database
- High CPU use
- Network problems

For the database, perform the following checks:

- Library cache hit ratio
- Data dictionary cache hit ratio
- Database buffer hit ratio
- From the V$SYSSTAT view
    - enqueue waits should be zero
    - dbwr free needed should be zero
    - redo log space requests should be zero (otherwise indicates the redo log_buffer is too small)
    - long and short table scans
    - table fetch continued row(indicates row chaining)
    - sorts in memory and sorts to disk (high number of sorts to disks indicates the sort_area_size may be too small)
- Buffer busy waits
- Check V$ROLLSTAT for waits
- A listing of initialization parameters
- Segments that have more than four extents (see below)

Monitoring and Maintenance

Over time, most systems begin to exhibit different operating behavior. Systems often get slower as they get larger. The main culprit of this degradation are queries that are no longer tuned to reflect the new sizes of table and indexes. The mix of data may also have changed since the database first became operational. (It is amazing how something like a Christmas sale can skew the distribution of data in some of the date indexes of a retail sales system.)

Some of the things you will want to look for on a regular basis are:

- Object growth (looking for data in the next extent)
- Fragmentation .
- Row chaining
- Database errors in the alert log and trace files
- Check the audit logs if you are auditing

You may find it helpful to distinguish between different types of database availability and down time. Too often, when a system is down, everyone associated with the system gets blamed. For good public relations, not to mention job security, develop a way to distinguish between the client being down, the server being down, the database being down, and/or the network being the source of difficulties. In addition, you may want to further break down database availability into such categories as unavailable because of scheduled maintenance; unavailable because of unscheduled maintenance; the database is up but certain data is unavailable because someone inadvertently dropped a table; and the database is down because of outside factors such as an operating system failure.

Alert Logs and Trace and Dump Files

While Oracle is running it writes various messages to certain log and trace files. These files should be examined, looking for any error messages generated by Oracle. Rather than hear from your users that your system is not operating properly, or not operating at all, you may be able to find out first from the errors in the log and trace files.

These alert and trace files are constantly growing and multiplying. Unless they are examined and deleted these files will grow until they take up the whole disk or partition. Develop a procedure—manual or automated—that examines these files and deletes them on a regular basis. Note, however, that these files can provide valuable information for Oracle Support if you call them when you are experiencing problems, so save the error messages.

Database Growth

Except for Parallel Server systems and striped tablespaces, one of our design tenants was to build the INITIAL extent large enough to hold a specified period's worth of data. The MINEXTENTS was set to two to help in database monitoring. The basic premise is that when data is added to the second extent, it is time to look at resizing and reorganizing the table(s). At least two extents were allocated to prevent dynamic allocation while the database is running.

The following query (Figure 7.18) will show any segment that has more than one extent and the segment's total size. This query uses the USER_SEGMENTS view, so it only shows the segments for the user that is executing the query. To see all the segments regardless of owner, use the DBA_SEGMENTS view.

For systems with heavy transaction volumes, i.e., systems that generate a lot of redo log activity, you may want to monitor the location of the ARCHIVE_LOG_DEST. If the disk where the archive log files are written should be filled, the system will stop.

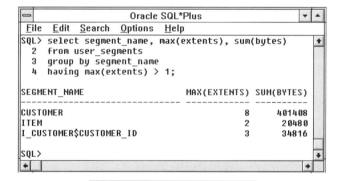

Figure 7.18 Creeping extents.

Analyze Tables and Indexes

If you intend to run your database using the cost-based optimizer, be sure to have in place procedures and routines to update the table, cluster, and index statistics on a regular or as needed basis. The biggest need will arise for changes in the number of rows in the database.

A side benefit of the ANALYZE command is that it will show if there is any row chaining occurring in the tables. Row chaining can significantly degrade performance, so checking for this information is a good reason to periodically run ANALYZE.

Tools Again

Finding the right question is usually harder than finding the right answer. With the users screaming, "The response time stinks!" it's often difficult to step back and ponder the problem. But you will want to perform a series of diagnostics (like the quick check presented earlier) to find out what the problem is before you try and tune anything.

All of this effort is immeasurably easier if you have a tuning or monitoring product to help you.

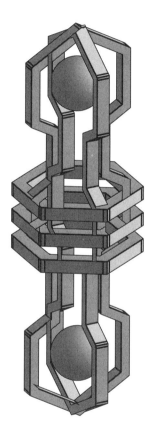

PART FOUR

OTHER ISSUES

Chapter 8: Policies and Procedures

Chapter 9: Special Issues

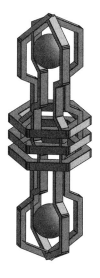

Policies and Procedures

"There are no technical problems any more, just political ones." This chapter and the next explore the people and management issues that must be blended with the technology to make your efforts pay off. This chapter covers several non-technical issues that must be addressed in every database environment, regardless of size. These issues are more important than the technology itself and will go further in determining the long term cost, flexibility, and productivity of any and all systems that you build or support.

As hardware and software change it is important to have an organization that can recognize, quantify, adopt, and support the ineluctable nature of change. If you build the ability to support change into your processes, then the inevitable changes that do come can create opportunities rather than burdens. The whole point of the three schema architecture is to reduce the trauma of change, because you can never eliminate it.

Policies, procedures, and standards must be written and distributed. If seasontotaste is ok for your important things like naming standards or backup procedures that's fine. But, if you would like to have some things done consistently and correctly, write the recipe in detail. In other words, if it is not written and disseminated, then policies become folk lore and no one can be blamed for not following them.

Personnel

In the database arena there are numerous tasks that must be performed once or on an on-going basis. These tasks can be grouped by some common job titles or functions. The tasks may be performed by one or many people. In some shops a single person may perform all of the tasks. In larger organizations several people may perform the tasks within a single group. The purpose here is to list many of the common tasks and suggest ways to divide the labor. I am not insisting that every Oracle shop must have at least three people on staff to perform these tasks; but someone needs to perform them. An organization may wish to contract for some of the tasks, especially those that are one-time or require a very high level of expertise.

The three general job functions are Data Administration (DA), Database Administration (DBA), and Systems Administration (SA). Some of the tasks covered by these functions include backups, security, tuning, design, naming standards, etc. Some of these tasks are performed by only one group, but most have some overlap or pass from one group to another. Ultimately, you must decide who is to do what, as well as when and how they should do it. Identifying the technical issues and resolving the political ones will be more important to your success than any amount of hardware or software.

At the end of this section there is a matrix that shows how the tasks and functions relate.

Data Administration

Data Administrators (DA) are the keepers of the conceptual schema. It should also be DA's responsibility to develop, publish, and, in some cases, enforce policies regarding data and some database operations like security and archiving policies. In a large organization with multiple projects and multiple databases the DA job is critical.

DA is one of those things in database like database programming, discussed earlier, and naming standards, covered in the next section, that I term as front loaded tasks or functions. Front loading means that there is a lot of work required in the early stages of a project that has most of its pay off, or pay backs, in later stages or later projects. This initial cost and late pay back often results in a temptation to scale back or discontinue the DA function during or shortly after the first project. (Remember the comparison between the tactical nature of external schema development and the strategic nature of conceptual schema development discussed in Chapter 1. DA is a strategic position or function.) If your organization is one that must support on-going development efforts, then DA will be extremely important in helping ensure that past efforts are leveraged in building new ones. The DA group is the one charged with keeping an eye on long term systems integration.

There is a clear need for data stewardship in terms of managing data just like any other organizational asset such as cash, inventory, and personnel. There is a data life cycle, just as there is a product life cycle. The stages include:

- Identification — Identify what data is important to the organization.
- Standardization — Develop standards for new and existing data definitions.
- Acquisition — Determine how data is accumulated.
- Maintenance — Determine how data is maintained. Maintenance includes updates to the data itself, as well as the security and backup issues related to the database.
- Archival — While the trend is towards larger and larger systems, it is seldom necessary or desirable to keep data on—line forever. At some point, someone needs to decide what data can go, where it should go, and how it will get there.
- Disposal — While very similar to the archival stage, disposal, as its name implies, specifies how data and definitions are removed from the systems.

Several of these stages present some significant problems in terms of organizations and technology that are worth noting. For truly integrated systems (those that cross organizational or functional boundaries) data acquisition, or data entry/update can create special headache, heartache, and opportunities. You will find this especially true in projects that are part of a reengineering effort.

A mantra for most integrated development efforts is "one-time data entry." This is one of the great promises of relational technology. The goal is to enter the data once (and there could actually be many points of entry) and then have that data accessible to all authorized users. Achieving this goal should produce significant tangible and quantifiable cost saving in data entry and support for multiple sets of the same data. Less tangible but probably more significant are the opportunity and productivity costs associated with a single timely and consistent set of data.

The difficulty in realizing this goal lies in moving from what was to what will be. In the non-integrated environment there was a diverse set of data entry screens that were needed to support a particular department, function, or application — a particular external schema. What is needed is an understanding and consensus about how data needs to be entered and maintained for the entire organization — the conceptual schema that realizes the goal of one-time data entry. What quickly becomes apparent with this organizational view is that individual departments do not have the resources or budgets to support the "burden" of collecting all of the data at one of these single points of data entry. A department only needed to collect a certain subset of data in a format that only needed to support its own internal functions. There were or are no incentives for the order-entry staff to support the needs of accounting, manufacturing, product development, distribution, or strategic planning, just to name a few of an organization's other functions.

The issue boils down to, or blows up, at the point where more work is required to fill in the new screens that support more than one department. Again, this will be especially true where a reengineering effort is under way. This problem (and the solution) is not a technical one; in fact, it is the technology that shines a bright light on the problem. As new systems are developed and screens shown to prospective users, I hear over and over again; "Hey, I never had to collect all of this data before...I don't have the time or the need to collect this stuff....The old system didn't require me to format the data in this way either. This is more work. I'm not going to use it. You didn't do a very good job in building this system."

What to do? The solution(s) lies in vision, education, incentives, preparation, and in good management and political skills. As keepers of the conceptual schema, it is incumbent on DA to address and resolve these issues. DA has to proselytize, educate, and negotiate. Individuals and departments need to understand why things are changing, how they affect the entire organization, and then they must be given the incentives, budgets, and resources to perform the new tasks. The infighting and solutions will revolve around the incentives, budgets, and resources. Simply telling someone (although it sometimes ultimately comes down to this) that you **will** do things this way seldom makes for happy campers. It's an idea that has to be sold. **DA organizations that** simply act as the data police are more often part of the problem rather than part of the solution.

Another delicate issue is often data archival and disposal. The issue is especially acute for government or other regulated organizations that have rules that define data retention and maintenance requirements. An example will best illustrate this issue. I have worked for both justice and environmental organizations. Both had legislation that stated what data was to be collected and how it should be disposed of. What comes to mind are rules about expungement and data retention. *The American Heritage Dictionary* defines expunge as: "To erase or strike out...To eliminate completely." A person can go to court to get their records expunged. This is common in cases involving juveniles, and people or organizations that have been exonerated or acquitted of charges or accusations.

So, what happens? Well, in a solely paper-based system, the person with the expungement order goes to the clerk of courts, and/or some other records keeping body, and people go through ledgers with black makers and strike out references to the case, then they go and destroy any other documents related to the case.

Where computers are involved, however, the problem becomes **much** more complex. Most regulated institutions also have strict rules on data backup and archiving. These rules usually specify so many years of data retention. For computer systems the data is usually backedup and/or archived to tape. The question becomes, How does one locate and destroy all reference to a particular case if the data is stored on potentially dozens if not hundreds of tapes? And what happens if the data is stored on CD-ROM? I have yet to see these issues effectively addressed, let alone solved, by any state legislature, mostly because of the complexity, procedures, and costs involved.

This example is intended to illustrate the kinds of issues that should be addressed by DA with regard to data archival and disposal. Sometimes these issues become hideously complex and do not lend themselves to any kind of a solution — yet.

DA should define how data is handled during each stage, as well as, who is responsible for the work. One of the hardest tasks is determining data ownership. Many people or departments will quickly say that certain data is theirs and that they should control it. What they do not want to do, however, is have to maintain the data. The situation manifests itself when a department steps ups and says, "We are responsible for the XYZ lookup codes. We control what the values are, and we will determine who can use them.......What? you want us to define and maintain the values? What? someone in our department actually has to do some work for this? Forget it, DA, that's too much work for us. We have real work to do; you maintain the values." I find that one of the most daunting tasks in building integrated systems is developing the consensus necessary to define and develop lookup codes and tables.

Database Administration

Database Administrators (DBA) are the keepers of the internal schema. They are responsible for the physical database design, implementation, and maintenance. They are also the ones primarily responsible for implementing many of the policies and procedures defined by DA.

Besides the initial physical design efforts, DBA's on-going task is to support the various database environments. On the design side, DBAs work closely with the DA group to translate the LDM to an effective physical database. For maintenance and support the DBAs work more closely with the systems administrators. There is significant overlap and interdependence in backups, system security, performance tuning, and recovery. This overlap can give way to finger pointing when things go wrong and with missed efficiencies if not properly planned and assigned.

In the scenario where more code is put in the database rather than the application, a new function arises which is essentially database programming. This could mean that some programmers, proficient in PL/SQL, get shifted to the DBA group to write and maintain code for triggers, functions, stored procedures, and packages.

Systems Administration

Systems Administrators (SA) are responsible for the operating system and machine side of an organization's computer system. They may also be responsible for the networks, telecommunications, and performing backups as well. They are usually responsible for machine and network security, allocation of machine resources, and performance monitoring and tuning as well. SAs usually work closely with DBAs in database design.

SA usually provides the "operators" who perform many of the routine maintenance and monitoring tasks such as, loading tapes and performing backups, and monitoring network traffic, system status, and resource utilization.

Table 8.1 is a matrix to show where some of the tasks may fit various roles.

Table 8.1 Personnel Matrix

Task	Data Administration	Systems Administration	Database Administration
Capacity Planning	X	X	X
Change Control & Migration	X	X	X
Data Archiving	Define	Perform	
Data Modeling	X	X	
Database Backups	Define	Develop	Perform
Database Design		X	X
Database Installation		X	X
Define External Interfaces	Logical	Physical	
File System Backups			X
Maintain External Interfaces		X	X
Maintain Database User	Define	Maintain	
Maintain Machine Security			X
Naming Standards	X	X	
Performance Monitoring		X	X
Performance Tuning		X	X
Installation & Upgrades		X	X

Naming Standards

Good naming standards are critical to the ease of maintenance of an Oracle database, especially when there are multiple developers on a project and multiple projects. Conversely, complex naming standards can be a pain. Simple guide lines will go further than strict voluminous standards tomes. So, the first rule is to keep it simple. A corollary to the rule is that which isn't published can't be followed. Be sure to document the standards before you try to enforce them.

Gary Milsap of Oracle developed the Optimal Flexible Architecture (OFA) which should be followed for naming and placing directories and files. Not only does this save you from reinventing the wheel, it also provides instant documentation. Following the OFA will also make it easier to work with Oracle Support and, hopefully, those third-party vendors that adhere to the same standard. This directory and file naming issue also illustrates an area of significant overlap between DBA and SA functions, especially since there are usually operating system specific requirements to naming things at this level.

For objects within the database, Oracle will let you name most schema objects using up to thirty characters. You will find it much more practical to keep names much shorter. In an effort to keep names short do not make them cryptic. Clarity is still better than brevity, which is why Oracle gives you thirty characters. There is an economic argument for brevity, and it is simply that it takes longer to type longer names, and there will also be more chances for mistakes with longer names. Put another way, shorter names should translate into more words per minute and higher productivity.

To help end users with clarity, some shops have two names for objects. They use short names for internal schema objects like tables and columns to make programming easier. Then they create views that have longer names for the tables and columns, and these longer names are for the external schema and end users.

Reserve words need special note in some Oracle or client/server environments. The problem you will encounter is that all of the reserve word lists that you will need may not be consistent across all products. A reserve word in one product may not be a reserve word in another product, and vice versa. You will find it useful to compile a list of all of the reserve words for all of the products you use and distribute the list.

There are two types of words that you will want to make a concerted effort to find and eliminate or at least document and control. These are homonyms and synonyms. (This discussion does not pertain to Oracle synonyms which are used to create aliases for tables to facilitate control and/or access.) Homonyms are words that have the same sound or spelling but mean different things. For example, the word bill should not be permitted to refer to both customer and supplier invoices, otherwise, how can you tell which is which by the name bill.

Synonyms are different words that have the same meaning. Do not, for example, use both supplier and vendor in the same system to refer to the same thing. Be consistent. Controlling these types of words will help control ambiguity.

SQL

Oracle will reuse or share SQL statements that are exactly the same. When a query is submitted to the database Oracle first checks the Shared SQL Area to see if the query is already in memory. If Oracle finds an **exact** match it will use the query that is in memory. To facilitate this sharing capability it is wise to develop SQL coding standards.

A simple standard would be one where all SQL statements are in all capital (or lowercase) letters and there are no indentations.

```
SELECT EMPNO, ENAME, HIREDATE
FROM EMPLOYEE;

     or

select empno, ename, hiredate
from employee;
```

To enhance readability the word case is often switched between commands and objects as in the following example:

```
SELECT empno, ename, hiredate
FROM employee;
```

As with any standard the key is to keep it simple so people can follow it. Simplicity is especially important here because so many different people could be writing SQL statements. So, however legible changing cases and using indentations may make the statements, remember that performance could suffer (or not be optimal) as many comparable SQL statements are forcing swaps in the Shared SQL Area because the statements are not **exact** matches.

Abbreviations and Acronyms

Develop a short list of standard abbreviations and acronyms. The abbreviations should not be names in themselves. Acronyms, however, are often words that help people associate their meaning to a particular system, process, or object. The list of abbreviations need not be exhaustive. For internal schema objects consider always using the abbreviations in place of the full spelling even when there is room for the full spelling. For external or conceptual schema objects, full spelling, where room permits, may help in communications. The following example illustrates the two different naming conventions. Figure 8.1 shows the longer names that would be used for the conceptual and external schemas. Figure 8.2 shows the names that would be used in the database.

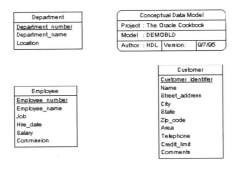

Figure 8.1 Longer names used for conceptual and external schemas.

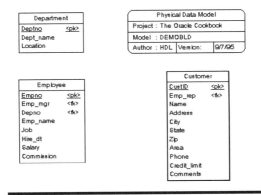

Figure 8.2 Shorter names used in the database.

Consider the following abbreviation examples:

amount	amt
average	avg
date	dt
identifier	id
number	num
standard	std
total	tot
volume	vol
year	yr

Keep the list short and manageable. Do not give people the excuse not to use it because it is lengthy and burdensome.

Some CASE tools (unlike the S-Designor product used here) may not support different names for entities and tables, or attributes and columns. If this is the case, you should probably go with the shorter names because they will be used much more often over the life of a system.

Where there is not a standard abbreviation, a simple rule for creating abbreviations is to first eliminate vowels (except leading vowels) and double consonants. If there are still too many letters in the word try to eliminate the remaining letters while still preserving the meaning of the word.

The following are some suggestions for naming different objects both within and outside of the Oracle environment.

Entities

Entity names should be singular, and they should clearly define the objects they represent. These names should be completely spelled out to eliminate any ambiguity.

Relationships

Relationships should be used to state business rules, however, there is usually not enough room to say much on an ER diagram. The relationship name that appears on the ERD is only a part of a complete business rule. It is these business rules that help check the quality and integrity of the model. (Defining the relationships at the very beginning of a project is a good way to find the entities that will need to be included in the system. Defining the relationships first can help identify the entities.)

By combining the entity names, the relationship names, and the cardinality you can produce a full sentence that states the business rules for the two entities. The relationships in the ERD below actually states the rules that, Each DEPARTMENT may **contain** zero, one, or many EMPLOYEEs, and when read the other way, Each EMPLOYEE must **work in** one and only one DEPARTMENT. (Figure 8.7.)

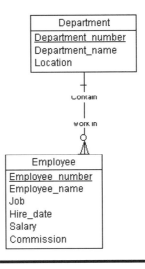

Figure 8.3 The relationship between two entities.

The Oracle CASE tools can produce these rules automatically. With most other CASE tools the rules must be produced by hand. Regardless of the method used to produce the rules, it is an extremely worthwhile endeavor to list them because it is the best chance you will have for the user to understand and decipher the little lines, crows' feet, circles, arrows, or other dohickeys and what-do-you-call'ems on the ER diagrams. Additionally, you can recite the rules to the users and ask them if the rules are true. For example:

```
Is it true that each employee must work in one and only one
department?
Is it true that each department may contain  zero, one, or many
employees?
```

A simple yes or no, or even an, I don't know, in response to these questions is a quality check of the highest kind because it is in a language the uses can understand. Most end users just don't get all of the lines on the ERDs, but they can comprehend a simple question, even if they don't know the correct answer.

Incidentally, these relationship rules are the main reason that entity names should be singular. With singular names the rules are grammatically correct, but they aren't with plural entity names.

Domains and Attributes

Make sure the names mean what they say. For example do not call an attribute a number when the attribute can contain letters or symbols. If a customer is identified as E324 then the attribute should not be called CUST_NUM but CUST_ID.

Most CASE tools now support domains. Using domains for attributes that occur multiple times is a wonderful way to ensure data consistency, and control ambiguity. Domains can also save quite a bit of typing by not having to retype the properties of an attribute.

Avoid the temptation to define domains simply as datatypes. In the relational model, domains define objects of interest to the organization and these objects show up as attributes in tables. An important characteristic of domains is that they describe the join potential between two objects. Simply because two fields share the same datatype and length, does not mean that they share the same meaning.

By creating domains as meaningful objects, rather than just a datatype and length, you can create a framework for a requirements traceability matrix that allows you to find all of the occurrences of a specific column/field, even if the column has different names in different tables.

Tables

Tables are the structures created in an Oracle database to hold data. They should have short meaningful names. Where full spellings are used for table names, and in most other instances, the names should be plural. The Oracle CASE tool creates plural names for all of the tables generated from entities. The Oracle sample databases, however, used singular names.

Columns

Certain schema objects in an Oracle database use qualifiers to uniquely identify the object. For example, several different users could each create a table called EMPLOYEE. These EMPLOYEE tables could, in fact, be exactly the same structure for each user. The question is: How does Oracle, or the various users for that matter, keep track of the different tables? Oracle can keep track because each table is qualified with the name of the user that created and thus owns it.

The following example shows a table that was created by user SCOTT/TIGER, then a table by the same name created by user HARRY/HARRY. The table name is SAME_TABLE. (Figure 8.4.)

Figure 8.4 Table names and owners

In order for someone other than the table owner to access either of the SAME_TABLEs, the table name must be qualified with the name of the table owner. The example below shows the user SYSTEM/MANAGER trying to select from the table SAME_TABLE without using the owner qualifier. Oracle says that the table does not even exist. To perform the query the table names must be qualified with the name of the table owner. (Figure 8.5.)

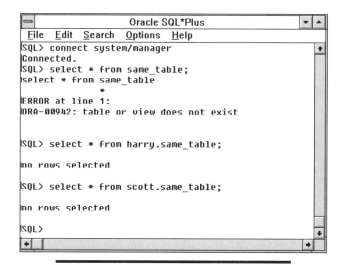

Figure 8.5 SELECTs using the table owner

We have seen how the use of synonyms can simplify some of the naming/ownership/qualification issues.

Just as table names are qualified by the table owner, the column for each table is qualified by the table name, and if necessary (as in Figure 8.6) by the table owner as well.

```
┌─────────────────────────────────────────────────────────┐
│ ▬               Oracle SQL*Plus                    ▼ ▲ │
│ File   Edit   Search   Options   Help                   │
│ SQL> select owner, table_name, column_name          ↑  │
│   2   from all_tab_columns                              │
│   3   where table_name = 'SAME_TABLE'                   │
│   4   order by owner, table_name;                       │
│                                                         │
│ OWNER        TABLE_NAME        COLUMN_NAME              │
│ ----------   ---------------   ---------------          │
│ HARRY        SAME_TABLE        COLUMN1                  │
│ HARRY        SAME_TABLE        COLUMN2                  │
│ SCOTT        SAME_TABLE        COLUMN1                  │
│ SCOTT        SAME_TABLE        COLUMN2                  │
│                                                         │
│ SQL>                                                 ↓  │
│ ◆                                                    →  │
└─────────────────────────────────────────────────────────┘
```

Figure 8.6 Naming qualifications

In the example above the column HARRY.SAME_TABLE.COLUMN1 is different from SCOTT.SAME_TABLE.COLUMN1 even though the table names and column names are the same.

Where this discussion of qualification leads is, simply, you need not preface non primary key columns with the table name. For example, if you have a table called CUSTOMER, do not name the non-key columns CUST_NAME, CUST_ADDRESS, or CUST_PHONE. The use of qualifiers makes the actual names of these fields:

```
CUSTOMER.CUST_NAME
CUSTOMER.CUST_ADDRESS
CUSTOMER.CUST_PHONE
```

If you would use the columns name, address, or phone multiple times in a single table, then you would have to qualify the columns because a given column name can only appear once in a single table. This is common where there are columns like a SHIP_TO_ADDRESS and a BILL_TO_ADDRESS in a single table.

Since these are guidelines and not rules, the above guideline may require exceptions where columns in tables are often used with similarly named columns in other tables. If the columns NAME and DESCRIPTION were used in several tables that were often joined together, then it may be helpful to qualify the columns with a table name or other descriptor so the resulting queries are more meaningful.

The primary key should include the table name because it will be referenced, or used in one or more foreign keys. For primary keys, use names such as CUST_ID, or INVOICE_NUM. When the CUST_ID is used as a foreign key in the sales order table it is easily recognized as a foreign key.

When a column is a foreign key, it should have the same name as the column, or primary key column to which it points. Where several foreign keys in a table point to a single primary key you may want to add a qualifier to the foreign key column names. This extra qualifier can make it more meaningful or distinguish it from other columns that are also foreign keys pointing to the same primary key. In the example below the SALES_ORDER table has two foreign keys that point to the CUSTOMER table. In this case the names must be qualified because CUSTOMER_ID could not be used twice in the SALES_ORDER table. (Figure 8.7.)

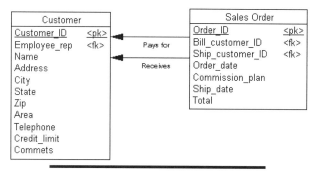

Figure 8.7   Qualified foreign key names

Indexes

Indexes are perhaps the most difficult object to name, especially when they contain multiple columns. If an index contains just a single column consider concatenating, or linking the table name with the column name. This concatenation may work for several columns as long as the table and column names are short. Figure 8.8 shows an index called CUSTOMER_ZIP created for the ZIP_CODE column in the CUSTOMER table.

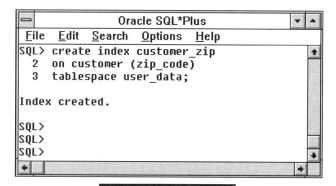

Figure 8.8   Index naming

Remember that you do not have to explicitly create indexes for primary keys. Indexes for primary keys are created when the primary key constraint is created or enabled. See below for more information on naming constraints.

Constraints

Some of this material on constraints was covered in Chapter 2. The focus there was how the constraints worked; the focus here is how to name them.

There are five kinds of integrity constraints in Oracle created with the CONSTRAINT clause. They are:

- CHECK
- FOREIGN KEY
- NOT NULL
- PRIMARY KEY
- UNIQUE

These constraints can be created for individual columns in a table or for multiple columns in the table. They can be defined as part of the CREATE TABLE statement or they can be created separately with an ALTER TABLE statement. Of the five constraints listed, it is most important to explicitly name PRIMARY KEY and UNIQUE constraints. These two constraints are important because they automatically create indexes. You may find it helpful to name all constraints because Oracle returns the constraint name when a rule is violated (except for NOT NULL constraints), as illustrated below.

PRIMARY KEY, and UNIQUE constraints automatically create indexes for the tables and columns specified. (Yes, it's worth repeating.) Be sure to explicitly name these constraints. If you do not specify a constraint name Oracle will name the constraint using the form SYS_Cnnnnn. Figures 8.9 and 8.10 illustrate this point by showing a table created without naming the primary key constraint, and then a table that has the primary key constraint named as **test2_pk**. In Figure 8.9, note the error returned which shows the Oracle generated name for the primary key constraint. Is that a user-friendly name or what? SYS.C00366 is also the name of the index that was created for the primary key.

In Figure 8.10, note the error which clearly shows the object that is causing the problems, the primary key constraint. As above, TEST2_PK is the now more meaningful name of the index on the primary key.

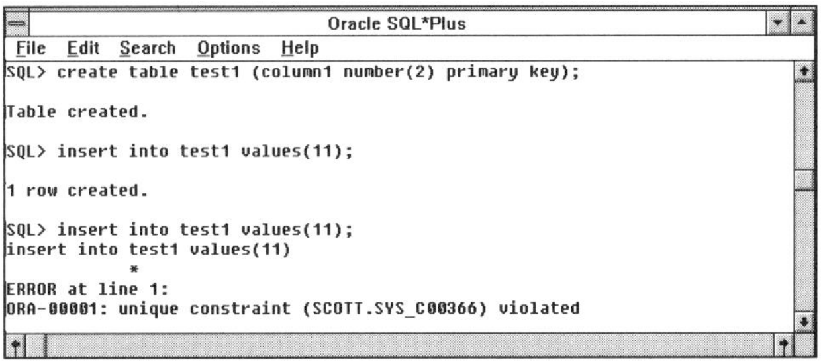

Figure 8.9 Oracle generated constraint name

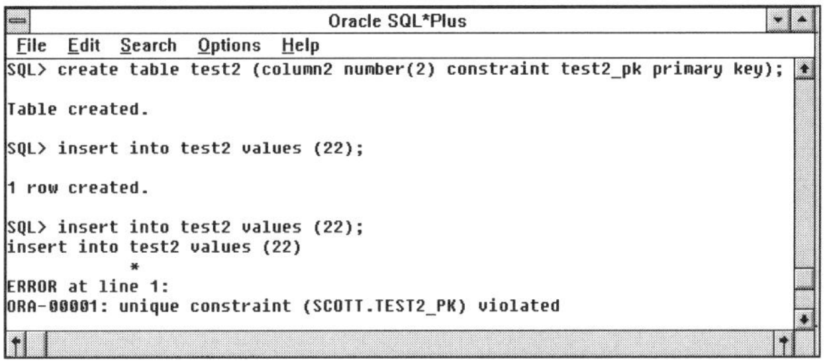

Figure 8.10 Named primary key constraint

A simple standard for naming PRIMARY KEY constraints is to prefix or append the letters PK to the table name as in the example above or like PK_TEST2.

When adding PRIMARY KEY and UNIQUE constraints which create indexes, you should also include the USING INDEX clause to control the placement of the indexes. Storage clauses can also be added with the USING INDEX clause.

The first TABLESPACE reference (TABLESPACE user_index) is for the index that is created for the PRIMARY KEY constraint. The second TABLESPACE reference (TABLESPACE user_data) is for the table that was created.

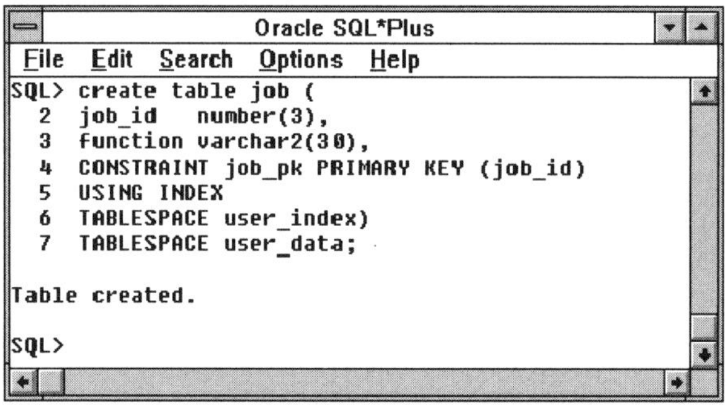

```
                  Oracle SQL*Plus
 File  Edit  Search  Options  Help
SQL> create table job (
   2  job_id   number(3),
   3  function varchar2(30),
   4  CONSTRAINT job_pk PRIMARY KEY (job_id)
   5  USING INDEX
   6  TABLESPACE user_index)
   7  TABLESPACE user_data;

Table created.

SQL>
```

Figure 8.11 Constraint with USING INDEX

When declaring one or more columns of a table as the PRIMARY KEY, it is not necessary to also declare these columns as NOT NULL since the PRIMARY KEY constraint does not permit nulls. This is different from UNIQUE indexes which will permit null values as part of a UNIQUE key.

FOREIGN KEY constraints can be derived by combining the source table and target table names as in EMP_DEPT_FK. This is another good reason to use short table names.

Directories

Follow the Oracle Flexible Architecture standards for naming directory structures.

Files

As with directories, follow the OFA standards for file naming conventions. (Some operating systems, or Oracle for certain platforms may have other naming restrictions. Check your *Installation Guide* for details.) These include:

.log for log files

.dbf for data files used for tablespaces

.ctl for the control files

If your files have a numeric designator in similar file names, use 01 instead of just 1 to facilitate sorting of the file names. This means that datafiles with names like data_01, data_02 would show up in proper order if the list reaches data_11, and data_12.

Lookup Codes

Even though lookup codes are not an Oracle component per se, they can affect your system's design. The use of lookup tables is driven by normalization and space requirements. For example, it is not a good idea to store the full product category description in every row (that is, do not have lookup codes at all, but just store the whole description wherever it is needed) because of the insert, update, and delete anomalies we covered earlier. All too often I have seen this desire to save space manifested in a table like Figure 8.12:

Product Category	
Product code	N2
Description	VA20

Figure 8.12 Lookup table model

The data in such a table often looks like the Figure 8.13:

PRODUCT CATEGORY

Product code	Description
01	Bath
02	Oral Hygiene
03	Shaving
04	Hair Care
05	Fragrances

Figure 8 .13 Lookup table values

The Product codes may be assigned to thousands of products. Notice all of the space we save by using only two characters for the category code. The questions that need asking are,

- Yes, we save space, but how much disk I/O must we waste doing table lookups to see which code we need to use? Is it 02 for Fragrances or 05? - Don't look!

- How much I/O must be performed for reporting purposes just to translate the codes?

- How long does it take new users to master the codes? (Did you ever see all of the code tables that data entry operators have taped to their walls?)

- Just how expensive is hard disk space when compared to operator learning curves, program lookups to produce a list of values, and machine time thrashing to do that last extra join so the category description prints out on the screen or report?

As an alternative to numeric codes how about using short abbreviations, mnemonics, or acronyms. Yes, they may take up more space but they should be easier for people to learn and use. The above example could look something like Figure 8.14:

PRODUCT CATEGORY

Product code	Description
BATH	Bath
ORAL	Oral Hygiene
SHAV	Shaving
HAIR	Hair Care
FRAG	Fragrances

Figure 8.14 Lookup value using codes

By using meaningful abbreviations, the SQL calls to get the full product category description might actually be a rare exception rather than the rule. And with even twice the amount of space used for abbreviations versus the numeric codes, the two extra characters would add a whole two megabytes to a million row table. The choice between using meaningful codes instead of meaningless numbers just seems so obvious to me.

Related to this idea of giving meaningful abbreviations to codes, brings to mind a story I once heard (perhaps apocryphal but it illustrates a point) about a system that was being converted from punch cards to interactive screens. On the old system, the users had become very proficient using the punch card machines to enter requisitions. The cards were 80 columns wide and each space had a meaning, which was usually conveyed by some numeric code or another. When items were requested, the data entry operators filled out the cards, and, of course, the experienced operators knew all of the codes by heart.

When these experienced users were asked what they wanted the new interactive requisitions system to look like, they didn't request a screen to look like the paper requisition form they were used to keying in. Instead, they simply requested 80 column lines across the screen that they could now edit instead of having to throw away the card and re-key it. Oh, and multiple lines on the screen would be ok, just don't clutter it up too much. They didn't need or want column names, or lookup tables, or any other kinds of tools to help them with their job. They just wanted a new way to punch cards, but one more forgiving with mistakes. (I think what they really wanted was job security. Mastering 80 columns of codes is no easy task. But, what if each field or column had a heading, and each field could display all of the current values for any new user, and what if the values actually made sense - heck, any body could do the job.) They did not realize that the paradigm had changed. The point is no longer to learn how to master data entry, the point is to help people perform their jobs.

Figure 8.15 The great leap forward?

Change Control

Change control is broadly

- A means by which users or developers can submit requests for changes to a system, requests for enhancements to a system, or report bugs or problems in a system.
- It establishes a predefined method to distinguish which type of request a "request" is, change, enhancement, or bug.
- It provides a method to prioritize the request.
- It provides a means to analyze the request and determine the impact of the request.
- It provides a means to assign and track resources, as well as progress and completion.
- It provides a reasonable and well defined context for users/customers and developers/vendors to discuss and negotiate the changes.

This section could be called "How to be a fire fighter with out wanting to be." Could you really be a master chief if you had to carry and use a fire extinguisher all the time? Change control is your friend because it provides all parties with a common set of policies and procedures by which to request, manage, and implement changes to a system.

You Control It or It Controls You

One of the things that makes systems difficult and expensive to develop and maintain is a lack of impact analysis. A user or programmer requests a change to a table or field, perhaps to change a column length or datatype. The question to answer is, where are all of the places that column is used? A system or method is needed to show all of the programs, modules, procedures, or whatever, that use that column. This is important where different external schemas access a common portion of the conceptual schema. It becomes critical in large systems where a bug fix or change request can have a ripple effect on other portions of the system.

I worked on a large Air Force system where every two database changes required an additional change because one of the initial requests inadvertently impacted other programs in the systems. The problems did not show up until a change was implemented to satisfy one program, which then caused other programs to crash.

To solve the problem, some programmers wrote parsing routines that showed what fields were used in every COBOL and IDEAL program. Then, when a request was submitted for a field change, I could look to see **all** of the programs that were affected. We were then able to show that a given request often had much greater impacts because the field was used in multiple programs. This multiple use, in turn, usually impacted the cost and priority of the request. Often, when confronted with the full impact and magnitude of a particular change request, the users would say "You have to change how many programs? And that's how many man-hours? Well, maybe that request is not so important after all. May be we can make the change later after some of these other problems have been addressed."

The point of impact analysis is not to get a particular user to back down on requesting (or demanding) changes. The point is to try to create an informed intelligent dialog in which all of the impacts are known and all of the costs are known. The point is to show what might happen to budgets and schedules, possible alternatives, and then make an informed decision.

To help with future impact analysis consider using or building CRUD matrices as part of the systems development process. A CRUD matrix shows where data is **C**reated, **R**ead, **U**pdated, and **D**eleted. The Oracle CASE tools use CRUD matrices to develop and generate applications, but the matrices can also be used for impact analysis, which, in large systems, can justify their cost. Where systems are developed with data flow diagrams, the data flows can also be used for impact analysis, because they show what modules use what data.

Besides the CRUD matrix, consider building a change control database that both users and developers can access to add and check on change requests.

Limit Access to Database Environments

Schedule regular maintenance times for any and all system changes. Instill a discipline that doesn't allow for unscheduled changes except for emergencies. This discipline should extend from the development environments to the production environments.

For systems that require extremely high availability, production changes become more difficult because it is not easy to shut the system down for backups and changes. Many large mission critical systems only allow for several hours of down time per quarter. If you can only plan for perhaps one full days worth of down time per year, you need to learn to make the best of that time.

Full Backups Before and After Any Production Database Changes

No matter how hard you try and how well you plan, something will go wrong whenever you try and make changes or corrections - it will. So the **only** prudent approach to any database changes is to perform a full database backup before the changes, and another full database backup after the changes are installed and checked/tested.

After the changes are installed the database should be started and the changes checked or tested. After they are verified shutdown the database and perform a full backup. Skip this step and you may be very, very sorry. You have a fifty-fifty chance of adding a new bug for every bug you fix. It may be easy to spot the fact that the new bug fix does indeed fix the bug it's supposed to, however, the new bug may not show up for hours or even days. Don't worry, this **will** happen to you, so the only thing you can try to do is have something to fall back on, like your backups.

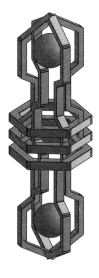

CHAPTER 9

Special Issues

There are a number of issues in managing relational databases that have nothing to do with a particular brand of database. They are larger issues that will, however, affect the success of database development efforts.

Project Management

While closely linked to change control, project management (PM) is an art unto itself. My view about PM can be summarized with the following points:

- Any project of any size must have formal project management controls.
- Project management must be formally assigned to someone.
- The project manager must know something about project management.
- The project plan must be shared with development staff and users.
- There must be formal delivery, review, and sign-off on deliverables.

While this may seem to belabor the obvious I have seen more projects fail for not following these points that for any other fault or shortcomings. Without formal PM, you are driving blind.

Project management is as much about risk management as about schedules and budgets. As part of PM, risks must be identified and managed.

The following is a partial list of some common risk factors:

- If it ain't fixed, don't automate it—Too many people look to computers to solve their business problems. If your business processes are not well defined, your development costs will be horrendous as you try to figure it out. Get the processes down before you begin development.

- Size and scope—the larger the effort, the greater the risk.

- Size and scope of individual tasks—the larger the formal tasks, the greater the risk. If a large project had a single task called "Design Database," that task would have substantially higher risk associated with it than if it were broken down into all the tasks listed in Chapter 5.

- Number of days assigned to an individual task—the larger the number of days for any one task, the greater the risk. With more days between tasks it's too easy for developers to get into the "I'm 80% complete" rut before you find out you're behind schedule.

- Data conversion—any time you deal with loading data from legacy systems there is a substantial amount of risk. The older and larger the system, the greater the risks.

- Personnel—all users and developers are not created equal. System development requires a lot of teamwork, communications, and knowledge. Occasionally, you will even run into users who deliberately try to stonewall efforts as part of some personal agenda. Also look out for people who are "too busy" to help you get your job done.

- Tools—If you are trying new CASE tools, new programming languages (is this your first crack at PL/SQL?), a new network, a new operating system, or a new database for the first time (and woe to those trying all five for the first time), be sure to plan for training and mistakes.

- Management and leadership—be sure there is someone around who can make **and** enforce decisions.

It's helpful to think of risk as the profit margin on a project. (Whether a system is being developed for profit or not, there are always budget factors.) Each task should have a margin of risk assigned to it. If a task is completed successfully, you are within budget and you make (or don't lose) money.

In financial markets, higher risk translate into higher interest rates. In PM, higher risks should translate into higher risk margins. The risk margins translate into days, personnel, and costs. Something like data conversion should carry a higher risk margin (more days and/or more people) than the development of training materials for the new system. Ultimately the risk factor or margin is nothing more than a "fudge factor."

Risks are identified and managed through scheduling (of time and resources) and the management of the project. What follows are my personal observations of what works and what doesn't in the context of PM.

Projects are driven by completed tasks, not set dates. And while every project and task will have begin and end dates, the only truly meaningful date(s) is for the task(s) at hand. When a task or phase is nearing completion, that is the only realistic time to assess and set the real target date for the next task. If one task gets behind schedule, especially if it is on the critical path, the entire project end date will slip and get pushed farther into the future.

Driving the entire development effort to a single end date is a bad idea. Many projects never see the light of day, and almost all are behind schedule and over budget. When someone says that the new system has to be delivered by a certain date (no ifs, ands, or buts), they generally have no concept of the complexities at hand. The point is to set general goals and be prepared to adjust your schedule based on outcomes. Work should be broken up into short sections that have clear deliverables that allow judgments as to their success or failure and closure.

This single end date fixation can also have some devastating side effects. Take, for example, an organization that has planned to reassign or lay off staff when the new system goes in production. What happens to all those personnel plans when the system is three months, or six months, or even a year late? Where is plan B?

Look out for things that are "outside the systems development effort" that can impact the effort. This could be anything from the purchase of PCs for the new end users to cabling for the LAN or the arrival of new machine tools that will work in conjunction with the new shop floor control system. Know who has responsibility for these "outside" factors, what their schedules are, and where they stand. I once worked on a project where the "project manager" drove our team to a completion date even though the building had not even been wired for the new LAN, let alone all the PCs purchased and working on everyone's desk. What was the point?

Be sure every project has decision points built into the schedule. At these points, one of four choices should be made:

1. Proceed as planned because things are going as planned.

2. Make adjustments to the plan to reflect the reality of the project's progress.

3. Cancel the project; know when to cut your losses. If this is the choice be sure to conduct a project review. Without a review the money and effort spent will be truly wasted.

4. Put on rose colored glasses and do nothing, confident in the belief that the team will catch up during the next phase.

Unfortunately, too many people choose the fourth option and too few choose the third. The norm should be to go with number two.

Given these comments, you may begin to think that I think there is no hope of success on any project. Quite the contrary. The following are some suggestions to help in PM.

An aggressive schedule may actually be better than a longer one in that it demands more focus and attention. But the aggression should be limited to the current phase and the planning to be aggressive on the next phase will depened on the outcomes of the current phase. Pushing anything beyond the next phase is like pushing on a rope. How aggressive you can be will depend on the number of days assigned to the task. The more well-defined or detailed the tasks, typically, the shorter they are. Short time frames and well-defined tasks lend themselves well to focus, accurate assessment (is it finished?), and completion on time and within budget.

Be sure to educate your users about the complexities of the development process and PM, and prepare them for schedule slips. People will not be as angry with a schedule slip if they know it's happening and why.

Develop deliverables that users can touch and feel, especially with screens and reports. This will make them comfortable with the progress and provide feedback to the project. You are better off knowing early on that a given screen does not fit their needs.

Prepare detailed to-do lists. As you get further into the project, more and more tasks will become visible, and their scope and resource requirements will become clearer. These changes/clarifications will affect schedules. The project leader should maintain these lists in great detail and make sure tasks are assigned and accomplished. This isn't to say that requirements won't or shouldn't change—they do change, and you need to be prepared for change.

A few words about project managers. Project managers are a special breed. They are not like operations people who work to streamline a particular task or job. Operations people go to the same work every day and try to increase productivity. They do it day in and day out. Their goal is a smooth operation that gets better every day by increasing productivity and reducing costs. But every project is different, and the personnel are always different. A project manager must constantly deal with change and adversity. As a result, a good line person may not make a good project manager.

The best project managers I have seen are those that focus on solutions rather than problems and that can motivate their people to do the same. They hate surprises, and I mean **really** hate suprises. Problems—sure everyonehas problems. A problem can usually be solved but a surprise is a betrayal of trust. Project managers want and need to know the bad news and the good news.

It may not even be important for project managers to be extremely well versed in a particular technology. The PMs' specialty is the plan, not the technology. They plan the work and work the plan. They gain the respect of the workers by relying on them to provide technical expertise. Project managers seldom tell a developer when they are to complete their tasks, they ask how long it will take. Project managers let the technicians do their thing; they just want to know how it's going.

Prototyping

The speed with which you can create an Oracle database and the tools that are available for creating screens and reports all point to rapid prototyping as one of the best means of developing applications.

Rapid prototyping is a method of development that attempts to show users a system as it is developed, rather than requiring users to describe their needs before development begins. It's like asking a restaurant patron to decide on dessert by choosing one from the dessert tray or reading a description on the menu. It is a lot easier for users to say that a working screen is what they want rather than just trying to verbalize what they want.

Trying to solve operational or political problems with technology is difficult. It might work in a very autocratic environment or one where off-the-shelf software can provide most of the required functionality, and the business adapts. Before trying to automate, be sure any new business processes are understood and ready for implementation.

Prototyping can be done in three broad phases. Each phase takes longer than the preceding because more details are known and more functionality is added as the system develops. The last phase is the longest, but customers often expect it to take the least amount of time. It is important to establish reasonable expectations up front.

> **Phase 1.** The analysis and get acquainted phase, or how to get everybody singing from the same page. This phase should not take more than six months. It is important for the team to show something as early as possible.
>
> **Phase 2.** Seeing is believing. This phase is longer than the first and may take four to six months because it includes more details.
>
> **Phase 3.** Deliver the product. This last phase may take up to six months because it includes all of the tasks necessary to move the system into production.

Actual time frames will, of course, depend on the scope of the project and the resources available. For extremely large projects, consider the following. Break the project up into several projects. If you have the resources, these projects could happen concurrently, although coordination among them may increase the length of each. If time is more available than resources, you have several options. Break the project up into several separate development efforts and perform them one after the other. Or develop the scope so that you deliver the system in several versions, each of which contains more functionality than the previous one.

Of the two alternatives (and, there are, no doubt, many variations) that extend the time line, the first (separate efforts), may seem more obvious than the second (creating multiple versions). I think the second is safer because requirements are always changing. I also feel it is important to get something into the users' hands that they can actually work with. Once they start working with it, they usually end up saying, "Gee, wouldn't it be nice if...." They always want more, and it is easier to accommodate them if you can say, "OK, we'll add that in version two."

One of the interesting things I find about prototyping is that the more time there is allocated to each phase, the more difficult it can become to complete the work. The problem is trying to accomplish too much. You will have more success if you deliver two versions of a single system rather than trying to put everything into a single version. If time frames seem too short, you may be trying to do too much.

Phase 1

In Phase 1 you need to perform the following tasks:

- Set up teams of users and developers to work on various portions of the system and develop the project plan for this phase. Creating more teams is one way to shorten time frames, but this can add complexity and communications that must be managed.

- User participation is probably more critical than the developer participation for success of the project. There are consulting firms that can get you many qualified developers, but, they won't know the business— or the politics. Without qualified users (those who really know the business) there will be no gas in the oven when you're ready to cook the meal.

- The users on the project should be the best the company has to offer, not the new kids on the block or those waiting to retire. Hopefully they will have a vision of what could be, not just what is needed to get by.

OK! You've assembled the teams , now what? Now several things have to happen, and most of them happen and more of them happen in parallel, so I'll just list them (the following holds whether there is one team or four; the only thing that's added is complexity, and you will need more coordination):

- Conduct interviews and read all the material you can get. Even though you have users on each team, you still need to get out in the field for more information. Try to develop a consensus about what the new system should do, how it should do it, and who will do it. Remember, the main emphasis of this phase is to gather requirements and do analysis. Even though the project started with some sort of requirements or goals, these activities should tell you what the **real** requirements are.

- Develop the core set of screens. Don't worry about all the screens, just the ones that are most visible/important and the ones you think might create some controversy. (More on the controversy issue later.) This set of screens (and the reports in the next bullet) should clearly define the scope of the system in terms of functionality, not the number of screens. You need not spend any effort getting the screens to work except to show how they might open and close or flow. These are basically pictures to find out what the system will do. They will most likely change based on the first demo, so don't waste effort if you don't have to. Building a working demo is the goal for Phase 2.

- End users develop reports. Have the users sit down with paper and pencil and draw what they want. They can use a word processor or spreadsheet if they want to get fancy. If they have current reports they would like to see duplicated or modified, have them supply those as well.

- Develop a logical data model. Each team should have someone who has the big picture, that is representative of the conceptual schema. Use the screens, reports, and interviews to develop the data model. Bring all the teams together on several occasions to review and refine the model. (You are using the CASE tools, right?)

- Slap together a database. This may or may not be necessary, depending on your application development tools. If you can develop the screens without a database, then you may want to skip this step. You want to avoid a situation where developers get locked into data structures that were never intended to represent the final database. No one should be under the illusion that the database developed here will be the final one! The most important part of database development in this phase is developing the data model, not the database.

- Develop the menu structures. Be able to show, at your first demo, how the work flows and how screens and menus support that flow.

- Begin to look into data conversion, populating lookup tables, and getting sample data. The amount of effort expended here will depend on the size of the conversion effort. If you are working on a new system that will have little or no legacy data, you're lucky. If your effort is part of a major conversion effort, dedicate a lot of resources *now*! Some of the things you want to watch out for on the lookup data are some of the problems described earlier, such as time constraints and ownership issues.

- Prepare for the first demonstration. This may seem simple, but it is one of the most critical steps, and it requires extensive planning and rehearsal.

This first demo can be tricky; it needs to be orchestrated very carefully. There are several major issues here. The first is that, even though you have had users on your teams, this will be the first time that "everyone" gets to see the prototype. The demo should be **extremely** stable. Your audience will quickly lose confidence if the system keeps crashing. You should use some sort of projection system **and** pass out screen prints to everyone. The demo should be scripted and follow the work flow.

Several things must be made very clear to the audience. The first is that they must understand that this first demo represents the team's interpretation of what it thought the end users said they wanted. This statement must quickly be followed by the statement that this first demo is the starting point for serious development. The point of this demo is not to say how things are, but for everyone to say how things should be.

Often the users are dismayed and they say, "That's not what I wanted!" There is a tendency for both users and developers to get defensive. Be sure the users understand that this is just a starting point and that the whole reason for getting together is to discuss the issues and reach an understanding. Let them know that their recommendations and concerns will be addressed; that's why they are there.

You will need to discuss the screens and reports. Find out what's right and what's wrong, and record the changes. (Please note that I have not mentioned formal change control yet; that will come later.) You will need to discuss new/additional screens, and reports, and the menu structure. Discuss user roles and security. Most importantly, assign people to tasks to address issues and answer questions raised during the session.

The result of the first demo should be a clear definition for **all** the screens and reports, which includes changes to existing screens and a list of all new, or remaining, screens and reports. What you are doing is formally defining the scope of the system.

After the demo, conduct a review with the team to discuss the demo. At this point you need to develop the plan for the second phase. Assign tasks to the various teams and find out how long each task will take.

Phase 2

Phase 2 adds substance to the form. You should have all the ingredients, now, let's make something.

The goal of this phase is to create a working demo that uses a real database with real data. The first phase produced a picture of the new system that described what the system should do. The second phase completes the picture and shows how things will work. Most importantly, this second phase should encompass the **entire** scope of the system. This phase will define the system's baseline and any change after this phase must go through formal change control procedures.

Tasks for Phase 2 include:

- Develop the "real" database. Map all the screens and reports to the data structures. Normalize the structures. Define all your constraints and implement as many as you can. Collect data and begin to work on the data loads. Size the database. Include some of the security covered in Phase 1. Hopefully, by the end of this phase you will have all your lookup tables populated.

- Adjust the existing screens per the users' feedback.

- Develop all remaining screens. Most of the screens should function to the point where the users will be able to tell how they will work, including some examples of error trapping. The error trapping should include Oracle generated errors as well as program and operator errors. Include examples of inserts, updates, and deletes. Building all the functionality is for Phase 3. Remember that there is another demo coming, and things will change again, so try to limit your exposure/effort.

- Develop all the reports. The database should include data, so the reports should have some data on them.

- Make all the menus functional, including some of the roles and security issues covered in Phase 1.

- **Thoroughly** debug the system and prepare for the demo.

While this may look like fewer tasks than Phase 1, it is actually a lot more work. At this demo, someone should be able to sit down and actually do some work. Users should be able to add data using valid lookup codes, perform updates, and produce reports using their data. The system won't be fully functioning, but the users will get a good idea of how it all works and fits together.

The demo for the second phase will go a little bit differently from the first. Everyone will expect more—after all, you said you were going to fix everything, right? This should be the entire system and much of it should work.

As you perform the demo (or better still have one of the team members who is a user perform it), people should get a good idea of how work will flow in the new system. New systems usually require changes to the way different groups work and work together. If the system is intended to focus on and accomplish one-time data entry, a few in the audience may finally realize how much the work flow changes and how much work a few individuals may have to perform.

This is where the reality sinks in and turf battles start. "Why do I have to do all of this data entry? I never had to do it before. I don't have time for all this stuff." Of course they don't know, or perhaps even care, that four other people used to type some of the exact same information into four other systems. Remember the reference to management and leadership as a risk factor in project management. Well, this is the reason. I have seen projects fall apart at this point. Not officially, of course, but for all practical purposes the project was at least stalled, if not doomed. The sad thing is that the projects continued and finally came to a halt when the users said they wouldn't (they always say they can't) use the new system. To be forewarned, is to be forearmed.

If you reach a consensus on the workflow, the other major task for the demo is to finalize/negotiate the scope. Everyone should be made very aware that any "changes" to the system from here on (other than the ones covered as part of the demo) will be subject to formal change control. You must draw the line in the sand.

Sometimes these two issues, workflow and scope, are too difficult to solve and you may decide to repeat Phase 2. The distinction between Phases 2 and 3 is the formal scope agreement. Proceeding to Phase 3 without everyone understanding their new work responsibilities and without a formal agreement will actually increase the risk of failure. Don't throw good money after bad: hash it out and get an agreement, repeat the phase, or stop the project. If you really want the project to continue, you should be willing to repeat Phase 2. By repeating the second phase you limit your risk to trying to fix what you have, not completing something that is not right.

Don't forget to discuss the screens, menus, reports, and security at the second demo.

Phase 3

You have collected and prepared the ingredients, now it's time to start cooking. The third phase has most of the work. Everything has to work, data must be loaded, systems tested and tuned, training material prepared, documentation completed, and the rollout planned (installation of the production system, training, conversions, etc...) This is a lot of work.

One of the challenges of prototyping is setting users' expectations. This phase will have the highest expectations. The users saw a "working" demo at the end of Phase 2, and they get the real thing in just a few more weeks. They can't, and you need to let them know that.

If things have gone smoothly so far, this phase should go well, despite the amount of work.

CASE Tools

CASE tools are computer–aided software engineering tools, although some folks say *systems* instead of *software*. But, a fool with *a tool is still a fool*. CASE is first and foremost a management tool to help you control the design and development processes. CASE requires a lot of discipline, and if you can't (or won't) manage the environment, the tools, the methods, and the people, then you will usually be better off forgetting them. A stroke of the brush does not guarantee art from the bristles.

CASE tools deserve the same praise I lavished on database tuning/monitoring tools. Tools like S-Designor, which I used for this book, are dirt cheap when compared to the costs of performing the same tasks by hand. The days and weeks I used to spend writing and editing DDL by hand, now are only minutes with a good DDL generator.

The cost of designing, building, maintaining, and documenting a system should be much less than the cost of the same tasks without using CASE tools. Any one of these tasks may cost less without a CASE tool, but any two or more should cost less with CASE tools than performing the same two or more tasks without CASE tools. However, going back to the bold print at the beginning of this section, if CASE tool users are not trained or do not follow prescribed procedures, use of a CASE tool can cost substantially more.

Would you buy a cookbook that did not explain its recipes? Would you buy a cookbook that displayed photographs but didn't list recipes? Would you buy a cookbook that only listed ingredients but no measures or cooking instructions? I think not! I am constantly amazed at the number of organizations that don't have any documentation about their databases other than what is out on the disks or in the data dictionary. Even sadder are the organizations that have very expensive CASE tools, and all they use them for is to draw pretty pictures.

CASE tools are a must for any database development project.

Off-the-Shelf Software

Off-the-shelf (OTS) software packages are application packages built by third-party vendors to perform specific tasks or functions. Rather than build systems from scratch, many organizations buy packages and either adapt to them or modify them to suit their particular purposes.

Many of the larger packages are designed, like Oracle, to be portable. The software can often run on a variety of hardware and operating system platforms, and they will often run on top of multiple databases. Numerous packages support Sybase, Informix, Ingress, and DB2, as well as Oracle. Where these packages support multiple databases you may discover several problems, including the following:

- The SQL code in the applications is generic so it can run with multiple databases. Generic code is usually unoptimized code.

- Similar to the generic code issue is the lack of support for some of Oracle's most powerful features such as stored procedures, sequences, outer joins (that little + sign that can do so much for you in Oracle), or even primary and foreign keys.

- Indexes may be inappropriate to support your mix of data and processing. There are sometimes too few indexes, but often too many indexes as the package is installed. There is a tendency to put indexes on all foreign keys, which is generally not a good thing when they reference small lookup tables.

- The DDL for the database and all the tables and indexes often take the Oracle defaults. The biggest problems are the result of defaults used to create the database. The default setting for PCTINCREASE is 50%. Most of the tables and indexes for the new system should have their own STORAGE parameters. Another problem is the MAXDATAFILES setting, which is often too low, especially if you will be running multiple instances. The default data block size (DB_BLOCK_SIZE) is also often too low.

- Vendors sometimes don't understand the concept of spreading I/O across multiple drives, and as a result often create a single tablespace to hold all of the tables for the entire application.

- Users are often not created with a DEFAULT or TEMPORARY tablespace assigned. If users are not assigned a temporary tablespace, sorts will take place in the SYSTEM tablespace. This is bad.

Most of these issues are discussed in detail in Chapter 5 "Getting Down to Business." Most of these problems can be addressed and fixed before you install the database, including sizing the tables and indexes. The sizing and object placement will be **much** easier if the data model is accessible with a good CASE tool.

The issue that may cause the most problems, generic SQL in the applications, may be hardest to solve. Some very clever applications will build or generate SQL on the fly based on end user input to prompts on the screen: pick one from column A, two from column B, etc. This may be great for the end users, but don't expect optimized SQL to pop out of the application.

If yours is one of those companies that is going to modify the OTS package to suit your needs, ask yourself several questions first. What are you going to do when the next version of the package is released? The first question begs the next, which is; What are you going to do when the new version comes out and the contractor or employee who made the changes is no longer around?

The answer to the second question is easier than the first. If anyone modifies the software and/or database, make sure you budget for and they thoroughly document the changes. For every change, they should document what the change was, where is, and how it works.

Regarding the first question about versions, you need to ask yourself just how different your business is that it cannot adapt to the new software. Sometimes you can lean on the vendor to include the changes you want in its software. In effect, you act as a beta site for a future release. If you require a lot of changes, there is a good chance you will be out of luck when the next version is released. If you anticipate a lot of modifications you should look very closely at developing the system yourself or having someone help you develop it. While probably more expensive up front, at least you will be able to grow with the system, and perhaps you will save money in the long run.

If you are buying software from a third party (or you are having a third party build or customize software for you) do not give them a check until they give you a well documented data model, a data dictionary, and all the DDL for the system. If a company cannot provide this documentation, you should consider their design and development practices suspect.

Very Large Databases

Very large databases (VLDBs) provide special opportunities to show your skills of design and implementation. Getting a system to fit on the target hardware, getting acceptable response time, and even trying to back up such systems have already been discussed in some detail. These topics are expanded on here as well. One of the toughest problems associated with VLDBs is just getting or having enough time to build and load such a beast.

The following will require special attention when building VLDBs.

Creating Databases, Tablespaces, and Other Objects

The issue with VLDBs in creating the actual database is that Oracle has to preallocate all the space specified in the size parameter of every file for every tablespace. The speed of this allocation is machine dependent, but the bigger the database, the longer it will take.

A database smaller than 100 MB shouldn't take much more than several minutes. When you get to several gigabytes, the time will probably become noticeable, perhaps an hour. If you are considering 50 to 100 GB or larger, it may take a day or two. It can take a long time to allocate a lot of space.

Creating the tables in a large database will present the same waits, although it does not take as long to build the initial extent(s) as it does to build the actual data files. With VLDBs, it may take several days just to just build the data structures.

Sometimes you may have objects that do not fit on a single disk, or the objects are accessed by many users simultaneously, albeit in a random (as opposed to a sequential) fashion, or you might just take my advice and put several files on a single drive rather than one large file. All these issues point to *table striping*, which allows you to spread a single object over several files and drives. When you are table striping, it is best to create a single tablespace to hold the object being striped.

The following set of DDL illustrates table striping. This example creates a single tablespace for a single table. The CREATE TABLESPACE builds eight separate files for the tablespaces. Note that the path specification should be added for every file. The total tablespace is 4 GB. The CREATE TABLE statement creates eight extents, one for each datafile. There is some system overhead so each extent should be slightly smaller that the target data file.

```
CREATE TABLESPACE customer
DATAFILE 'path/customer_01' SIZE 500M,
         'path/customer_02' SIZE 500M,
         'path/customer_03' SIZE 500M,
         'path/customer_04' SIZE 500M,
         'path/customer_05' SIZE 500M,
         'path/customer_06' SIZE 500M,
         'path/customer_07' SIZE 500M,
         'path/customer_08' SIZE 500M;

CREATE TABLE CUSTOMER
(CUST_ID       NUMBER(10),
 NAME          VARCHAR2(30),
 ADDRESS       VARCHAR2(40),
 PHONE         NUMBER(9))
TABLESPACE CUSTOMER
STORAGE(
INITIAL     495M
NEXT        495M
MINEXTENTS  8
MAXEXTENTS  8
PCTINCREASE 0);
```

The amount of space you allocate for the striped files should match the size of the object except where you are creating space for future growth. As Oracle loads the table it will start with the first file and fill it before it begins to fill the second file. To effectively utilize the above striping example, you should have almost four gigabytes of customer data, unless you were saving room for more data.

To create this tablespace, Oracle will go out and allocate all 4 GB specified as the total of all the datafiles. You get to wait while this happens. If you are talking about 100 or 200 GB, you get to wait a long time.

Data Loads

Loading a VLBD can often take significantly longer than building the data structures. The time can be significantly reduced, however, by using the **parallel data loader** option available with the Parallel Query option.

With the parallel data loader (Figure 9.1), multiple SQL*Loader processes are run in parallel, that is, simultaneously, to load the same table. As with other PQO processes, the parallel data loader works best when multiple data files are used to load a table that is striped across multiple-disks.

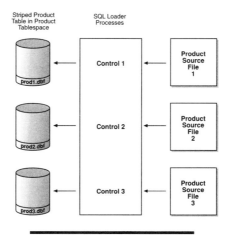

Figure 9.1 Parallel data loads.

Backup and Archiving

Where does anybody get the time to back up huge amounts of data? A better question might be, do you really need to back it up or back it all up. Decision support systems (DSSes), may not need backup at all if they are built with data from other systems and the source data is either readily available from other production systems or if the DSS is built with data loaded from tapes and the tapes are archived. If there are no updates, why back it up at all?

If your DSS does perform updates, such as creating summary or exception data, try to put the tables that are updated into one or just a few tablespaces. With this data separated into its own tablespace you can just back up that tablespace and leave the other data alone.

Hardware is Cheap Relative to Labor

Users and managers need to realize that relative to the cost of labor, adding hardware is often cheaper than spending time on a particular problem. Oracle can respond extremely well to proper and slight additions of hardware.

Denormalization

Some folks think that databases must be denormalized to get decent performance (I, personally, have never done it). Others prefer to wait and see if there is a performance problem before considering denormalization.

Normalization is not within the scope of this book, because it is a process that occurs during data modeling. It is a series of steps that are used to break complex data views into their component parts. Consider the data view shown in Figure 9.2 that represents a customer invoice.

Through the process of normalization, the invoice can be broken up into the pieces shown on the ERD in Figure 9.3.

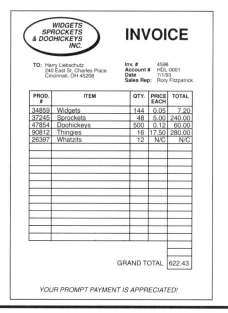

Figure 9.2 Data view of a customer invoice.

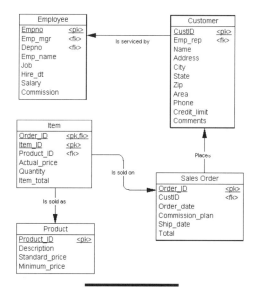

Figure 9.3 ERD.

The view is normalized (into the resulting table structures) to prevent what are called insert, update, and delete anomalies. The anomalies occur where data that is changed in one place can have undesirable affects in other places. For example, if we stored the customer's address on every single invoice, and only on the invoice, then what would happen when the customer submits a change of address? Do we have to change every invoice to reflect the new address? By putting the customer's name and address information into a separate, normalized, table, we would only need to change the address in one place, and thereby prevent an update anomaly. The goal of normalization is to create our table structures such that data is stored in only one place. It is not a good idea to have the same information stored in many places in the database.

The problem with normalization is that the original customer invoice view, once it is broken apart, or normalized, must, at some point, be put back together. The users want to see an invoice, not a bunch of tables. This reconstruction is accomplished by joins in one or more SQL statements. Unfortunately, joins can cause severe performance problems, especially if there are multiple joins across large tables.

Denormalization usually takes what was broken apart during analysis and design and puts it back together in the database to eliminate some of the joins. The denormalization then requires additional code, or programs, to keep the multiple copies of the data synchronized. Also, while denormalization may have solved one performance problem for one application, it often causes more severe performance problems for other programs that must access the same information. So choosing between normalization and denormalization requires a detailed understanding of the trade-offs throughout an entire environment, not just one application.

Oracle provides several ways to deal with the problems that result from normalization. If the tables are fully normalized, consider clusters and the parallel query option (PQO) to help with performance. Triggers or stored procedures can be used to help maintain denormalized tables.

As discussed earlier, clusters can be used to store data from several tables in the same physical data block. This is, in effect, a stored join that may eliminate the need to denormalize.

With proper hardware and database design, PQO can help improve performance for certain kinds of queries. The PQO can use multiple processors when performing queries that perform at least one full table scan. These queries work best when the data is located or striped across multiple disks.

Sometimes just adding more hardware, such as more memory or disk drives, can reduce, or eliminate the poor performance that results from multiple joins.

Denormalization should only be considered when an application environment is stable, that is, there is no other on-going development that will access or affect the tables considered for denormalization. Other methods, such as clusters, should have tried unsuccessfully to fix the problem.

And finally, if you must denormalize, provide very thorough documentation as to what was done, where it was done, and why it was done. Be sure to list all the tables, columns, and programs affected by the denormalization.

Obsession with Detail

I've heard it said that no amount of genius can overcome a preoccupation with detail. In the Oracle arena, getting close is often as good as or better than getting it perfect. This is especially true when getting it perfect takes a lot more time. For example, if you feel it is necessary to size every single table in a new database to the exact size because there might not be enough disk space, buy another disk drive. If your gross size estimates indicate there might be a problem, burning man-hours to get an exact figure is probably less productive that adding one or more disk drives. In addition to, the hardware versus labor costs, you will probably need more space later anyway (which means even more work later to size and move things about on the disks), and Oracle generally performs better with more disks.

The Mathematics of It All

Lets say you have a performance problem and a consultant is hired to fix it. It may might take only a day to fix a simple problem and a week for a complex one. Costs might run $100 to $200 per hour (plus travel) for the consultant and another $50 per hour for the in-house support. A best case scenario is eight hours of labor ranging between $1200 and $2000 a day for the high-dollar consultant and the internal support.

Maybe we can't buy too much hardware for $1200, but this was just an "easy" fix. The week-long tuning exercise could cost between $6000 and $10,000 plus travel and expenses. And this is just for one problem.

Hardware can hide a multitude of sins in an Oracle environment. It can be a shame to spend time and money only to prove you need more hardware.

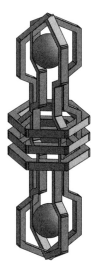

Sample Database

Oracle does not provide a logical data model or conceptual schema for the database provided with the installation medium, but if it did, it might look something like Figure A.1.

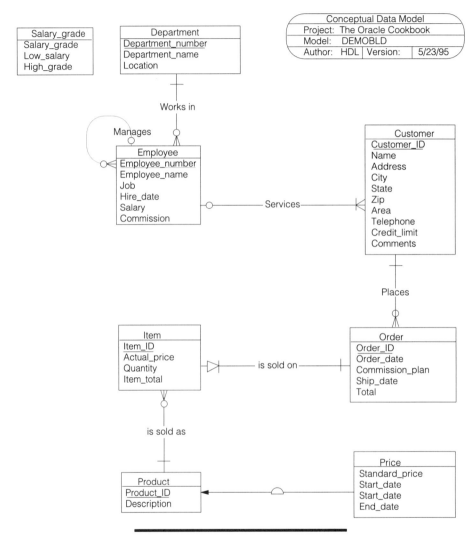

Figure A.1 Sample Logical Data model.

Figure A.2 represents a physical data model of the Oracle sample database.

The following three diagrams are different sets of the views in the Oracle data dictionary. These views are generated by the CATALOG.SQL script that should be run immediately after creating a database. They are something I wish

I had long ago, because it's difficult to have to constantly flip through the *Oracle7 Server Administrator's Guide* looking for the right view.

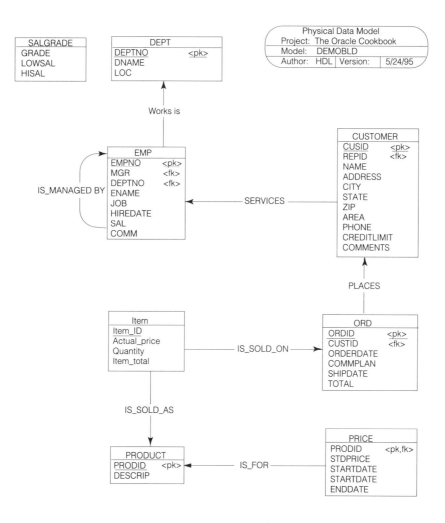

Figure A.2 Sample physical data model.

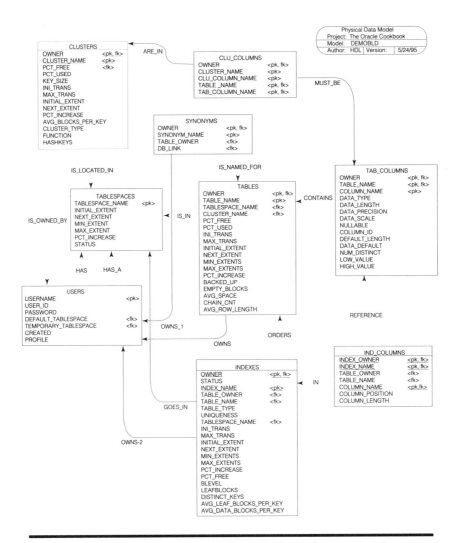

Figure A.3 Oracle data dictionary table, tablespace, cluster, and index views.

Figure A.3 shows most of the views that show information about tables, indexes, and clusters. The second diagram shows the views that provide information about users. The third diagram shows the views that provide information about the physical objects, data files, tablespaces, segments, and extents.

Figure A.4 illustrates the data dictionary views that provide information about users, roles, privileges, and grants. Relationships are not included in this diagram because it became unreadable when I tried to confine it to a single page.

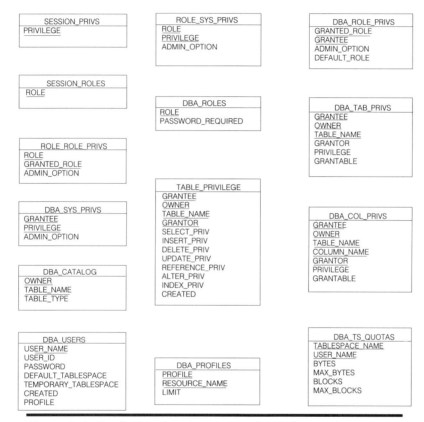

Figure A.4 Oracle data dictionary, user, role, privilege, and grant views.

Figure A.5 shows the data dictionary views that provide information about tablespaces, data files, segments, and extents.

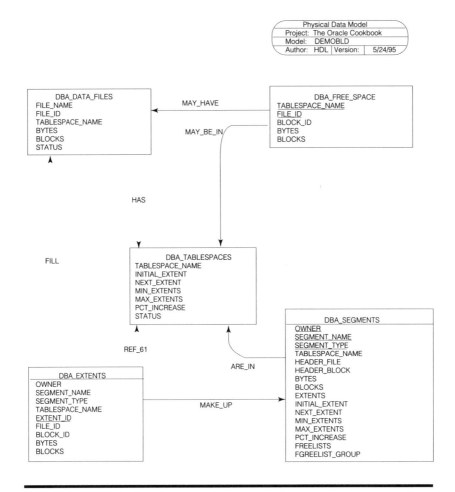

Figure A.5 Oracle data dictionary file, extent, tablespace, and segment views.

init.ora Parameters

The following is a list of many of the initialization parameters that will affect the performance of the database. Included with some of the parameters are considerations about how they may affect or be affected by different types of processing. In addition, some of the parameters include queries that can be run to check or tune the setting. Full details about tuning are in Chapter 7.

When you start an Oracle instance, Oracle reads the **init.ora** file specified in the `pfile=` parameter, or uses an **init.ora** file associated with your user account. This file contains parameters that determine how the database operates and how to allocate memory to various processes or memory caches.

Oracle provides sample **init.ora** files as part of the installation, and these may be fine to create your test database(s). For production systems you will want to create your own **init.ora** file that reflects your experience and tuning efforts with the system.

When creating a database you will need at least two versions of the **init.ora** file. You will need a special **init.ora** for creating the database and at least one that reflects the structures and size of your new database. You can edit a single file using comment characters (#) to comment out lines, or you can create different **init.ora** files and specify which to use with the `pfile=` parameter when starting the database.

Assuming a single instance on the machine, plan to allocate 30 to 50% of the machine's memory to the SGA. The more memory in the machine, the more space you can allocate to the SGA. I find small machines often have too much memory allocated to the SGA, and large machines do not allocate enough. The SGA should not be so large that it gets swapped from memory or causes other objects to get swapped.

There is a limit to the size of an **init.ora** file that Oracle can open; therefore do not create an **init.ora** file that lists every available parameter. In addition, realize that comments may make the file too large. Include only the parameters you wish to control and/or alter from the defaults. Comments can be included by placing the symbol # at the beginning of the line.

Some operating systems have trouble dynamically allocating or reallocating memory while the system is running. After collecting performance statistics you may want to change some of the SGA memory parameters to allocate more or less space to the SGA. After restarting the database so that the new parameters are used, you may find that the size of the SGA has not changed. If this is the case, you have one of those systems that may require you to re-boot the operating system before changes to the SGA take effect.

Some of the parameters are grouped by common functions or relationships. In the following sections, values after the = are intended as examples only. Every machine is different. Be sure to provide your own values for each parameter.

General Parameters

These are settings that affect CREATE DATABASE.

```
DB_NAME = SID
```

The database name is also specified in the **CREATE DATABASE** command.

```
INIT_SQL_FILES = (SQL.BSQ, CATALOG.SQL, ....)
```

This parameter lists files containing SQL statements that are executed during database creation. The script SQL_BSQ is the database bootstrap script that creates the data dictionary. Be sure file paths are accurate. This line serves no function once a database is created.

File Destinations or Locations

```
CONTROL_FILE = '/path1/controlSID1.ctl', '/path2/controlSID2.ctl',
'/path3/controlSID3.ctl'
```

This parameter designates the location of the system's control files.

Every Oracle database should have multiple control files, and these files should reside on different disks. By default, Oracle creates a single control file. You can manually create multiple control files or simply specify multiple control files in this CONTROL_FILE parameter. There should be at least two control files, and they should be located on separate disks. For safety's sake, create three control files and put them on different drives.

```
IFILE =
```

An *IFILE* is a file that can be referenced during startup. This file can contain additional parameters. This parameter is common in OPS environments, which require some of the **init.ora** parameters match across all instances.

The following dump-destination parameters tell Oracle where to write a variety of messages that it produces while it is processing. Sending these to a common directory will make it easier to monitor these files and delete them periodically.

```
BACKGROUND_DUMP_DEST = /user/oracle/rdbms/dump/log
```

The destination for trace files and messages produced by the background processes LGWR, DBWR, and others.

This is also the location of the ALERT.LOG, which is where Oracle logs a variety of events, such as every database startup and shutdown. The last value is a file name not a directory name.

```
USE_DUMP_DEST = /user/oracle/rdbms/dump/log
```

The directory where SQL_TRACE and user processes will write trace or dump files. The last value is a file name, not a directory name.

```
MAX_DUMP_FILE_SIZE =
```

The maximum size, in operating system blocks, of any trace file that the system may write. If trace outputs are truncated, increase this value.

```
LOG_ARCHIVE_DEST = /path/
```

This parameter should be set if LOG_ARCHIVE_START = TRUE. This is the location or destination of the archived redo log files. Since the database will stop if it cannot archive the redo log files when operating in ARCHIVELOG mode, the destination directory should have enough space. That way, there is no danger of the directory filling and additional writes failing.

Buffer Settings

These parameters determine the size of various components of the SGA.

```
DB_BLOCK_SIZE = 4K
```

This parameter determines the Oracle block size. It is used only once, when a database is created. After the database is created, changing this parameter will have no effect.

The Oracle block size should be the same size as, or a multiple of, the operating system block size.

```
DB_BLOCK_BUFFERS =
```

This is the total number of database buffers allocated for this instance. The number of buffers should be monitored and adjusted upward or downward after several iterations of tuning and testing. Be careful not to make this value (or any other parameter value) too high, lest the entire SGA, or other processes, get swapped out to disk by the operating system. If the block size were 8K 10,000 equates to 82 MB of total memory; 5,000 is approximately 41 MB.

The following query will show the database buffer "hit ratio." This number indicates the percentage of time that Oracle was able to find requested data in memory.

```
SELECT a.value + b.value "Logical Reads",
    c.value "Physical Reads",
    round (100*(a.value + b.value - c.value)/
          (a.value + b.value)) "Hit Ratio"
    FROM  v$sysstat a,
          v$sysstat b,
          v$sysstat c

    WHERE a.name = 'db block gets'
    AND    b.name = 'consistent gets'
    AND    c.name = 'physical reads';
```

```
LOG_BUFFER = 32K
```

This parameter, specified in bytes, determines the amount of memory allocated to the redo buffers. The default is set at 4 times the machine block size. For systems that will be primarily read-only, the redo buffers need not be large, and the default may be OK. For systems that perform a lot of updates, consider making this value at least 64K, regardless of the block size. Larger redo buffers should reduce log file I/O.

Monitor the value of redo log space waittime in the V$SYSSTAT table. If there are any waits, consider increasing the value for this parameter.

```
SHARED_POOL_SIZE =
```

This is the amount of memory allocated for shared SQL and PL/SQL blocks, as well as the data dictionary cache.

This parameter should be tuned before the DB_BLOCK_BUFFER, because the recursive calls associated with these buffers affect performance more than other buffers. To get the maximum use of these shared buffers, equivalued SQL statements must be spelled *exactly* the same in order for Oracle to recognize them as equivalent.

Systems that are short on memory tend to have too much space given to the shared pool. Systems that have abundant memory often have too little space allocated to the shared pool.

```
SORT_AREA_SIZE =
```

This is the amount of memory available for a sort in memory. This amount of memory is allocated to each sort and could, therefore, consume a lot of resources if there are many simultaneous sorts. If the sort cannot be performed in memory, Oracle uses space in the temporary tablespace on disk to store interim results. Increasing this value should reduce I/O to the temporary segment related to sorts.

```
SELECT NAME, VALUE
  FROM V$SYSSTAT
  WHERE NAME IN
('sorts(memory)','sorts(disk)');
```

The preceding query will show the sorts performed in memory and those performed from disk. If there were a lot of sorts on the disk, you should increase the sort area size.

For a DSS, this value may actually be larger than the database buffers.

```
SORT_AREA_RETAINED_SIZE =
```

This is the amount of memory that should be retained after a large sort. A value less than SORT_AREA_SIZE will free up memory after sorts but may degrade performance if there are a lot of large sorts because memory would constantly have to be reallocated.

Performance Gathering and Monitoring Parameters

The following parameters can be used to gather data to help tune the database.

```
DB_BLOCK_LRU_EXTENDED_STATISTICS =
```

This parameter is used to evaluate the performance gains that might be realized if the number of DB_BLOCK_BUFFER was increased. A value greater than 0 specifies the additional number of buffers for which statistics are gathered. The view X$KCBRBH is used to monitor results.

There is overhead associated with gathering these stats.

DB_BLOCK_LRU_STATISTICS =

When set to TRUE, this parameter enables statistics to help determine potential performance gains by reducing the number of block buffers. The view X$KCBCBH is used to monitor results.

There is overhead associated with gathering these stats.

SQL_TRACE = TRUE

Set to TRUE to enable the SQL trace facility for all sessions. This allows server processes to write to the trace file for things other than internal errors.

There is overhead associated with running this facility.

This parameter can be changed during database operations with the command
ALTER SESSION SET SQL_TRACE = TRUE or FALSE.

    TIMED_STATISTICS = FALSE

TRUE enables certain SQLDBA MONITOR screens.

There is overhead associated with running this facility.

WARNING

File I/O Parameters

The following parameters affect files and I/O.

    DB_FILE_MULTIBLOCK_READ_COUNT =

This parameter sets the number of blocks that can be read during each I/O. The range is 0 to 32, with a default of 8. This value should be set higher if often performing table scans because it can reduce the number of I/O operations that is necessary to read an entire table.

    DB_FILES =

This parameter specifies the maximum number of data files that Oracle can open. If this parameter is set too low, your database may run out of room because you cannot add any data files to your tablespaces.

    DB_BLOCK_MAX_SCAN_CNT =

This parameter determines how far up the LRU list a user process will search for a free buffer before it signals DBWR to write the dirty buffers to disk.

```
DB_WRITERS =
```

This parameter determines the number of DBWR processes that can be active. It should be set equal the number of disk drives on the target machine. This parameter is not valid with all operating systems, e.g., NetWare

The following LOG parameters affect archiving and the redo log sizes and speed.

```
LOG_ARCHIVE_START = TRUE
```

A value of TRUE will place the database in ARCHIVELOG mode once the archiver is enabled with the command ALTER DATABASE ARCHIVELOG.

```
LOG_CHECKPOINT_INTERVAL =
```

This value is the number of operating system blocks that will trigger a checkpoint; 1000 = 4 MB if the O/S block size is 4K. This parameter is one of the things that establishes the trade-off between performance and recovery. Increasing this number will reduce the number of checkpoints and should help run-time performance. Reducing this number will increase I/O activity but provide better recovery time. If set to a number greater than the redo log size, the checkpoints will only occur at log switches. If the interval is less than the size of the redo log file, then at least one extra checkpoint will occur between log switches.

```
LOG_CHECKPOINT_ITIMEOUT =
```

This parameter is similar to LOG_CHECKPOINT_INTERVAL, except that it specifies the time between checkpoints, regardless of the number of blocks written. This parameter is specified in seconds.

```
LOG_SIMULTANEOUS_COPIES =
```

This is maximum number of redo buffer copy latches that can be used to write log entries. Value can be double the number of CPUs.

```
CHECKPOINT_PROCESS = TRUE
```

TRUE enables a background process called CKPT, which relieves the log writer process, LGWR, of overhead associated with checkpoints. With CKPT enabled, LGWR does not have to update all the data file headers during a checkpoint.

Operating Parameters

```
OPEN_CURSORS =
```

The valid range is 5 to 255; it represents the maximum number of cursors that a single user process can have open at one time. Cursors should be controlled in the applications by closing them after their use. Setting a limit with this parameter will force developers to properly open and close their cursors.

```
OPTIMIZER_MODE = RULE/COST
```

This parameter explicitly determines whether Oracle will run with the cost-based optimizer or the rule-based optimizer.

This parameter can be changed for a session with the command **ALTER SESSION SET OPTIMIZER_MODE**.

```
OS_AUTHENT_PREFIX = "OPS$"
```

This parameter is set to allow users to log onto Oracle without having to enter a user name or password. It is intended to eliminate the need for a user to log onto the operating system with a user name and password and then having to type another user name and password to log onto Oracle. Normally a user would have to type the following string to log onto SQL*Plus:

```
SQLPLUS USERNAME/PASSWORD
```

With the OS_AUTHENT_PREFIX set, a user can log on by simply typing:

```
SQLPLUS /
```

If the OS_AUTHENT_PREFIX were set to OPS$, then the characters OPS$, must be prefixed to any user name added to the database that you want to use this feature. A user should be created by entering:

```
CREATE USER OPS$newuser IDENTIFIED BY password;
```

A null string is also allowed and is specified with open and closed quotation marks—"". Using "" would eliminate the need to prefix any Oracle user account that you wanted to allow to log onto the system. The downside to "" is that every one can log onto Oracle without specifying a user name and password, as long as they have a valid Oracle user name. If this parameter were set to OS_AUTHENT_PREFIX="", then any user created could log onto Oracle just by typing **a** / rather than their user name and password.

```
PROCESSES = 100
```

This is the maximum number of concurrent logons (or operating system processes) plus 5 for the background processes. At startup, Oracle will grab as many semaphores as indicated by this value.

```
ROLLBACK_SEGMENTS = (rb1, rb2, rb3, rb4, rb5, rb6,...)
```

This is the list of private rollbacks that an instance will acquire at startup. Remove rollback segments that are in the system tablespace from this list. Do not drop these system rollbacks, just remove them from the **init.ora** file.

When creating a database, this parameter should not be used since there are no rollbacks segments until you create them. A SYSTEM rollback segment is created by Oracle during the CREATE DATABASE statement, but that rollback segment should not be listed here.

Create one rollback segment for every four concurrent users.

```
SEQUENCE_CACHE_ENTRIES =
```

This is the number of sequences that can be cached in the SGA for immediate access. This value should be set for the total number of sequences used plus 5 for the background processes.

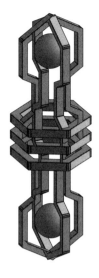

Glossary and Acronyms

archive log file Copies of the on-line redo log files. These copies are created when the database is in ARCHIVELOG mode.

archiver One of Oracle's background processes referred to as ARCH. ARCH copies the last filled on-line redo log files to the archive log destination after a log switch.

attribute A descriptor. Attributes of a table describe the properties of that table. In the relational model, an attribute is the occurrence of a domain in a table.

buffer An area in memory used to store data. Sometimes referred to as a *cache*.

cache hit Data that is requested and found in memory.

cache miss Data that is requested but not found in memory.

check constraint A constraint used to validate, or check, the values or format of data in a particular column.

checkpoint	A point where data in memory is synchronized with the data on the disk. A checkpoint forces the DBWR to write all buffers that were modified since the last checkpoint to the database.
checkpoint process	An optional background process, *CKPT*, that updates file headers during a checkpoint. This job is normally performed by the LGWR process. When the **init.ora** parameter CHECKPOINT_PROCESS=TRUE, the task of updating the file headers is shifted from the LGWR process to the CKPT process.
CKPT	*See* **checkpoint process**.
client/server	A computer system, application, or operating system architecture in which are split between those submitting requests, clients, and those that service or process requests, servers. Client processes send messages to the server processing work and/or data. The server process performs the work and returns a response to the client. Clients and servers can exist on one or more machines. Client processes are usually on separate machines from the server processes, and the communication is conducted across a network.
cluster	**hardware cluster**. Two or more computers or other hardware peripherals that are coupled or clustered together to increase processing power. **Oracle Cluster**. A storage structure that allows for greater control in placing and accessing data in a physical file.
commit	A statement that makes changes to the database permanent.
conceptual schema	One of the components of the three-schema architecture. The conceptual schema represents an organizational view of the data as opposed to a view of an individual user or application. The conceptual schema is totally independent of any hardware considerations or implementations.

constraint	Defines limits to the type of data or manipulations that may be performed on specific rows or columns in a database.
control file	A file in an Oracle database that defines the database file structure and other information about the database. Every Oracle database must have at least one control file, but there should be multiple control files.
CRUD	Acronym for create, read, update, and delete.
CRUD matrix	Shows where and how data is used by one or more applications. It has processes or modules along one axis and data elements along the other axis. One or more CRUD letters can be placed at the intersection of a process and a data element to show how data is used by that process.
CURRVAL	A pseudo column that shows the current value for a given Oracle sequence.
data administration	A job title or job function. This function is responsible for designing and maintaining logical data models, naming standards, and other policies and procedures that relate to an organization's data.
data block	The smallest unit of physical storage in a file. In Oracle, they range from 512 bytes to 32 KB in size.
data control language	The portion of SQL used to control access to objects and/or commands.
data dictionary	A set of tables and views in an Oracle database that describes the logical and physical components of the database.
data model	A formally defined structure or description of a system.
data type	Each column or attribute has a data type. It defines the type of data that may be stored in the column. The four

general types of data that can be stored in an Oracle database are: character, numeric, date, and binary.

database   A collection of files used to store data and information about the data.

database administration   A person or group of people responsible for the design and maintenance of one or more databases.

database link   A defined connection between databases in a distributed environment. It is created with the SQL command **CREATE DATABASE LINK**, and it defines the database name, path, logon account, and protocol used to connect to the remote database.

data warehouse   A database generally used to store historical data. Data is usually accumulated, or drawn, from on-line/transaction systems and used for analysis. These systems are also referred to as *decision support systems* (DSSes).

database writer   One of Oracle's background processes responsible for writing data to the database. Referred to as *DBWR*.

DBA   *See* **database administrator or database administration**.

DBWR   *See* **database writer**.

DCL   *See* **data control language**.

DDL   *See* **data definition language**.

decision support system   *See* **data warehouse**.

denormalization   A process or method of combining normalized data structures to improve performance. Performance should be increased by reducing the number of joins between tables created through the normalization process.

dictionary cache   One of the buffer caches in the SGA used to hold data that is read or modified by user processes.

dirty buffer　　　　A database buffer that has been changed.

dispatcher　　　　One of the Oracle processes used with the multithreaded server. The dispatcher routes user requests between the user process and the request and response queues.

distributed lock manager　　　　A host process used to control resource locks among parallel database instances.

distributed iprocessing　　　　Processes that occur between two or more database nstances.

DLM　　　　*See* **distributed lock manager**.

DML　　　　*See* **data manipulation language**.

Domain　　　　An item of interest to an organization. The occurrence of a domain is an *attribute*.

DSS　　　　*See* **decision support system**.

Dynamic performance views　　　　The V$ views that are created and populated by Oracle when an instance starts. The views are updated with various performance data while the database is running. These views are used for tuning and collecting other database statistics.

entity　　　　An item of interest to an organization. Entities are composed of rows/tuples and columns/attributes.

entity integrity　　　　A rule in the relational model that states that every row/tuple in a table/relation must be unique.

entity relationship diagram　　　　A diagram, or diagramming technique, used to depict a logical data model. It consists of entities, attributes, relationships, primary keys, and foreign keys.

ERD　　　　*See* **entity relationship diagram**.

export　　　　An Oracle utility that is used to make a copy of a database or a portion of a database.

export file   The file that contains the data that was extracted during an Export.

extent   A set of contiguous blocks used to define the size of a table, index, cluster, temporary segment, or rollback segment.

external schema   A definition, or user's view, of an organization or system.

foreign key   An attribute or group of attributes that share the same domain as a primary key. Foreign keys provide the links, or relationships, among tables.

fragmentation   Fragmentation occurs when multiple extents (sets of contiguous blocks) for a single object are located on different parts of a disk drive or on different drives. The extents are not located next to each other and thus there are gaps between them. These gaps can cause poor performance because the disk heads may have to move to different portions of the disk to locate data for the object.

freelist   Each table, cluster, and index has one or more freelist. A freelist is a list of all data blocks that have space available to insert new data.

freelist group   Freelists associated with specific manually allocated extents. Freelist groups are used with the Oracle Parallel Server to reduce freelist contention on objects accessed by multiple instances in a parallel environment.

function   A set of PL/SQL code that returns a value based on a predefined input. The function is like a black box that performs calculations, conversions, or some other task on the input value and produces an output.

hash cluster   A cluster that uses a hashing function to place and locate data. It converts a value into a physical address.

homonym   Words with the same sound or spelling that have different meanings.

index	A physical structure used to order and speed access to data in a table.
instance	A set of Oracle processes and memory structures used to access and manipulate data in a database.
internal Schema	A definition of the physical components and access methods for a database.
LCKn	*See* **lock process**.
LGWR	*See* **Log Writer**.
library cache	A portion of the shared pool in the SGA that contains information about SQL statements submitted to the database.
lock process	A process used by the Oracle Parallel Server to coordinate the parallel cache manager and the distributed lock manager.
log group	A set of mirrored on-line redo log files. Each log group contains two or more redo log files. Data is written to both files simultaneously.
Log Writer	One of Oracle's background processes, referred to as *LGWR*, that writes data from the redo buffers to the on-line redo log files.
logical data model	A representation of a system that is independent of any physical implementation details. LDMs are created before a physical data model is created. They are usually depicted as entity relationship diagrams and are produced using CASE tools.
LRU	*See* **least recently used**.
meta data	Data about data. The information in the Oracle data dictionary is meta data in that it contains data about the database. This information includes data about the table, indexes, users, files, tablespaces, and so on.

MPP	*See* **massively parallel processor**.
NEXTVAL	A paused column used to retrieve the next value from a particular sequence.
normalization	A formal set of steps used to break down complex objects into their component parts. Normalization is used to split complex user views, such as invoices or purchase orders, into separate tables to eliminate redundant data.
Null	The absence of information.
OLTP	*See* **on-line transaction processing**.
On-line redo log	A set of two or more redo log files that contain changes made to the database.
On-line Transaction Processing	A type of processing consisting of mostly short, well defined, and repetitive transactions, usually used in the day-to-day operations of a business.
OPS	See Oracle Parallel Server
Package	An Oracle program unit consisting of a package and package body. The package references the procedures or functions defined in the package body.
parallel data loads	An option in Oracle that allows multiple SQL*Loader processes to run on multiple CPUs.
parallel index creation	An option in Oracle that allow indexes to be created using multiple CPUs.
parallel processing	A type of processing where tasks are subdivided and processed simultaneously or in parallel.
parallel query processing	An option in Oracle that allows certain types of queries to be divided and executed on multiple CPUs multaneously, thus increasing the speed of the queries.
PGA	*See* **program global area**.

PL/SQL	Oracle's procedural language extension to SQL. PL/SQL is based on the programming language ADA.
PMON	*See* **process monitor**.
PQO	*See* **parallel query option**.
primary key	An attribute or group of attributes that uniquely identify a row in a table.
privileges	Rights granted to users or roles.
procedure	An Oracle program unit that contains PL/SQL.
process monitor	One of Oracle's background processes that monitors user processes connected to the database. If a user process fails, PMON cleans up transactions and the areas of memory used by that process.
program interface	One of the processes that controls communications between an application program and an instance/database.
RAID	*See* **redundant array of independent disks**.
RDBMS	*See* **relational database management system**.
recoverer	One of Oracle's background processes in a distributed environment to recover or resolve in doubt transactions that have resulted from a failed instance or network connection.
recursive call	A call made by Oracle to its data dictionary to find out information about the database. Recursive calls occur when Oracle cannot find the necessary information in the dictionary cache.
redo buffer	The redo buffers are an area in the SGA that contain changes made to the database. Data in the redo buffers is written to the redo logs.

redo log   A physical structure in an Oracle database that contains changes made to the database. The redo logs are used to reconstruct the database in the event of a failure.

referential integrity   One of the rules of the relational model that states a foreign key's value must reference a primary key value.

relation   The eponymous components of the relational model that describe certain types of tables used in the model. Relations are made of tuple/rows and attributes/columns. While relations are two-dimensional tables, they cannot have duplicate rows or columns, and there is no order to the rows or columns.

relational model   A model for large shared databases developed by Dr. E.F. (Ted) Codd. The model applies mathematical principals to data structures to define how data should be structured, integrity constraints, and how data should be manipulated.

relationship   A link between two tables in an entity relationship diagram, usually implemented with foreign keys.

rollback   A SQL command used to undo, or roll back, a transaction

rollback segment   A data structure that contains "before images" of data.

ROWID   An Oracle paused column that shows the physical address of a row in a table.

ROWNUM   An Oracle paused column that produces the number of each row returned in a query.

schema   A stored definition or description.

schema object   The logical structures in an Oracle database, including tables, indexes, clusters, sequences, views, program units, synonyms, and database links.

segment   Any one of four types of objects in an Oracle database differentiated by the type of data contained. There are

	segments for user data, indexes, rollback data, and temporary data. Segments comprise one or more extents.
sequence	An object in Oracle used to generate numbers.
SGA	*See* **system global area**.
shared pool	One of the components of the SGA. The shared pool contains the library cache, which contains the execution plans for SQL statements, and the dictionary cache, which contains data dictionary information.
SQL	*See* **Structured Query Language**.
SMON	*See* **system monitor**.
SMP	*See* **symmetrical multiprocessor**.
Structured Query Language	A language use to create and access databases.
stored procedure	A set of PL/SQL stored in the database.
synonym	An alias assigned to a table or other object.
system change number	A number assigned by Oracle to a transaction.
system monitor	One of Oracle's background processes, referred to as *SMON*.
symmetrical multiprocessor	A computer that uses multiple CPUs. Each CPU can perform any task.
table	A two-dimensional table made of rows and columns.
tablespace	An Oracle structure that holds tables, clusters, indexes, and rollback segments. A tablespace is made of one or more data files.
trigger	A program stored in the database that is activated, or fired, when a certain action is requested for the table associated with the trigger.

tuple   One of the components of the relational model that represent rows in a relation/table. A unique row in a table. Tuples differ from rows in that there can be no duplicate tuples in a relation.

UNIX   An operating system developed by AT&T that runs on many different computer systems ranging from PCs to mainframes.

very large databases   Databases that range from several gigabytes to more than a terabyte (1,000,000,000,000 bytes) in size.

view   A virtual table. Views are created with the SQL command **CREATE VIEW**. Views can be used to limit access to specific rows and columns in one or more tables.

VLDB   *See* **very large databases**.

Index

A

Abbreviations, 248

Abort, 109

Acronyms, 248

ADA, 34

AdHawk, 214

After image, 42

Alert log files, 234

Alert logs, 59, 295

ALTER TABLE Adding constraints, 173

ANALYZE, 103, 152, 156, 202, 236

ARCH, 52

Archive log files, 59

ARCHIVE_LOG_DEST, 52, 124, 235

ARCHIVELOG, 55, 59, 122, 124, 170, 199

Archiver process, 52

Archiving, 119, 124

Starting archiving, 199

Attributes, 21, 251

AUDIT_TRAIL, 189

Auditing, 189

AUTOEXTEND, 172

B

Background processes, 48

BACKGROUND_DUMP_DEST, 295

Backups, 119

Backup script, 126

Very large databases, 282

Before image, 42

Begin backup, 126

Blind key, 24

Block size, 77, 150, 151, 156

C

CACHE, 165

Cache hit, 222

Cache miss, 42, 222

Cascade delete, 92

CASE, 15, 135, 145, 153, 249, 251, 266, 276, 278

317

CASE tools, 276

CATALOG.SQL, 96, 197, 288

CATAUDIT.SQL, 189

CATDBSYN.SQL, 197

CATEXP.SQL, 197

CATLDR.SQL, 197

CATNOAUD.SQL, 189

CATPROC.SQL, 197

Change control, 262, 275

Changing passwords, 188

Character datatype, 81

Check constraints, 92, 93

Checkpoint, 49, 50, 52, 301

Checkpoint Process, 52

CHECKPOINT_PROCESS, 52, 301

CKPT, 52. See Checkpoint process

Client/server, 45

Cluster ,key, 63

Clusters 63, 152

Codd, Dr. E.F., 20

Cold backups, 123

Column constraints, 89

Columns, 252

COMMENTON COLUMN, 99

COMMENT ON TABLE, 99

COMMENTS, 99, 100

Commit, 42, 80

COMPRESS, 131, 132

COMPUTE STATISTICS, 105

Computer Aided Software Engineering, 276

Conceptual Schema, 13, 175, 222

Concurrent users, 137

CONNECT INTERNAL, 106

Connect privileges, 183

CONNECT role, 182

Constraints, 89, 153

    Check, 92

    Foreign Key, 90

    Naming constraints, 256

    Not null, 94

    Primary Key, 89

    Unique, 95

Contention, 228

Control files, 58

CONTROL_FILES, 58, 174, 191, 295

Cost-based optimizer, 101

CREATE DATABASE, 171, 177, 190, 294

Create database script, 192

CREATE DATABASE LINK, 73

CREATE SCHEMA, 173

CREATE SEQUENCE, 67

CREATE SESSION, 187

CREATE TABLE, 32, 157, 173

    Table striping, 280

CREATE USER, 184, 303

CREATE.SQL, 192

Creating a profile, 186

CRUD matrix, 263

CURRVAL, 87, 89

D

Data Administration, 16, 240

Data blocks, 76

Data Control Language, 33

Data Definition Language, 31

Data dictionary, 19, 40, 74, 96, 290

Data dictionary Model, 98

Data files, 55

Data loads, 203

    Very large databases, 281

Data Manipulation Language, 32

Data types, 81

    CHARACTER, 81

    DATE, 83

    LONG, 86

    LONGRAW, 86

    NUMBER, 82

    RAW, 86

    VARCHAR2, 81

Database, 35, 54

    Alert log files, 59

    Archive log files, 59

    Control files, 58

    Data files, 55

    Dump files, 59

    Files, 54

    init.ora files, 58

    Redo log files, 55

    Size limits, 78

    Trace files, 59

Database Administration, 18, 240, 244

Database buffers, 40

Tuning, 224

Database environments, 174

Database Exporter, 130

Database Importer, 132

Database links, 72

Database programming, 30, 70

Database writer, 42

DATE datatype, 83

DB_BLOCK_BUFFERS, 40, 296, 297

DB_BLOCK_LRU_EXTENDED_STATISTICS, 298

DB_BLOCK_LRU_STATISTICS, 299

DB_BLOCK_MAX_SCAN_CNT, 42, 49, 51, 300

DB_BLOCK_SIZE, 40, 77, 191, 278, 296

DB_BLOCK_WRITE_BATCH, 49, 51

DB_FILE_MULTIBLOCK_READ_COUNT, 300

DB_FILES, 171, 191, 300

DB_NAME, 191, 294

DB_WRITERS, 301

DBA, 18, 182, 244

DBA_DATA_FILES, 125

DBMSSTDX.SQL, 197

DBTune, 214

DBVision, 214

DBWR, 42, 48

dbwr free needed, 50

DCL, 33

DDL, 31. See Data Definition Language

DDL Generators, 276

    Scripts, 172

Dedicated server configuration, 44

Default column constraints, 95

DEFAULT TABLESPACE, 76, 160, 185

Defragementing tables, 131

DEMOBLD.SQL, 5

DEMOBLD7.SQL, 5

Denormalization, 200, 282, 284

Design objectives, 166

Development environment, 175

Dictionary cache, 40, 222

DIRECT PATH loads, 206

Directory structures, 114

Dirty buffer list, 49

Dirty buffers, 41

Disk maps, 139, 141, 168

    To support DSS, 170

    To support OLTP, 168

Disk mirroring, 139

Dispatcher process, 53

Distributed Processing, 109

DML, 32

Domains, 21, 251

DSS, 120, 136, 146, 161, 170, 225, 282

DUAL, 84

Dynamic allocation of extents, 162

Dynamic performance tables, 37, 97

E

EcoTOOLS, 214

End backup, 126

Entity, 249

Entity integrity, 26

Entity relationship diagrams, 24

Environment variables, 112

Environments, 137

ESTIMATE STATISTICS, 105

Exclusive mode, 108

Executable code, 35

EXP_FULL_DATABASE role, 182

EXPLAIN PLAN, 102, 153, 214, 215, 216, 217

    Results, 218

Export, 120, 129, 131, 134

Extents, 79

External Schema, 12, 175, 222

F

File naming, 258

FLOAT datatype, 82

FORCE startup, 109

Foreign Key, 25, 90, 143, 148, 254

    Recursive foreign key, 25

Fragmentation, 234

Freelists, 42, 158, 164, 230

Contention, 230

Freelist groups, 165

G

Grants, 179

    Columns, 179

    PUBLIC, 179

    Table, 179

    Using views to limit access to tables, 180

H

Hash clusters, 63, 64, 66

Hints, 104

I

IDEF1X, 24

IDLE_TIME, 186

IFILE, 295

Immediate shutdown, 108

Impact analysis, 263

Import, 129, 132, 134

Indexed clusters, 63, 66

Indexes, 29, 62, 152, 155, 255

   Sizing, 155

init.ora file, 37, 40, 58, 174, 191, 293

init.ora parameter listing, 293

INIT_SQL_FILES, 192, 196, 294

INITIAL extent, 160, 235

INITRANS, 159

Installation, 111

Instance, 35, 36

Instance failure, 120

INTEGER datatype, 82

Internal Schema, 17

K

Kernel, 36

L

Latches, 228

LDM, 20, 142, 149. See Logical data model

Least recently used list, 41

LGWR, 52, 55. See Log Writer

Library cache, 222

Limiting table access with views, 182

Lock process (LCKn), 53

Log sequence number, 55

Log switch, 56

Log writer, 43, 52

LOG_ARCHIVE_DEST, 59, 296

LOG_ARCHIVE_START, 125, 191, 301

LOG_BUFFER, 43, 226, 297

LOG_CHECKPOINT_INTERVAL, 50, 301

LOG_CHECKPOINT_TIMEOUT, 50, 301

LOG_SIMULTANEOUS_COPIES, 301

Logical data model, 9, 142

Logical data modeling, 19

Logical structures, 61

Logical volumes, 139

LONG datatype, 86, 150

LONG RAW datatype, 86

LONGRAW datatype, 150

Lookup codes, 259

LRU list, 41, 49, 50, 51

M

Maintenance, 213, 233

Manipulation, 29

Martin, James, 24

Massively Parallel Processing computers, 136

Master-detail relationship, 68

MAX_DUMP_FILE_SIZE, 296

MAXDATAFILES, 171

MAXEXTENTS, 79, 162

MAXSIZE, 172

MAXTRANS, 160

Media failure, 120

Members (log group), 57

MINEXTENTS, 162, 235

Mirrored redo log files, 57

Monitoring, 213, 233

Most recently used list, 41

Mount startup, 107

MPP, 136, 165

MRU list, 41

MTS, 45, 53. See Multi-threaded server

MTS_MAX_SERVERS, 47

MTS_SERVERS, 47

Multiple instances, 109

Multi-threaded server, 45

N

Naming standards, 245

NEXT extent, 162

NEXTVAL, 87, 89

  Inserts, 88

NOARCHIVELOG, 127

Nomount startup, 107

Normal, 108

Normalization, 282

NOT NULL constraints, 94

Null, 26

Nulls versus blanks, 27

NUMBER datatype, 82

O

Object oriented programming, 34

Obsession with detail, 285

OFA, 141, 246

Off-the-shelf software, 277

OLTP, 136, 146, 160, 168, 225

Online backups, 124

Online transaction processing system, See OLTP

Open database, 107

OPEN_CURSORS, 302

OPS, 108, 121, 138

  Pinging, 165

OPS$, 303

Optimal Flexible Architecture, 246

Optimizer, 101

Optimizer goal, 104

Optimizer mode, 104

OPTIMIZER_GOAL, 104

OPTIMIZER_MODE, 104, 302

Oracle architectures, 109

Oracle Backup Manager, 127

Oracle CASE, 21

Oracle configurations, 110

Oracle Database Manager, 105

Oracle Parallel Server, 53, 121, 138, 165

Oracle Recovery Manager, 128

Oracle User Manager, 188

ORACLE_HOME, 112, 114

ORACLE_PATH, 113

ORACLE_SID, 107, 113

OS_AUTHENT_PREFIX, 302

P

Packages, 70

Parallel, 108

Parallel Data Loader, 281

Parallel data loads, 206, 207

Parallel Processing, 110

Parallel Query Option, 138, 206

PCTFREE, 150, 157, 158

PCTINCREASE, 162, 163

PCTUSED, 157, 158

Percent increase, 163

Personnel, 240

Personnel Matrix, 245

PFILE, 106

PGA, 47

Pinging, 165

PL/SQL, 34, 69, 149

PMON, 52

PQO, 138

Precision, 82

Primary Key, 23, 89, 143, 152, 254

    Naming constraints, 256

    Updating, 28

    USING INDEX, 258

Private rollback segments, 80

Private SQL area, 39

Procedures, 70

Process Monitor, 52

PROCESSES, 303

Production environment, 177

Profiles, 178, 185

    Creating a profile, 186

Program Global Area, 47

Program interface, 44, 47

Program Units, 69

Project management, 265

Prototyping, 269

Pseudo columns, 86

    CURRVAL, 87

    NEXTVAL, 87

    ROWID, 86

    ROWNUM, 86

Public rollback segments, 81

Q

Qualifiers, 252

Quotas, 185

R

RAID, 121

RAW datatype, 86

Raw devices, 139

Read consistent image, 80

RECO, 53

Recoverer process, 53

Recovery, 119, 122, 128

Recursive call, 40

Redo buffers, 42

Redo latches, 229

Redo log buffers, 225

Redo logs, 55, 122

    Log groups, 57

    Log switch, 59

    Mirrored redo logs, 56

Referential integrity, 27

    Cascade delete, 28

    Default, 28

    Nullify, 28

Restrict delete, 28

Relation, 21

Relational Database Management Systems, 9

Relational Model, 19, 62

Relationships, 25, 249

Reserve words, 246

RESIZE, 172

Resource privileges, 183

RESOURCE role, 182

Restrict delete, 91

Restricted mode, 108

Roles, 178, 182

   CONNECT, 182

   EXP_FULL_DATABASE, 182

RESOURCE, 182

Rollback, 42

Rollback segments, 75, 80

   Private, 80

   Public, 81

   Tuning, 228

ROLLBACK_SEGMENTS, 81, 191, 303

Row chaining, 150, 151, 234

ROWID, 62, 77, 86

ROWNUM, 86, 87

   Used to limit query results, 88

Rule-based optimizer, 101, 102

S

Sample database, 287

Sample Logical Data Model, 288

Sample Physical Data Model, 289

Scale, 82

Schema, 10, 61

Schema objects, 61

S-Designor, 24

SDP Technologies, Inc., 24

Security, 178

Segments, 80

SEQUENCE_CACHE_ENTRIES, 303

Sequences, 67, 153

Server processes, 43, 50

Session, 43

SGA, 37, 38, 43, 49, 58, 139, 165, 177, 222, 294, 296

Sizing, 294

   Tuning, 222

Shared pool, 38, 222

Shared SQL area, 39, 247

SHARED_POOL_SIZE, 38, 224, 297

Shutdown, 105, 108

   Abort, 109

   Immediate, 108

   Normal, 108

Single instance, 109

Single task configuration, 44

Sizing Index Spreadsheet, 156

Sizing objects, 137, 154

Sizing Table Spreadsheet, 155

SMON, 53, 120

SORT_AREA_RETAINED_SIZE, 298

SORT_AREA_SIZE, 298

   Tuning, 226

Spreading I/O, 167

SQL, 9, 105

   Hints, 104

   Naming standards, 247

SQL TRACE, 214

SQL*DBA, 106

SQL*Forms, 76, 113

SQL*Loader, 205, 206, 281

SQL*Net, 45, 46

SQL*Net listener process, 53

SQL.BSQ, 96

SQL_TRACE, 220, 299

SQLTRACE, 153

   Outpu\t, 221

STANDARD.SQL, 197

Starting archiving, 125, 199

Startup, 105, 106

   Exclusive, 108

   Force, 109

   Mount, 107

   Nomount, 107

   Open, 107

   Parallel, 108

   Restricted, 108

Storage parameters, 157

Structured Query Language, 30. See SQL

Synonyms, 71, 247

SYS, 188

SYSDATE, 84, 95

System Global Area, 37. See SGA

System inventory, 137

System Monitor, 53

System tablespace, 74

Systems Administration, 240, 244

T

Table constraints, 89

Table striping, 74, 280

Tables, 62, 150, 251

   Defragmenting, 131

   Sizing, 155

Tablespaces, 73, 160, 171, 257

   AUTOEXTEND, 172

   Data, 74

   Default, 76

   Index, 75

   RESIZE, 172

   Rollback, 75

   System, 74

Temporary, 76

Temporary tablespace, 76, 185

Test environment, 176

Third normal form, 142

Three Schema Architecture, 10, 175

TIMED_STATISTICS, 220, 232, 300

TKPROF, 153, 214, 220

tkprof.exe, 220

Trace files, 59, 234

Training environment, 177

Triggers, 69, 149

Tuning, 213

   A quick check list, 232

Tuning I/O, 227

Tuple, 21

Two task, 44

U

Unique

   Constraints, 95

   Indexes, 29

   Naming constraints, 256

Unique constraints, 152

UNIX, 113, 139

USE_DUMP_DEST, 295

USER function, 181

User processes, 44, 47

USER_DUMP_DEST, 220

Users, 96, 184
    Default tablespace, 185
    Passwords, 188
    Profiles, 185
    Quotas, 185
    SYS, 188
    SYSTEM, 188
    Temporary tablespace, 185
USING INDEX, 258
UTLBSTAT, 214, 232
UTLESTAT, 214, 232
UTLMONTR.SQL, 97, 197
UTLXPLAN.SQL, 216

V

V$LATCH, 230
V$LOG_HISTORY, 122

V$ROLLSTAT, 233
V$SGASTAT, 38
V$SYSSTAT, 50, 224, 231, 233
Validate logical data model, 142
VARCHAR2 datatype, 81, 150
Very large databases, 279
Views, 68, 180

W

WORM drives, 126

X

X$KCBCBH, 299
X$KCBRBH, 299

ABOUT THE DISKETTE

The SQL scripts and Microsoft Excel spreadsheets included on the enclosed diskette are covered in detail in the the book. There are seven SQL scripts and six Microsoft Excel spreadsheets on the diskette. The QUERIES.TXT file, also on the diskette, lists as well as explains what each script does. The following SQL scripts are on the enclosed diskette:

```
dbchit.sql
sysstat.sql
extents.sql
explan.sql
tabstp.sql
create.sql
creana.sql
```

In addition, there are six Microsoft Excel spreadsheets included on the diskette. The tables.xls and indexes.xls are used to size and locate tables and indexes. The four disk map spreadsheets are used to locate tablespaces and other files on the target machine. Those files that have a 4 in the name are for machines with four disk drives and those with a 6 in the name are for machines with six disk drives.:

```
tables.xls
indexes.xls
dssmap4.xls
oltpmap4.xls
dssmap6.xls
oltpmap6.xls
```